MORE ADVANCE PRAISE FOR
THE BLACK–WHITE ACHIEVEMENT GAP

"Secretary Paige and Dr. Witty brilliantly dissect the last civil rights issue in America: the education achievement gap between black and white children. We can close that gap, they rightly argue, if black leadership embraces innovation, creativity and commitment to really put kids first. Our black leaders need to embrace an 'unwavering sense of moral purpose' to lead and not follow on the issue of finding solutions to the education disparities that plague the black community. This is a book whose time has come."

—Kevin P. Chavous, former member of the Council of the
District of Columbia; and Chair of the Council's
Committee on Education, Libraries, and Recreation

"Paige and Witty have called our attention to a problem that our nation and our leaders have too long ignored. They offer an insightful and compelling argument for the necessity of urgently closing the black–white achievement gap. This book is a must-read for anyone interested in civil rights and social justice in America."

—Anthony Williams, former Mayor of Washington, D.C.

"There are no leaders—other than Paige and Witty—who are closer to the reality of the problem that African Americans will face in the future global competition if the achievement gap is not bridged."

—The Honorable Dr. Rev. Floyd H. Flake,
U.S. Congressman, Retired

"This book unveils the reasons why the black–white achievement gap is the major civil rights barrier of today, and charges the African American leadership with responsibility for closing it. While providing a candid and unapologetic look at the status of African American student performance in schools today, this book lays out a hopeful path to improvement. African American leaders must embrace the challenge to take up arms and move this issue to the top of their agendas. No other action can do more to help us reach the goals of racial equality and social justice in society today. This book is a must-read for everyone who thinks of himself or herself as a leader."

—Yvonne B. Miller, State Senator, Virginia

"Paige and Witty have appropriately placed the achievement gap between white and black K–12 public education students in the context of the period following *Brown v. Board of Education,* and they have thrown down the gauntlet for strong leadership to tackle solving this extremely grave problem."

—Barbara J. Holmes, former Director of Policy
Studies, Education Commission of the States

The Black–White Achievement Gap

Why Closing It Is the Greatest Civil Rights Issue of Our Time

ROD PAIGE

ELAINE WITTY

AMACOM AMERICAN MANAGEMENT ASSOCIATION
New York ▸ Atlanta ▸ Brussels ▸ Chicago ▸ Mexico City
San Francisco ▸ Shanghai ▸ Tokyo ▸ Toronto ▸ Washington, D.C.

Bulk discounts available. For details visit:
www.amacombooks.org/go/specialsales
Or contact special sales:
Phone: 800-250-5308
Email: specialsls@amanet.org
View all the AMACOM titles at: www.amacombooks.org

Library of Congress Cataloging-in-Publication Data

Paige, Rod.
The Black–White achievement gap : why closing it is the greatest civil rights issue of our time / Rod Paige, Elaine Witty.
    p. cm.
Includes bibliographical references and index.
ISBN-13: 978-0-8144-1519-1
ISDBN-10: 0-8144-1519-9
1. Education—Demographic aspects—United States 2. Academic achievement—United States 3. Educational equalization—United States I. Witty, Elaine P. II. Title.
LC205.P35 2009
379.2'60973—dc22

                                                                      2009026386

About AMA
American Management Association (www.amanet.org) is a world leader in talent development, advancing the skills of individuals to drive business success. Our mission is to support the goals of individuals and organizations through a complete range of products and services, including classroom and virtual seminars, webcasts, webinars, podcasts, conferences, corporate and government solutions, business books and research. AMA's approach to improving performance combines experiential learning—learning through doing—with opportunities for ongoing professional growth at every step of one's career journey.

Printing number
10 9 8 7 6 5 4 3 2 1

This book is dedicated to the men and women of years gone by who gave of their devotion, courage, sacrifice, and, in some cases, their lives, to advance African Americans toward racial equality and social justice in America.

CONTENTS

FOREWORD

On February 7, 2003, D.C. Mayor Anthony Williams, former Milwaukee Public School Superintendent Dr. Howard Fuller, and I met with U.S. Secretary of Education Rod Paige in his office. At the time I was a member of the Council of the District of Columbia and Chair of the Committee on Education Libraries and Recreation.

While it was largely reported that we met to discuss the federally funded Washington Opportunity Scholarship Program (OSP) proposed by President George W. Bush and Secretary Paige, we actually talked about far more than that. In fact, we spent a substantial portion of the meeting talking about the education deficits of children of color in this country and the lack of outrage in response thereto. Both Secretary Paige, a former superintendent of the Houston Public Schools, and Dr. Fuller spoke about their experiences as leaders of large urban school districts. They lamented the fact that there was a collective lack of urgency about the growing achievement gap between African American and white schoolchildren. That complacency, they suggested at the time, had led to an acceptance of the status quo, which is destroying the educational outputs of our kids. What's worse, Dr. Paige emphasized, is that our leadership has a head-in-the-sand response to these growing deficits.

That meeting, which involved four African American men, helped pave the way for the first federally funded scholarship program for low-income District of Columbia children. As a result of that program, 2,000 children have been able to attend selected private schools of their choice in the District and, thus, receive the quality education that they might not otherwise receive. One notable scholarship recipient was Tiffany Duston, who graduated valedictorian of her class at Archbishop Carroll Catholic High School in D.C. Tiffany, who now attends Syracuse University, frankly states that she would have never made it to college without the scholarship that allowed her to attend Archbishop Carroll.

Whether one believes in vouchers or not is a secondary issue. The main point is that African American leaders have responsibility to take ownership of the education reform issue and promote measures that enhance the educational advancement of our children. Measures, I might add, that do not preserve the status quo.

Since leaving the District Council, I regularly travel around the country and speak with parents, educators, policymakers, and elected officials about what ails our schools. The winds of change are blowing and the current outputs for African American children are no longer acceptable. People are, in the words of Mississippi civil rights activist Fannie Lou Hamer, "sick and tired of being sick and tired."

The key missing ingredient to wholesale change in our schools is leadership. Folks intuitively know that what we are doing isn't working, but our leaders are either unwilling or feel unable to lead the fight for change. Adult interest, personal political goals, and historical alliances often paralyze our leaders from doing what's right for kids.

In their book *The Black–White Achievement Gap: Why Closing It Is the Greatest Civil Rights Issue of Our Time,* Secretary Paige and his sister, Dr. Elaine Witty, brilliantly dissect the core tensions associated with solving what is indeed the last great civil rights issue in America: the education achievement gap between African American and white children in this country. We can close the gap, they rightly argue, if African American leadership really commits to putting children first. In short, the solutions to this problem, whatever they are, will have longstanding value if they are embraced and championed by authentic African American leaders, no matter what the cost. The challenge is in getting those leaders to, in fact, lead.

For that to occur, African American leaders must adopt the tenets and approach followed by Frederick Douglass, Dr. Martin Luther King, and Nelson Mandela, to name a few. These men led passionately, righteously, and with, as Drs. Paige and Witty point out, an unwavering sense of moral purpose that guided their every move. In order to close the achievement gap between African American and white children, we need leaders to place every other interest behind that of the children. The goal should be to educate our kids by any means necessary.

I am sure that some will bemoan the critical tone of Drs. Paige and Witty's book. Self-analysis is not an easy exercise, particularly when it is much easier to point fingers outward. But those criticisms aside, the reality is that these are our kids. If we don't take ownership of their education, who will?

Legend appropriately holds that each generation is ultimately judged by how it treats its children. In *The Black–White Achievement Gap,* Rod Paige and Elaine Witty issue a clarion call to today's generation of African American leadership. Their book urges that these leaders move beyond the historical vestiges of slavery by leading the fight to make certain that our children learn and excel in school. I hope our leaders take on the fight. No other issue is more important than the commitment to truly serve our children.

Kevin P. Chavous

PREFACE

THE TWO OF US

We approach this work not from a political or social-activist point of view, nor from an academic point of view, but from our personal perspectives as two educational practitioners. The opinions and thoughts expressed herein are drawn from a combined ninety years of experience at all levels of the educational spectrum in an array of positions: U.S. Secretary of Education, deans of colleges of education, school board trustee, superintendent of the nation's seventh largest public school district, all the way up the education hierarchy to the single most vital position of classroom teacher. Decades of teaching, serving in educational administration, and operating in education policy circles have shown us that education is, in fact, a highly politicized issue. However, while political matters are addressed as a matter of necessity in this book, our primary interest here is not in politics. It is in education. More specifically, our goal is to address the barriers to closing the black–white achievement gap—of which contemporary African American leadership, or *lack* thereof, is one.

When we talk about African American leaders, we are referring to elected officials in national, state, and local government, and those in leadership positions in nongovernmental organizations, faith-based organizations, commissions and committees, civic organizations, and other large state and national social organizations.

Of course, it's impossible to entertain any consideration of the work of African American leaders without some reference to political matters. African American leaders are a definite part of the conglomerate of factors and entities that together form the United States educational system. Every other factor in the educational system that influences student outcomes has already been scrutinized, criticized, and subjected to detailed public discussion—all except our political and community leadership. It is now time to examine leaders' behavior as it relates to the black–white achievement gap.

Before we begin, let us tell you why each of us is so passionate about this issue.

▶ ▶ ▶

REFLECTIONS BY ROD PAIGE

Before delving into the history behind my interest in the subject addressed in this book, I wish to first express how much this book, or rather the process that led to the book, means to me. On a personal note, this book has allowed me the pleasure to collaborate on a project with my sister, whom I have admired all of my life. Not only was she the inspiration that lead me to continue my studies in the field of education, but she continues to inspire me through her wide-ranging contributions to the area of teacher education, and the field of education in general. Her impeccable character as a person and as a professor of education is one of the driving forces that has guided me not only to believe that we can improve our educational system, but also to push for the necessary changes that will allow all students opportunity for an equitable education. I am motivated by her will and desire not only to close the black–white achievement gap, but also to provide a strong education for all children.

Now to reflections regarding our book, which is about what I believe to be one of our nation's most overlooked, urgent, persistent, dangerous, mismanaged, and most correctable domestic problems. Our book is about the black–white achievement gap. It's also about leadership. Specifically, it's about the qualities of leadership embedded within the African American culture and how that leadership, both through omission and commission, is part of the achievement-gap problem. This book is about how the African American leadership culture not only fails to properly address the problem of the black–white achievement gap but also how it may be contributing to the problem's intractability. In short, this book is about finally identifying the causes of the achievement gap and proposing a real solution for closing it.

The thoughts and ideas contained in this book are offered to a general audience, to the everyday American citizen who is interested in a better America, to those who wonder sometimes why the time-honored African

American journey toward racial equality and social justice seems to be getting more difficult for many, and for some, even stalled. There has been much written about the black–white achievement gap in the academic literature, and it has been the subject of a great deal of discussion in academic circles. We believe that it is time to broaden the awareness, understanding, and concern about the this gap, so that the level of dissatisfaction with it intensifies to the point of action—no, not just action, but *productive* action. For that reason, through this book, we hope to reach outside the academic world and engage the general public in the struggle to confront and defeat what we believe to be today's most urgent civil rights issue, the black–white achievement gap.

I can trace my interest in this matter back to the spring of 1986 when I was teaching a class in testing and measurement at Texas Southern University (TSU). We were working on an assignment on percentiles and percentile rank.[1] I had asked each student to bring a data set to class that represented actual measurements of some commonly measured variable. Part of the assignment was to rank order the data, compute the median, the first and third quartiles, and the percentile rank of certain selected variables.[2]

As we reviewed the data in class, one student raised her hand and asked for assistance in interpreting the material. When I went over to her desk, she handed me a sheet of paper listing school-by-school scores from the Houston Independent School District (HISD) on the most recent administration of the Texas Assessment of Basic Skills (TABS).

As I examined her work, the first thing I noticed was that almost all the schools that I identified as having a majority enrollment of African Americans were in the lowest quartile of the distribution. This, of course, interested me. I took a closer look, and it verified my initial conclusion. Of the better than 180 schools in the distribution, I recognized only one African American school in the top quartile. There was one African American school in the third quartile, two in the second quartile, and all the others were in the bottom 25 percent of the distribution. This was a curious phenomenon, I thought. I filed that observation in the back of my mind and continued with the class.

Later in the semester, I planned a unit on correlation coefficients. While preparing for this unit, I decided to conduct a review of the lesson by computing the coefficient of correlation using an actual set of data. Browsing through the file of students' assignments to find an appropriate data set, I came across the percentile-rank data mentioned earlier. Recalling that almost all African American schools were in the lower rankings, I decided to use those data and correlate school rankings on the TABS with the percent of enrollment of African American students.

Wow! To this day, I can still physically feel the shock I experienced when I saw the numerical relationship between those two variables. The data revealed an extremely high correlation between the percentage of African American students enrolled, and their schools' rankings on the TABS. In other words, the more African American students that were enrolled in a school, the more likely that school would be ranked in the lower quartiles of the school-by-school TABS performance distribution.

This was a very troubling discovery. On numerous occasions, I had run across references in professional literature to the gap in academic achievement between African American students and other ethnic groups, but at the time, it simply had been an academic matter for me. This experience of analyzing the data myself seemed to make it much more personal.

I didn't take steps that day to act on the results of my computations, shocking though they were. Like many in the African American leadership community, I moved on—safe in the view that this was somebody else's problem. But the experience gave me a high level of sensitivity for the gap in academic performance between African American students and students of other ethnic communities.

A few years later, in April 1990, I successfully ran for a seat on the Houston Independent School District Board of Education (HISD). The incumbent gave up her seat to run for the Eighteenth Congressional District made vacant by the death of Representative Mickey Leland. I had reluctantly yielded to pressure from several prominent members of the African American faith-based community to seek the position on the school board and was elected for a four-year term.

As a member of the school board of a large, urban, multiethnic school district, I had firsthand access to a gold mine of student performance data: SAT, ACT, district-by-district and school-by-school, state-mandated tests, rising junior tests—you name it, HISD had it. This was hog heaven for me. I spent hours digging into this information. It wasn't long before I realized that there was something strange about the student performance data. No matter what set of test data I analyzed, no matter what statistical technique I used, one thing remained the same: on average,

African American students performed below their white and Asian peers, and in many cases, below their Hispanic peers. I found no way to escape the reality that the black–white academic performance gap was real, it was large, and more perilously, in some instances, it was getting larger.

Four years went by; and before I knew it, I had served my first full term as a trustee and successfully campaigned for a second four-year term. Early in my second term, I was asked by my colleagues to become the district's superintendent of schools. After careful consideration and consultation with trusted friends, I agreed; and on February 18, 1994, I was appointed superintendent of the Houston Independent School District.

The perspective from the superintendent's office is altogether different from that of a university professor or a school board member. With regard to the black–white achievement gap, this new perspective changed everything. As a university professor, I could find solace in the belief that the achievement gap was somebody else's problem; as superintendent, I realized that it was now my problem and must be managed along with the myriad of other problems that confront superintendents of large urban public school systems.

It had taken eight long years of many up-close-and-personal encounters for me to realize that the achievement gap was not just a problem in and of itself. During those years I had come to believe that the gap gave support to the theories espoused in Herrnstein and Murray's widely popular book *The Bell Curve*, and that since it retarded African American economic advancement, it was a major barrier to African Americans' long quest for racial equality and social justice in America. This brought me face to face with the reality that if I were indeed interested in African Americans achieving equality in this country, this gap was a problem that I must work toward solving.

Moreover, I have come to believe that the black–white achievement gap is not only my problem, but because it has such strong influence on the nature of race relations in America, it is every American's problem. Even more, this gap is especially every African American's problem, particularly those who consider themselves leaders. I believe that African American leadership in the resolution of this problem is an absolute necessity if we are to close the gap.

That's really our point. African American leaders have for too long been absent from the battlefront of the black–white achievement gap. And for too long, I was among them in their absence. Given this reality, I can only offer understanding and even forgiveness of other African Americans in leadership positions for not accepting the black–white achievement gap as our problem.

Still, even today, far too few members of the African American leadership community accept the achievement gap as their problem. In truth, it is, or it should be, our entire nation's problem. Yes, it is a national problem of major proportions, but it is most especially a problem for each and every member of the African American community. I make this point because after careful study of this phenomenon, I have become convinced that the achievement gap is now the most important challenge for African Americans. In the following chapters we will argue that as a barrier to African American advancement toward our twin goals of racial equality and social justice in America, the black–white achievement gap now ranks ahead of our old nemeses of racism and racial discrimination.

Because I believe that the goals of racial equality and social justice in this country can never be achieved in the presence of a large, constantly present achievement gap, especially one of the current magnitude, I think it deserves the full attention of the African American leadership community. For those of us in leadership positions, acknowledging that the black–white achievement gap is our responsibility is only the first step. The next step is to do something about it. This will require African American leaders to put forth a concerted effort to truly understand the problem. I use the term understand here purposely, as I want to emphasize the need to go deeper than just mere awareness.

There is plenty of lip service, superficial discussion, and random and isolated activity about the black–white achievement gap. Yet, this book is a call for African American leaders to do more—much more. For those African American leaders who retort, "We have been working on the achievement gap for years," I would respond, "Of course you have." There have been countless workshops, seminars, and roundtable discussions on African American education issues, sponsored by groups such as African American fraternities, sororities, social groups, the Congressional Black Caucus (CBC), the National Association for the Advancement of Colored People (NAACP), the National Urban League (NUL), and others. But where is the evidence that any of these efforts has had even a modicum of success in reducing the achievement gap? For the most part, these activities have merely skimmed the surface of a deep, stagnant river.

The gap is still here. The problem persists in all its complexity and tenacity, despite years of such efforts to eradicate it.

Considering the intractable nature of the achievement gap, I believe African American leaders must confront five important and difficult questions:

1. Why do African American students, on average, consistently score lower on academic tests than their white counterparts?

2. What are the long-term economic, social, and racial consequences for African Americans in the event of a continued—and possibly growing— achievement gap between African American students and their white peers?

3. Why have past African American efforts to close the achievement gap between African Americans and their white peers resulted in such utter failure?

4. If African American leaders do not take responsibility for finding the solution to the black–white achievement gap, who will?

5. What are the implications of a continued black–white achievement gap in terms of prolonging the racial stigma of African American intellectual inferiority?

This book challenges African American leadership to address these questions with the sense of urgency and commitment that was used to confront past civil rights barriers. We make this challenge because we have every confidence that if the black–white achievement gap becomes a point of focus of African American leadership, it will travel the same path to the scrap piles of American history as have so many other barriers to African American advancement. We are where we are today because of the potency of African American leadership. We are where we are now because past African American leadership identified the major barriers to African American advancement, devised appropriate tactics to overcome them, adopted a full-court-press attitude toward them, and stayed the course until the battle was won.

As we applaud such leadership, we nonetheless caution that the barriers that retarded advancement in past years are not the same barriers that retard us today. Contemporary African American leadership must take a

new look at today's realities, identify today's primary barriers to advancement (we argue that the achievement gap is *the* primary barrier), devise
effective tactics, and confront the problem with the tenacity of past civil
rights efforts. Overcoming yesterday's barriers with yesterday's tactics was
fine to accomplish the important work that's gotten us to where we are
today. Although these tactics and the focus of leadership got us here, they
won't get us the rest of the way because the remaining challenges require
a different approach and different style. The game has changed, and we
must change also.

In the following chapters, we criticize the current African American
leadership culture for its role in the existence, magnitude, and intractability of the black–white achievement gap. At the same time, however, we
avoid condemning the good intentions, good will, and good work of individual African American leaders. In fact, we deliberately use the term
"leadership culture" to represent the generally accepted beliefs, values,
and assumptions that best characterize the current African American leadership landscape. This was intentionally done to steer clear of criticizing
individual personalities.

The phrase "African American leadership culture" does not perfectly
capture the range of beliefs, values, and assumptions that exists within the
entire African American leadership community. Clearly, no term could do
that. African American leaders represent a wide spectrum of beliefs, values, and assumptions. But while they can be found all along the political
spectrum from liberal to conservative, it is hard to dispute that the vast
majority congregate toward the left of the political continuum. The phrase
"African American leadership culture" as used in this book is, therefore,
intended to describe the beliefs, values, and assumptions of this majority.

Let me be more explicit. The African American leadership culture
described herein can be characterized by its strong liberal ideology, its
view that all African American problems are caused primarily by racism,
and its strong aversion to self-criticism. It is important that I am clear here
because there appears to be a new African American leadership culture
emerging in this country of which I wish to be supportive. All across the
country I have noticed what appears to be an increase in the number of
mostly young African Americans who are beginning to engage in African
American leadership matters.

Up until now, the African American leadership culture and the leadership direction it espouses have barely been scrutinized with respect to

their role in the black–white achievement gap. Every part of the education system has taken its share of criticism for the existence of the gap—except African Americans who hold political and leadership power, and, therefore, have the capability, and I believe, ultimately the responsibility to make a real contribution to ending this problem. It is high time that this group takes its rightful place in the spotlight and shares the scrutiny and the responsibility. African American leadership will no doubt claim innocence and cry out for more resources or identify other causes. But this response to the problem is itself evidence of African American leadership's culpability.

There is absolutely no doubt in my mind that African American students can achieve at the highest levels, matching anyone of any skin color or ethnicity. I emphatically reject the notion that the achievement gap is a result of African American children's DNA, as a few have proposed along the way. The question is not whether they can do it but how we adults can help make that happen.

The successful African American students I have known and the schools that succeed despite the greatest of odds fill me with hope for eliminating the achievement gap. But doing so will require concerted action by an improved African American leadership culture. It is my hope that we can rally around this common cause.

▶ ▶ ▶

REFLECTIONS BY ELAINE WITTY

I was a sophomore at one of the nation's historically black colleges in 1954 when the Supreme Court issued the ruling designed to eliminate separate schools for black and white children. I was fully aware of the discrepancies between the school facilities for each of the races. I also had a deep suspicion that even though I was in the top 5 percent of students at my college, I was still not as well prepared for college work as I should have been.

With great relief I thought that, with the *Brown v. Board of Education* decision in place, black students coming to college after me would not have to worry about inadequate academic preparation.

For my master's and doctoral studies, I entered a previously segregated college. I learned that while I could perform well in class and on research projects, standardized examinations were still a challenge. Like those of most other black students, my test scores were much lower than those of my white peers. But focused study and a clear understanding of the importance of these standardized tests remedied the situation for me.

In the late 1970s, I took a semester of postdoctoral study at the University of Georgia. I studied under Paul Torrance in the area of education of the gifted. One of the presentations made by a guest speaker focused on identifying gifted African American students. At that time, only a few African American students were included in the special classes for the gifted. The presentation focused on a special scoring formula for a commonly used test designed so that some African American students would make the adjusted cut score for inclusion. In other words, the concept would be, "This is a good score for an African American student." Success with this type of identification would mean that African American students included in the classes for the gifted would actually have less knowledge and fewer skills than their peers in the general population, according to the test; but they would be the top-scoring students in the African American population. I viewed this as a dangerous and embarrassing concept for the students as well as for the teachers. Why not adjust the students' instruction rather than adjust the cut scores on the test? This alternative was not explored. Somehow, simply teaching the students so that they would master the necessary knowledge and skills was not seen as a viable option.

Questions about the difference in the test performance of white and African American students remained on my mind and came to the forefront of my work agenda in the 1980s when I was an administrator and professor at one of the historically black colleges and universities. Part of my job involved dealing with state-imposed mandates related to college admissions and teacher education program admissions criteria. The gap between SAT scores of white and African American students was apparent on both the quantitative and verbal sections of the test during every testing period. This same pattern occurred across the nation and in every state where the test was used for college admissions.

Even after participating in remedial basic skills courses and in transitional programs designed to sharpen their college readiness skills, African American students who completed their courses of studies found that their scores on the standardized tests used for teacher certification and licensing were still lower than those of their white peers. Again, this was true across the nation in every state where standardized tests were used for teachers. Even in 2006, only on those campuses where educators provided special standardized test preparation were African American candidates scoring as well as their white counterparts on teacher licensing examinations. Why, then, are all campuses not offering the same training and resources?

Obviously, achievement gaps between African American and white students do not miraculously appear when students enter college or begin teacher-education programs. The gaps are already apparent at the elementary school level. Yet, children are passed on from grade to grade without evidence that they have mastered the necessary skills. Surely, adults in the community must know when children are having a hard time reading. This must be evident in their daily lives and in Sunday school lessons. But there are no mass meetings about academic achievement, no alarm about the problem at all.

Underachievement is especially critical for African American boys. More than any other segment of the school population, these students are at risk of being misunderstood and undertaught. They make up a disproportionately large percent of school dropouts and later underemployed or unemployed citizens. These students are most often the ones I saw sitting in the principal's office when I supervised student teachers. They were usually there for disciplinary reasons. The questions that seemed to be in their faces were: "What is it about me that the teachers don't like?" or "Why can't they teach me?" These boys were the students most often placed in special education, where, again, they were not being taught.

I noticed that even in programs designed especially to improve academic achievement of disadvantaged students, African American students were being shortchanged. Many of these programs focused heavily on basic skill drills at the expense of thinking skills and enriching content. Especially bothersome were the lines of students waiting in the halls to go to the latest pull-out programs. While these programs were planned to help students bridge the gaps between their skills and the skills needed for success at their grade level, most programs actually led to greater disparities because students lost the opportunity to participate in whatever lessons teachers taught their classmates while they were out of class getting "special instruction."

Because the academic achievement of African American students is so critical to racial equality, it must now become the number-one goal for the African American community. Even as economic, political, and social barriers are being reduced, students whose academic skills are under par are left unable to profit from these societal changes. Leadership must be focused on creating a culture of academic support and expectation that makes it unacceptable for African American students to fail to achieve. Leaders must now work for those factors that replace African American students' fear of "acting white" with the joy of excelling. They must work in support of those factors that free African American students from low expectations for themselves and for their peers.

After a long career in teacher education, struggling with college students who fall far behind their white peers on standardized tests, I ask, why are African American leaders not launching nationwide programs to make underachievement in academics unacceptable? While there is still work to be done and miles to go in fighting racism, African American leaders must now move educational achievement to the top of their agenda.

I hope that this book provides a wake-up call and inspires African American leadership to launch the response that this urgent national problem demands.

ACKNOWLEDGMENTS

One of the special joys we experienced during our work on this project was the extraordinary pleasure we found in our collaboration with so many wonderful people who so freely gave of their time, energies, and talents to assist us. To each of them, we wish to express our enduring gratitude. Our problem now, however, is finding a way to acknowledge this gratitude without omitting anyone. We were assisted by many whose contribution was up close and personal, like the assistance we received from Lynn Jenkins, Amy Shah, Stephanie Nellons, Christal Burnett, Rosalind Young, Greg Forster, and Nell Cline, all of whom helped with research, editing, and other tasks so necessary in preparing for publication. Then there were others who offered ideas, feedback, and positive criticism, like Don McAdams, Wilbert Pete, Ron Tomalis, Paul Brunson, John Grimaldi, James Bryant, John Danielson, and Reverend Joe Samuel Ratliff. Equally helpful, too, were those who, through their research and writing, provided us with immeasurable inspiration, like Christopher Jencks and Meredith Phillips, James MacGregor Burns, Abigail and Stephan Thernstrom, William Julius Wilson, Glenn C. Loury, John McWhorter, Ronald Walters, Robert C. Smith, Roland Fryer, Ron Ferguson and too many others to name. To all of these magnificent people, we offer our everlasting thanks. We would also like to thank the entire staff at the Center for Reform of School Systems (CRSS). We are grateful to Aubrey Locke, Mary Triplett, Sharon Jacobson, Susie Crafton, Faith Edwards, Melanie Markley, Yolanda Guerrero, Glenda White, Gail Littlejohn, Stephanie Baker, and Vita Montalbano for each of their various contributions which often remained behind the scene, but that were essential to the completion of this book.

PATH TO A MORE PERFECT UNION

For the African American community, that path means embracing the burdens of our path without becoming victims of our past. It means continuing to insist on a full measure of justice in every aspect of American life. But it also means binding our particular grievances—for better health care, and better schools, and better jobs—to the larger aspirations of all Americans—the white woman struggling to break the glass ceiling, the white man who's been laid off, the immigrant trying to feed his family. And it means taking full responsibility for our own lives—by demanding more from our fathers, and spending more time with our children, and reading to them, and teaching them that while they may face challenges and discriminations in their own lives, they must never succumb to despair or cynicism, they must always believe that they can write their own destiny.

> Excerpt from Senator Barack Obama's remarks, "A More Perfect Union," Philadelphia, Pennsylvania, March 18, 2008

▸ ▸ ▸

ESTABLISHING A SYSTEM OF PUBLIC EDUCATION IN WHICH ALL CHILDREN ACHIEVE AT HIGH LEVELS AND REACH THEIR FULL POTENTIAL

Without question, education is the key to progress and prosperity in the United States today. Whether fair or not, educational opportunity and academic achievement are directly tied to the social divisions associated with race, ethnicity, gender, first language, and social class. The level and quality of educational attainment either open the doors to opportunity or close them.

Education starts at home, in neighborhoods, and in communities. Reading to children, creating time and space for homework, and demonstrating—through words and deeds—that education is important are the key first building blocks for high educational achievement. While schools are responsible for what children are taught, reinforcement at home is essential. As members of the black community, we must take responsibility for educating all our children—whether ours by birth or otherwise—to uplift our people as a whole.

Excerpt from Edmund W. Gordon's essay in *The Covenant with Black America*

THE BLACK–WHITE ACHIEVEMENT GAP

CHAPTER 1

The Greatest Civil Rights Challenge of Our Time

If racial equality is America's goal, reducing the black-white test score gap would probably do more to promote this goal than any other strategy that commands broad political support. Reducing the test score gap is probably both necessary and sufficient for substantially reducing racial inequality in educational attainment and earnings. Changes in education and earnings would in turn help reduce racial differences in crime, health, and family structure, although we do not know how large these effects would be.

—Christopher Jencks and Meredith Phillips,
The Black-White Test Score Gap

THE AFRICAN AMERICAN unfinished journey from chattel slavery to racial equality and social justice in America has been, and continues to be, a long and arduous struggle. Although many dangerous and deadly barriers have imperiled this journey, none has been able to stand up to the power and determination of authentic African American leadership. No barrier—whether embedded in law, rooted in social or economic custom, or enforced by racial terror—has been able to hold firm against the powerful and unwavering commitment to advancement of a determined, authentic African American leadership. One by one, each primary barrier standing in the way of African American advancement has been confronted and defeated by a resolute African American leadership culture. That is, until now.

Now, the African American journey to racial equality and social justice is jeopardized by a different kind of barrier. Perhaps because this is a different kind of barrier, it's virtually overlooked by contemporary African American leadership culture and has yet to be identified as a major civil rights problem. Now, the primary barrier impeding progress toward our twin goals of racial equality and social justice isn't the clearly visible objects of oppression of yesteryear. Today's primary barrier appears much more innocuous and much more subtle. In a way, it's almost invisible to society at large, and unlike segregation, slavery, and discrimination, which were imposed intentionally by a racist society, no one is forcing this barrier to exist—yet it's there. Today's primary barrier is the black–white achievement gap.

On almost every measure of academic performance, be it the SAT, ACT, or state-mandated examinations, African American student performance trails, by large margins, that of their white peers. The average African American public school twelfth grader's performance on academic measures approximates that of the average white eighth grader. Not only do African American students trail their white peers on academic tests, they also experience much higher college dropout rates and a tendency to shy away from majoring in the hard sciences and mathematics.

To overcome today's primary barrier, a new kind of thinking, a new kind of strategy, and a new kind of leadership will be required. To overcome the barriers of yesteryear, we had to confront and overcome clearly identifiable oppressive laws, tyrannical customs, and racially repressive practices. Today's primary barrier may, in a sense, be more difficult to confront than previous barriers, because defeating it will require African Americans to face up to and overcome an apparent unwillingness to look inward for solutions to problems. Contemporary African American leadership culture attributes almost 100 percent of African American disadvantage to outward causes. Effectively confronting today's primary barrier may be more difficult precisely because it will require African Americans to accept ownership of the achievement gap as a civil rights problem. It will require an understanding that the problem cannot be solved without authentic African American leadership.

There are many reasons why African American leadership must consider the academic achievement gap to be a serious civil rights issue. But of all the compelling reasons, two stand out. First, the black–white achievement gap provides major support to the theory of inferiority, i.e., the gap exists because black students are inherently academically inferior to white students. Second, it is a primary impediment to the development of African American wealth.

We chose to begin this chapter with a quote from Christopher Jencks and Meredith Phillips' powerful volume *The Black-White Test Score Gap* because it so succinctly conveys our central premise: closing the black–white achievement gap would do more to advance African Americans toward our long-sought-after goals of racial equality and social justice in America than any civil rights strategy available to us today. In part that is because of the hard and good work that has already been done. We have accomplished much. But there is more to do.

The achievement gap is not a new challenge. Almost a century has passed since the problem was first identified and quantified by the United States Army when it began to use large-scale mental testing to assess recruits. The results showed that white recruits outscored their black peers by substantial margins.

In the years since, countless studies and surveys have reinforced and expanded on these early findings. We know now, for example, that differences in language and math skills appear by the time that children enter kindergarten, and those differences persist into adulthood. And as we will see later, we know more and more each year about the gap's underlying factors and causes of these differences.

Despite our growing knowledge base about the gap in the academic community, little of this new knowledge has made its way into the general public, and consequently, the sense of public awareness of the gap's magnitude and consequences has created little sense of public alarm. This lack of intense public concern is, in our view, a major reason why on a national basis, we have made relatively little progress in closing the achievement gap. Results from the National Assessment of Educational Progress (NAEP) and other studies show that while the black–white achievement gap has narrowed in some subject areas since 1970, the average African American student still scores below 75 percent of white students on most standardized tests.[1] And while individual schools sprinkled across the nation have succeeded in eliminating the gap—proving that it can, in fact, be done—no large district or state has yet done so.

To remind ourselves of how a national thrust of education would help close the achievement gap, let us revisit the 1970s and 1980s, when on a national basis the gap began to close (unfortunately, the narrowing of the gap stopped in the early 1990s). The 1970s and 1980s stand out in American history as an important period in the nation's trek toward racial harmony. It was a period when many major national efforts to reduce poverty, equalize opportunity, and achieve social justice, which had begun just prior to this period, began to bear fruit:

- School desegregation driven by the 1954 *Brown v. Board of Education*

- The 1964 Civil Rights Act

- The 1965 Voting Rights Act

- The 1965 federally funded Head Start program

- The 1965 enactment of the Elementary and Secondary Education Act (the eighth reauthorization, in January 2002, is referred to as the No Child Left Behind Act)

- State and federally funded compensatory programs for elementary school with high enrollments of low-income children

- Affirmative action policies for admission to colleges, universities, and professional schools

The 1970s, 1980s, and the years leading up to them were rife with legislation and activity designed to equalize opportunity for all Americans, but arguably they benefited African Americans most. Consistent with the view that environmental factors are foremost in influencing academic performance, many scholars and researchers believe those changes in the economic and social environment of African Americans narrowed the gap during this period.

However, while having lived through this period as young African American adults who were deeply involved in the education of African Americans, we would like to offer a different point of view. We contend that, while African American students did in fact benefit from improvements in their economic environment during this period, the prevailing attitude about education in the African American community was the main driver of educational improvements. The attitude about education in the African American community at that time was much like that of the freed slaves just after the Thirteenth Amendment outlawed slavery in

1865. Recall that the freed slave's thirst for education was intense during this period. Freed slaves rushed into any educational institution they could find. Many, even most, of the historically black colleges and universities trace their origins back to that period when education was viewed as the key to freedom in the black community.

Although the period of the 1970s and 1980s was much shorter and the quest for education in the African American community was perhaps less intense, it was strong nonetheless. The African American community was still glowing from the high hopes emanating from the *Brown v. Board of Education* decision. Expectations were high for African American advancement. Freedom's bells were ringing. With the possibility for advancement in the air, more opportunities to vote, better funding for schools, and more African Americans running for elected offices, schools were beginning to address the "all deliberate speed" mandate, and school desegregation was picking up speed. It was a period of hope; and education, as Malcolm X stated, was viewed as the passport to freedom. The power of education rang from the pulpits of the black churches; it was discussed in black social settings and work sites. We offer no empirical evidence; this was just how we experienced that period. If you need more evidence, just ask other African Americans who lived through this period.

We should not be at all surprised, therefore, at the educational progress African American students made. During this period, African Americans' interest in education was heightened. It was a solution to oppression. So why did the air go out of the balloon during the early 1990s and how do we recapture it for contemporary students so that we can continue to narrow the gap? That is the challenge we face today.

Closing the black–white achievement gap is an urgent task. In Chapter 3 we provide extended justification for our belief that eliminating it would promote racial equality, sharply increase black college graduation rates, reduce racial disparities in men's earnings, probably eliminate racial disparities in women's earnings, and allow selective colleges and employers to phase out racial preferences.

Every one of these goals is critically important. If you are not so sure eliminating racial preferences is a good idea, recall that in its landmark ruling on affirmative action at the University of Michigan Law School in 2003, U.S. Supreme Court Justice Sandra Day O'Connor stated that within the next twenty-five years there would be no more need for affirmative action.[2] Since many major colleges and universities use affirmative policies to assist minority enrollment, losing these policies would reduce minority enrollment in these schools. This reduction in African American enrollment can only be offset by preparing African American students to compete and win admission to these prestigious institutions on the same bases as other students.

Think about it. Can you identify any other African American advancement strategy over which we have major control that would have such a powerful impact on the quest for racial equality and social justice in America? Indeed, racial equality and social justice have been the core goals of the African American community throughout its presence in this nation. From that fateful day in 1619, when nineteen Africans were thrust upon these shores as unwilling pilgrims, to this very day, African Americans have asked little more than this from this country: that the Constitution speak the truth and that racial equality and social justice exist as promised.

How Far We've Come

In pursuit of these twin goals, our trek has been long, the struggle has been painful, and the price we have had to pay for the progress we have made has been steep. Many enormous and seemingly intractable barriers have jeopardized progress toward these goals. Foremost among them were mean and brutal chattel slavery, the unfulfilled promises of Emancipation and the Reconstruction period, the heartlessness of the Jim Crow era, and the cold callousness of legally supported racial segregation, born during the last quarter of the nineteenth century and lasting right up through the first six or seven decades of the twentieth century. All these barriers have imperiled the path to racial equality and social justice for those bearing the mark of Africa. But, to quote the poet Maya Angelou, "And still we rise."

Yes, despite the best efforts of evil men and women full of hatred, mayhem, and terror, who fostered racist practices and policies, still we rise. We rise because our leaders have been up to the challenge. In every epoch, we have been blessed with powerful Negro, black, or African American leaders who have had the courage and leadership to point the way—refer to them as you will.[3] In every age, we have been blessed with committed, determined, courageous, capable, and *authentic* African American leadership. No matter the problem, notwithstanding the difficulty, these leaders have been equal to the task.

One might find the phrase "authentic African American leadership" puzzling. We wanted to find a way to unmistakably distinguish between the kind of African American leadership that is needed to close the achievement gap and the kind of leadership we currently see all too often. It is important to appreciate much about the leadership efforts of contemporary African American leaders, but one can conclude from the subtitle of this book that we deem such leadership culture clearly insufficient to lead us forward toward our twin goals of racial equality and social justice in America.

What Is Authentic Leadership?

The use of the term *authentic* to achieve this distinction was inspired by several sources, two of which stand out. The first source was Bill George, the author of several best-selling leadership books. His books, especially his 2009 *Leading in Crisis,* make a gripping case for the right kind of leadership. But his informative article entitled "Truly Authentic Leadership," which appeared in the October 30, 2006, *U.S. News and World Report* special report, "America's Best Leaders," was particular compelling. In this powerful piece George argues, "Authentic leaders know the 'true north' of their moral compass and are prepared to stay the course despite challenges and disappointments."[4] He contends that authentic leaders are "more concerned about servicing others than they are about their own success or recognition. This is not to say that authentic leaders are perfect. Every leader has weaknesses, and all are subject to human frailties and mistakes. Yet by acknowledging failings and admitting error, they connect with people and empower them to take risks."[5]

The second inspirational source for the term authentic came to us from the title of John McWhorter's powerful book, *Authentically Black: Essays for the Black Silent Majority.*[6]

By openly discussing why he feels that so many African Americans continue to define themselves by race and examining what he calls the "cult of Victimology, Separatism, and Anti-Intellectualism," McWhorter steps boldly into the turbulent waters of African American no-no's and directly confronts African American sacred cows which have heretofore intimidated less authentic souls.

For the purposes of this book we define authentic African American leadership as that leadership which meets our three-part test. First, it must be leadership which identifies and confronts major barriers to African American advancement, as opposed to merely addressing minor or simple news-grabbing issues. Second, it is leadership that is unselfish and intended for the betterment of others. Third and finally, it is leadership that is virtuous by generally accepted American standards. We will offer more on this matter in later chapters, but let us now turn to some of the most notable examples of authentic African American leadership from the past.

During slavery we had the authentic leadership of men like Frederick Douglass and women like Harriet Tubman and Sojourner Truth, who identified slavery as the primary barrier to advancement and confronted it head on. After Emancipation and during the Reconstruction period, we had the powerful leadership of W. E. B. Du Bois, Booker T. Washington, Thaddeus Stevens, Charles Sumner, and Benjamin Singleton, who need no introduction from us.

The period of racial prejudice and racial discrimination launched by the 1896 *Plessy v. Ferguson* trial attracted leaders like Justice John Marshall, Ida B. Wells, William Dean Howells, Mary White Ovington, Oswald Garrison Villard, A. Philip Randolph, and William English Walling, all individuals who identified and confronted in unselfish and virtuous ways the primary barriers to African American advancement of their times.

And during the 1950s and 1960s, men and women like Carter G. Woodson, James Weldon Johnson, Eleanor Roosevelt, Mary McLeod Bethune, Charles Hamilton Houston, Thurgood Marshall, and Martin Luther King, Jr., provided authentic African American leadership that shattered the legal foundations upon which racial prejudice and discrimination rested.

Notice that not all authentic African American leaders we name here are African American—another seemingly radical notion. Each of these exceptional people, regardless of the color of his or her skin, played a pivotal role in leading African Americans in the United States to our present advantages. In this book, we are addressing the concept of "authentic African American leadership" from the point of view of leadership aimed at African American advancement, not from the point of view of the ethnicity of the individual. Indeed, though many challenges remain, the advantages we have gained as a result of past authentic leaders have been truly extraordinary.

Courage, determination, and tenacious commitment to the goals of racial equality and social justice characterized every single one of these leaders. They differed from lesser leaders in a very fundamental and critical way: all confronted the primary barriers that stood in the way of the advancement of African Americans.

The word *primary* is carefully chosen. On the long, difficult road to racial equality and social justice, African Americans have had to—and we continue to have to—overcome numerous barriers. Some barriers have been larger than others, some more dangerous than others, and some more central to our advancement than others. Deciding what is a primary barrier and what is simply a hindrance and choosing which barriers to expend scarce resources on are major decisions. Furthermore, choosing which barrier to target defines the quality and the core values of the leaders who make those choices.

Put plainly, we believe that authentic African American leaders, regardless of their race or ethnicity, are those who lead by tackling the primary barrier of their time—the barrier that, if eradicated, offers the greatest potential for advancement toward our goals of racial equality and social justice in America.

The Primary Barrier to Equality

What then, is the major barrier today that keeps African Americans from achieving full racial equality and social justice? There is much disagreement on this point. Many, including a majority of the most powerful leaders in contemporary African American culture, would say that the major barriers continue to be racial prejudice and discrimination. In fact, almost all current civil rights strategies are based on this premise. Current strategies to end discrimination in wages, home ownership, incarceration rates, employment, and health care are typically based on this assumption.

Without a doubt, racial prejudice and discrimination *were* the primary barriers impeding African American advancement toward economic, social, and political parity with white Americans—until the 1960s and 1970s. Certainly powerful, sometime overwhelming vestiges of racial prejudice and racial discrimination persist even to this day. But are prejudice and discrimination the *primary* barriers impeding the progress of today's African Americans toward our goals of racial equality and social justice? We argue that the answer is no.

In today's America one would be hard pressed to identify a single area of American social, economic, or political life, in medicine, literature, music, the arts, or sports, in which African Americans have not ascended to the very top in their chosen fields. The doors to advancement in virtually every American profession or occupation are open to talented and qualified African Americans. Racism and discrimination still offer a layer of difficulty along the road to advancement for African Americans, but they are less potent as barriers than they were in past years. Educational underachievement is much more powerful.

On January 20, 2009, at about 12:00 noon, on the steps of the capital in Washington, D.C., racism and racial discrimination were demonstrated, in a most visible way, to be feeble barriers to African American advancement, as Barack Obama was sworn in as the forty-fourth President of the United States of America. This fact is highly visible evidence that racism and discrimination no longer represent a ceiling to African American success—not to mention Oprah; Tiger Woods; Dr. Ben Carson Sr., Professor of Pediatric Neurosurgery, Johns Hopkins Children Center; Sylvia Rhone, CEO Elektra Entertainment Group; Kenneth Chenault, CEO American Express; James A Bell, CEO of Boeing Company; Richard Parson, Chairman Citi Group Inc; Carl Horton, CEO of Absolut Spirits Company Inc.; Cathy Hughes, CEO of Radio One; and a host of others. There is a street saying that makes our point in a clear and inequitable way. It goes like this: *Racism and discrimination can slow you down, but lack of education can knock you out.* Enough said! That's why we assert that the black–white achievement gap is now the primary barrier impeding African American progress, just as Jencks and Phillips suggest. To be sure, it's not the only obstacle standing in the way of racial equality and social justice; it's just the primary one.

This assertion will spark intense arguments. We would be foolish not to expect resistance, even anger, in response. The notion that racial prejudice and discrimination are the key civil rights challenges impeding African American progress has deep roots in African American culture, and its grip will be loosened only with the greatest struggle. Given this reality, it can be expected that most current African American leaders will strenuously resist any suggestion that their basic assumption about the African American disadvantage should be reconsidered.

If you doubt this, consider the reactions to others who have suggested that something other than racial prejudice and racial discrimination was the most important barrier impeding progress. When Harvard sociologist William Julius Wilson wrote in his book *The Declining Significance of Race: Blacks and Changing American Institutions* that the significance of race was waning, the African American leadership community threw everything but the kitchen sink at him.[7] The publication of his book not only sparked outrage from many African American notables, it also sparked the withdrawal of invitations for Dr. Wilson to speak at prestigious African American events.

Recall too, reactions to conservative scholar Dinesh D'Souza of the Hoover Institution when he proposed "that we now live in a post-racist era and that policies based on the assumption that racial prejudice and discrimination are responsible for the current condition of the Black population in the United States do more harm than good."[8] In his book *The End of Racism*, D'Souza even had the audacity to criticize the civil rights movement's—in his words—"flawed assumptions about the nature of racism," arguing that the civil rights movement cleaves to the incorrect assumption that racism is an authentic expression of the true nature of the American society, not simply a departure from American ideals. As with others who have made such claims, he endured the wrath of African American leaders.

We do not support everything that either Wilson or D'Souza sets forth, although some of their perspectives resonate. The vestiges of racial discrimination and prejudice remain a large problem in our society. But by recognizing the gains that African Americans have made over the past four decades and the resulting advantages and opportunities that we now enjoy, we believe it is time for leaders to update their thinking about racism and its legacy by reassessing its contribution to African American disadvantage.

The Stigma of Racial Inferiority

Harvard economist Glenn Loury helps to illuminate this new direction. In the introduction to his commanding book, *The Anatomy of Racial Inequality*, Loury asserts: "I will argue that 'racial stigma' should be given pride of place over 'racial discrimination' as the concept which best reflects the causes of African American disadvantage."[9] He draws a careful distinction between the two terms. "[Racial] discrimination is about how people are treated," Loury explains, whereas "stigma is about who, at the deepest cognitive level, they are understood to be."[10]

Accepting Loury's sharp distinction between racial discrimination and racial stigma leads us to the conclusion that with respect to concepts that impede African American progress, stigma is the more potent of the two concepts. If stigma is, as most dictionaries define it, a negative connotation tied to a particular thing, individual, or group; a sign of social unacceptability; a mark of disgrace, reproach, or infamy; a moral blemish or other characterizations of unworthiness, and if, at the deepest cognitive level, an observer believes a subject to be stigmatized, there is little chance that the observer will view the subject as an equal. Viewing the subject as unequal provides the foundation for discrimination, how the subject is treated. This being so, we could view racial stigma as a, and maybe the, root cause of racial discrimination. Therefore, as Loury suggests, as a causal agent, racial stigma should be given pride of place over racial discrimination.

Almost twenty-five years ago, a similar view was expressed in a *New Republic* article, "Rumors of Inferiority: The Hidden Obstacles to Black Success in America," written by social psychologist Jeff Howard and physician and ordained Minister Ray Hammond. They wrote:

> We are convinced that Black people today, because of gains in education, economic status, and political leverage that we have won as a result of the civil rights movement, are in a position to substantially improve the conditions of our communities using the resources already at our disposal. Our thesis is simple: the progress of any group is affected not only by public policy and by the racial attitudes of society as a whole, but by that group's capacity to exploit its own strengths. Our concern is about factors that prevent Black Americans from using those strengths.[11]

Expanding on this theme, Howard and Hammond proposed that "rumors of Black inferiority" were a key factor thwarting African American progress. Put simply, they suggested that black people have a tendency to avoid intellectual competition primarily because they have internalized the larger society's image of black intellectual inferiority. This, in turn, perpetuates poor academic performance—and the cycle continues. "Intellectual inferiority," conclude Howard and Hammond, "like segregation, is an idea whose time has passed. Like segregation, it must be removed as an influence in our lives."[12]

This point of view meshes with our own beliefs. Whether you call it racial stigma, as Loury does, or rumors of inferiority, as Howard and Hammond do, this idea is deeply persuasive. Academic underachievement of African American youth perpetuates the stigma of intellectual inferiority, and this stigma—more than anything else—is the primary barrier impeding African American's progress toward the long-sought goals of full racial equality and social justice. We make our case for this point of view in Chapter 3.

The central questions are: What must we do to eradicate the rumors of African American inferiority once and for all? How can we remove the stigma? The best way, and perhaps the only way, is to raise the academic achievement of African American students—all of them—everywhere. And how can we accomplish this? The same way we have done everything else—through leadership. Determined, courageous, and committed authentic African American leadership.

What Is the Cause of the Gap?

If we want to move forward, leaders in the African American community must rally around the cause of closing the achievement gap. This change of direction will not be easy; it will demand difficult choices and a willingness to give up some sacred notions. Above all, a commitment to closing the achievement gap will require contemporary African American leaders to move beyond the concept that the African American disadvantage is entirely due to racial prejudice, racial discrimination, and the failures of government. This is not to say that these are not still problems, sometimes rampant, only that they are no longer the primary barrier to racial equality.

It will also require leaders with widely diverse constituencies and different points of view to come to consensus around intervention strategies targeted at improving the academic achievement of African American students. Given the fact that there are wide differences among African American leaders regarding civil rights tactics, strategies, and even goals, this, too, will be no simple task.

But the task should be aided by advances in research and statistical methods, which have given us a better understanding of many factors underlying the black–white achievement gap. What we know about *why* the gap exists, which we discuss in Chapter 4, must point the way to strategies and solutions for eradicating it.

That, of course, begs the next important question. What precisely do we know? From the very beginning, researchers and others have pondered the root causes of the gap. Is it the result of heredity or environment? The debate has been long and intense, with the pendulum swinging back and forth. The debate heated up in the 1920s and again in the 1960s when James Coleman and his colleagues published their influential study titled *Equality of Educational Opportunity* (more widely known as The Coleman Report), which found that black students in the United States scored substantially lower on standardized tests than white students did.[13] This finding strengthened the hand of those who contended that heredity was the root cause of the gap, while it invigorated the efforts to find fault with the Coleman study of those who supported the environmental argument.

The debate resurfaced in the mid-1990s, when Richard Herrnstein and Charles Murray published their controversial book, *The Bell Curve: Intelligence and Class Structure in American Life*. Their thesis suggests to us that blacks score lower than whites on tests (on average) because they are genetically inferior.[14] Whereas Herrnstein and Murray's book offended many readers, black and white alike, it at least spurred scholars to redouble their efforts to investigate and illuminate nongenetic explanations for the gap.

From the very discovery of the gap, scholars have disputed its causes. In 1995, Susan Mayer and Christopher Jencks organized a year-long workshop at the University of Chicago, bringing together scholars from many disciplines and universities to study "meritocracy." Although assessing the bell-shaped curve was not technically the goal of the workshop, a day-long session was included for scholars who were interested in studying the causes of the gap. Susan Mayer and Harvard's Paul Peterson arranged a similar conference in 1996. One of the major conclusions emanating from this scholarly activity was that "many common explanations for the test-score gap, including racial disparities in family income, school resources, and innate ability, did not seem to be as important as their proponents claimed."[15] From our review of the research we conclude that despite voluminous scholarly activity seeking to determine the gap's causes, explanations of the gap's existence vary widely even among experts. In Chapter 4 we will discuss some of the most common explanations of the gap's existence as well present some thoughts of our own.

Because of the public perception that schools hold the major obligation for educating children, schools tend to get the lion's share of the
blame for the achievement gap. It is not surprising then that when the
nation looks to ways to reduce or close the gap, the major attention tends
to be aimed at improving schools. Recent research has yielded a much
clearer understanding of the extent to which, and the ways in which,
school variables influence the achievement gap. The belief that good
schools have a powerful impact on student achievement was the driving
force behind the No Child Left Behind (NCLB) Act. In 2001, for the first
time in our nation's history, closing the black–white achievement gap was
determined to be of such importance to our national interest that it
became a matter of federal policy. The purpose of the bill was clearly
stated right up front on the title page: "To close the achievement gap with
accountability, flexibility, and choice, so that no child is left behind."[16]

There is no question that improving school quality is a necessary condition to closing the achievement gap. But is improving school quality a
sufficient condition, in and of itself, to completely close the achievement
gap? We argue that the answer is no. Improving school quality is a necessary condition, but it is an insufficient condition to completely close
the gap. Let us be clear here, because this point underpins our main
argument. To close the gap we need not just good schools, but great
schools. There are many examples where great schools have done exem-
plary work in narrowing the achievement gap, even closing it in a few
cases, and their accomplishments must be applauded (see Chapter 6).
But to completely close the achievement gap—not just in a few schools
or even a few districts, but on a national basis—will require support for
school achievement and cognitive development from students' home and
community environments as well. Schools are of course central to a
child's cognitive development, but absent strong home and community
support they are rowing against the tide. We need to close the gap on a
national basis, and that will require an effort on all three fronts: the
school, home, and community.

We are not alone in this view. Scholarly support for the importance of
non-school factors in a child's cognitive development is massive.
Preeminent among scholars who support this view is psychologist and
scholar Laurence Steinberg, who holds that a child's cognitive development is influenced not just by school quality but also by factors beyond
the classroom.[17] In his bestselling book *Outliers,* Malcolm Gladwell points

out how non-school factors impact a child's cognitive development.[18] He argues that what a child does during summer vacation impacts the child's test performance. Drawing from the research of Johns Hopkins University sociologist Karl Alexander, he points out that wealthier kids have organized academic learning experiences during summer months and return to school in September with improved academic skills, whereas poorer kids, with fewer organized cognitive learning activities during summer, return to school in September having actually lost ground cognitively. More aggressively, he suggests the possibility that poor kids may even outlearn rich kids during the school year only to fall behind during the summer months. This concept, that a child's summer activity impacts school performance, offers meaningful leadership opportunities for home and community assistance in closing the achievement gap.

What Do People Think Is the Cause of the Gap?

Teachers, school administrators, and others frequently argue that the achievement gap is so complex and entrenched that factors beyond the school must be a central part of any intervention strategy. Schools alone cannot close the achievement gap on their own. In fact, there is now considerable research supporting this position.[19] The general public apparently shares this view. According to the most recent results of the Phi Delta Kappa/Gallup Poll of attitudes toward public schools, the public generally blames the achievement gap on factors such as home life and upbringing (87 percent), the amount of parental involvement (90 percent), student interest or lack thereof (80 percent), and the community environment (66 percent).[20]

The influence of other socioeconomic factors such as income and wealth disparities, the legacy of slavery, educational disparities, discrimination, and other kinds of oppression are often cited as causes of the achievement gap. Columnist James Traub has argued in the *New York Times* that class and socioeconomic status are major predictors of a child's success in school.[21] And Traub's *New York Times* colleague, Richard Rothstein, in *Class and Schools: Using Social, Economic, and Educational Reform to Close the Black–White Achievement Gap*, argues that class and race are connected and these factors create disparities in schools and beyond.[22] His point that closing the achievement gap should not be viewed as solely the school's burden is, in our view, reasonable, but we find no room for agreement with what we understand to be his major premise: that these social and class conditions must be ameliorated before lower-class children can be taught to high levels. Rather we hold that teaching these children to high levels is the solution to the class and socioeconomic problem.

School-quality factors—which are at the core of the NCLB reform strategy—comprise only a portion of the variables, including family background and community environment, that affect student academic performance. There are many who feel that in fact the non-school factors outweigh school quality in predicting student achievement. We can, however, speak from personal experience as educators and administrators, and assure you that strong school quality has the power to overcome non-school factors that would otherwise harm a child's ability to be academically successful.

The Houston Independent School District (HISD) is a large inner-city district inside the fourth largest city in America. In the early 2000s the HISD had more than 280 schools, of which approximately 173 were elementary schools. It was not unusual for two or more elementary schools to be serving essentially the same communities, with similar demographics, similar levels of parental educational attainment, and similar community impact. Yet, in several cases where two or more schools served essentially the same populations of children, one of the schools experienced high rates of student success while the others struggled and had student performance records like those considered typical of schools serving poor children from inner-city environments. Because all of the children experienced the similar socioeconomic and sociopathological impacts, the difference in educational development experienced by the children had to be attributed to the school they attended. There is no doubt that negative non-school factors can make the education development of children more challenging. But these kinds of personal experiences emboldened us in the conclusion that great schools can go a long way toward overcoming many negative non-school factors.

We confess that our concurrence with some of these "beyond the school" assertions makes us a little nervous. Today, a few—yet too many—public educators feel they and their schools should not be held accountable for children's school performance. Citing non-school factors over which they have little or no control, they see no reason to exert themselves to eliminate the achievement gap. This kind of attitude endangers progress toward closing the gap. Recognizing that beyond-school factors are major determinants of student performance must in no way let schools off the hook. Any erosion of the school's responsibility for student academic performance will endanger student progress.

We have spent our lives in public and higher education and arguing passionately that schools should be held accountable for student performance, notwithstanding the student's poverty level, race, English proficiency, or ZIP code. Our mantra has always been, and remains, "No excuses! Teach the children to high levels." As public school administrators and university professors training individuals for teaching careers, we wanted those associated with leadership to accept responsibility for the achievement of students under their charge regardless of the student's socioeconomic status, limited English proficiency, or even when they came across the border. We felt that this no-excuses mantra, even in the face of some harmony with the fact that beyond-school factors hold some influence on student's school performance, was necessary in order to make the point that even though a child's non-school environment was not supportive of school success, we as teachers and school professionals would work our butts off to help the child to succeed.

Whereas we believe that, in the main, teachers and school professionals have accepted accountability for student learning and have taken on the no-excuses mantra, we know also that schools have not been able to close the achievement gap on nationwide basis. To close the achievement gap on a nationwide basis will require the active and effective involvement of leadership which can influence the home and community environments of African American children.

Still, superintendents and school board members must hold schools—and, by extension, school employees—accountable for their students' performance notwithstanding students' home circumstances. Again, no excuses! We echo this statement of Dr. Martin Luther King, Jr.: "The job of the school is to teach so well that family background is no longer an issue."[23]

Evidence, research, history, and common sense all make it abundantly clear that school quality is a major determinant of student performance and, therefore, a major determinant of the magnitude of the achievement gap. There are many places, in fact, where improving school quality alone has made a substantial difference in raising student performance and closing the black–white achievement gap.[24] Many are schools where almost 100 percent of the students come from low-income families, or where high percentages have limited English proficiency or learning disabilities, yet committed principals and teachers with the involvement of parents and community leadership have succeeded nonetheless.

Closing the achievement gap in a single school is one thing. But closing the achievement gap nationally is quite another. It simply cannot be done without the concerted, sustained efforts of local, state, and national leadership working together toward common goals. We, therefore, propose three goals.

First, African American leaders must embrace the view that home and family, community environment, and school quality are all important determinants of children's educational possibilities. Working together, we must design and implement gap-closing intervention strategies in the beyond-the-school factors as well as in the in-the-school factors.

Second, those of us in the education community must accept the point of view advanced by Dr. King and strive to create the level of school quality that can, in and of itself, close the achievement gap. We need to put away excuses and believe—honestly and deeply—that all children can learn, no matter their socioeconomic status or ZIP code.

Third, and finally, leaders who are African American must understand that this is *our* problem, and it is not going to be solved until we ourselves solve it. Leaders who are African American must engage in a way that inspires communities to become involved in the resolution of the problem. Rather than continue the age-old controversy about the causes of the achievement gap and how the responsibility for its intractability should be apportioned between the home, community, and school, we call on African American leaders to move forward with national intervention strategies on all three fronts.

These recommendations, we realize, represent a sharp departure from the current situation. At present, with the exception of a few courageous individuals, African American leaders are largely silent on the issue of the achievement gap. They mention it from time to time, but the priorities of national civil rights organizations are focused elsewhere.

It is encouraging that recently there have been small improvements in African American student achievement. Even as we appreciate these small improvements we can't accept them as major indications that the problem is being solved. With African American student academic improvement at the present rate it would be fifty to seventy years to close the gap even if the white student improvement is held constant. Furthermore, this small recent improvement has been due to improvement on only one front, school quality—and the leadership for that movement is almost entirely outside the African American leadership community. To actually close the gap, we will have need of effective movement on the home, family, and community fronts and this will require greater effort from African American leadership.

And so, this book is both a testament to a scarcity of authentic African American leadership on the achievement gap issue and a clarion call for a new leadership commitment. The achievement gap cannot be eliminated unless and until African American leadership begins to focus intently on addressing the unacceptable underperformance of black students relative to their white peers. We know these students can do better. They can perform as well as their white peers if they are provided the right learning environments, and they receive the messages of our high expectations that they in fact can succeed. Our challenge is to provide the leadership that is needed to make those opportunities happen.

Authentic leadership in the past has enabled African Americans to come so far. Though we have much to be thankful for, we have overcome much. It is time for today's leaders to address what is now the primary barrier to racial equality and social justice.

Summary

In this book, our premise is fourfold:

1. The black-white achievement gap is the primary civil rights issue of our time.

2. Currently, there is no civil rights strategy with greater potential to advance African Americans toward the longstanding goals of racial equality and social justice than closing the black–white achievement gap.

3. Because the achievement gap is a function of both in-school and beyond-school factors, it cannot be closed without an African American leadership culture that supports closing the gap as its primary goal.

4, Contemporary African American leaders must start engaging in activities that close the gap and stop engaging in activities that (whether intentionally or unintentionally) perpetuate the gap. In short, they must change both their perspectives and their strategies.

We want to stimulate a national discussion about the black–white achievement gap and how to close it. Although the ideas we propose may spark some controversy, even anger, this in itself is productive. It is through debate and dialogue that we will find intelligent and enduring solutions to the most difficult and pressing problems of our time.

Step forward and engage in this vital debate. Enlist in the cause of eliminating the achievement gap. Rally the leadership. It is only through shared commitment and deep resolve and a willingness to join together, despite our differences, that we will prevail in solving this pernicious problem—just as those great authentic African American leaders of the past have done. Our children's futures, and our long-term well-being, depend on it.

CHAPTER 2

The Facts of the Matter

Yes, leadership is about vision. But leadership is equally about creating a climate where the truth is heard and the brutal facts confronted.

—Jim Collins, *Good to Great*

SES not
controlled.

HERE, AT THE OUTSET, it is important to clarify exactly what we mean by "achievement gap," since it can be defined in many different ways. The achievement gap refers specifically to the difference between the performance of white students and black students on academic assessments such as SAT and ACT scores, and graduation rates. While there are interesting differences in academic achievement among other racial and ethnic groups—white and Asian students, black and Hispanic students, and so on—our focus here is on how black students perform when compared with their white peers. Admittedly, there is a need to improve academic performance of all American students. But African American students' underperformance, on average, is so pronounced, and lags behind the performance of white students to such an extent that special attention to this problem is warranted. The use of the performance of white students as a benchmark intends in no way to suggest conflict between the two groups.

In this chapter, we examine students' performance in reading and math as they move through the K–12 educational system and post-secondary institutions. We also explore differential rates of participation in higher education. Throughout, our goal is to lay bare what we call the facts of the matter.

To understand that the black–white achievement gap not only exists but also persists over time, it is necessary to review numerous sets of data, in the form of numbers and percentages. Although a chapter full of numerical data might be mentally cumbersome or just plain boring (we tend to agree with this point), we ask you to continue reading and familiarize yourself with the issue at hand. We promise that the remaining chapters will not be as numerically dense as this one.

Why is this important? Despite the escalating discussion of the black–white achievement gap in the K–12 educational community and in a few corners of academia—fueled in no small part by the implementation of No Child Left Behind—surprisingly few people have given much thought to this issue. Many people are vaguely aware that black and white students, on average, perform differently in school, but relatively few possess an understanding of the full magnitude of the problem.

Even among those who are aware of the gap's existence and its magnitude, there is often a belief, as we said in the last chapter, that the divide cannot be bridged until poverty is eradicated and all vestiges of racism in our society are eliminated. In other words, these observers view the gap with a kind of determined resignation, and see efforts to eliminate it as futile. Dan Seligman, for example, in the December 12, 2005, issue of *Forbes* magazine called attempts to close the achievement gap "a fool's errand,"[1] while William J. Mathis, in a *Phi Delta Kappan* special section on the achievement gap entitled "A Bridge Too Far," referred to such efforts as "an exercise in ritualistic magic."[2]

Of course there are even those who doubt that the black–white achievement gap exists. Those skeptics say it is an artifact of biased tests or is not as big as people say it is. But this is ludicrous. Performance disparities show up on virtually every measure of student achievement. It's obvious that the problem is real, it's undeniable, it's big, it's not going away, and, in some cases, it's getting worse.

In this chapter, we want to make it inescapably clear that the black–white achievement gap does exist. We will examine what the gap looks like, how it manifests itself, how large it is, and how it has changed (or, in some cases, not changed) over time.

Why is this scrutiny of the data so important? As Jim Collins observes in *Good to Great,* "One thing is certain: You absolutely cannot make a series of good decisions without first confronting the brutal facts."[3] This, no doubt, will be difficult to do, but confronting the brutal truths of the black–white achievement gap is a necessary condition to correcting the problem.

The Beginnings: School Readiness

It has been widely reported that by the twelfth grade, black students, on average, lag far behind their white peers academically. But this problem doesn't simply appear out of nowhere. When does it begin, and how does it evolve as students progress through school?

The Early Childhood Longitudinal Study, Kindergarten Class of 1998–1999 (ECLS-K), a national assessment program administered by the U.S. Department of Education, has been tracking the progress of a national sample of children who entered kindergarten during the 1998–99 school year. The results tell us whether there is a performance gap between black and white children when they begin school, and what happens as they grow older.[4]

Researchers analyzing the ECLS-K data have found that the reading and mathematics skills of black and white children do, in fact, differ at the point of school entry, but the differences are small.

One way to compare the achievement of young white and black children is to look at the extent to which they possess specific reading and math skills. As shown in Figure 2.1, white children entering kindergarten were more likely than black children to know their letters (74 percent vs. 59 percent) and to display an understanding of the correspondence between sounds and letters appearing at the beginning (36 percent vs. 21 percent) and the end (21 percent vs. 11 percent) of words. By the end of first grade, however, the achievement gap in these three areas was greatly reduced, as the vast majority of black and white children alike mastered these foundational skills.

The achievement gap in a more advanced reading skill area—recognizing sight words—looks different. Very few white or black children entering kindergarten were able to recognize common words in text by sight. By the end of first grade, 88 percent of white children displayed proficiency in sight word recognition, compared with 71 percent of black children. So, while there is little or no gap at the beginning of kindergarten, over the year, the gap grows to 17 percent.

In math (see Figure 2.2), the results are similar to those observed in reading. Differences between the percentages of white and black kindergartners

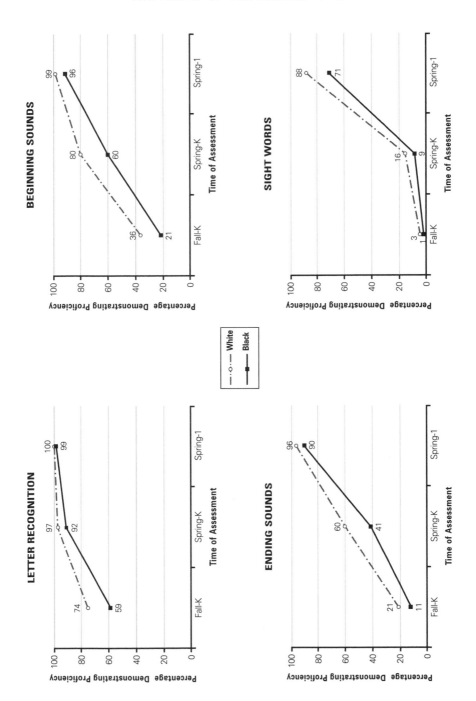

FIGURE 2.1. Percentages of black and white children demonstrating proficiency in specific reading skill areas. Source: U.S. Department of Education, National Center for Education Statistics, Early Childhood Longitudinal Study Data, Kindergarten Class of 1998–99.

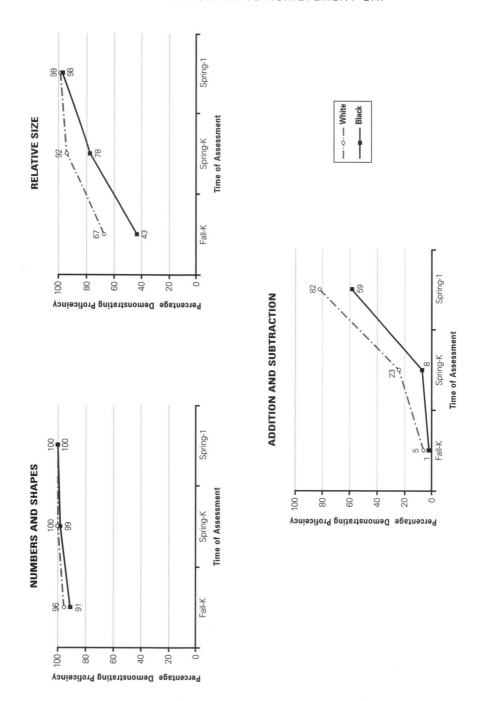

FIGURE 2.2. *Percentages of black and white children demonstrating proficiency in specific mathematical skill areas.* Source: U.S. Department of Education, National Center for Education Statistics, Early Childhood Longitudinal Study Data, Kindergarten Class of 1998–99.

who knew their numbers and shapes (96 percent vs. 91 percent) and who understood relative size (67 percent vs. 43 percent) diminished by the end of first grade, at which point the vast majority of students had mastered these skills. But in the more challenging area of addition and subtraction, the black–white achievement gap grew between kindergarten and first grade. Only 5 percent of white kindergartners and 1 percent of black kindergartners demonstrated proficiency in adding and subtracting. By the end of the first grade, this figure rose to 82 percent for white children but only to 59 percent for black children.

In summary, these data on our nation's youngest students show that, on average, white children tend to outperform black children in reading and math at the point when these children enter school—and that these gaps grow as children progress through their elementary school years. Thus, if we think of the elementary school years as a race, the distance that young black children have to travel in order to "catch up" with their white peers keeps widening. These are the facts of the matter.

The Early Years: Elementary School

In addition to analyzing the percentages of students who possessed particular skills, researchers have used the ECLS-K data to compare the overall reading and math achievement of various groups of students. To do so, they use scale scores, which provide a norm-referenced measure of performance.[5]

When one compares the overall reading performance of young white and black children, one sees that the average reading score of white kindergartners assessed during the fall of 1998 was 28 (on a scale ranging from 0 to 186), compared to 25 for their black peers—a gap of 3 points. By the time these same students reached the spring of their fifth-grade year, the gap between black and white students had grown to 17 points: 143 for white fifth graders and 126 for their black peers. Viewed differently, the average reading score of white children rose by 115 points between the fall of their kindergarten year and the spring of fifth grade. For black children, the gain was smaller, at 101 points (see Figure 2.3).

A similar pattern was found in mathematics, but the gap upon kindergarten entry was slightly larger than in reading and widened further with years of schooling (see Figure 2.4). The mean mathematics scale score for black kindergartners was 18 (on a scale from 0 to 153), compared with

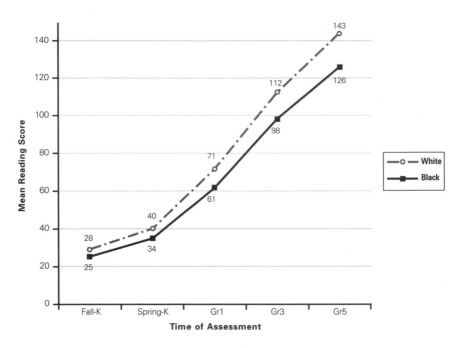

FIGURE 2.3. *Average reading scores for white and black children.* *Source: U.S. Department of Education, National Center for Education Statistics, Early Childhood Longitudinal Study Data, Kindergarten Class of 1998–99.*

23 for their white peers—a gap of 5 points. By the end of fifth grade, the gap had grown to 19 points. White students had a mean math score of 117, versus a mean score of 98 for black children.

Viewed from the "growth" perspective, the average math score of white children climbed by 94 points between the fall of their kindergarten year and the spring of fifth grade. For black children, the gain was significantly smaller, at 80 points.

So we know that the differences in the academic achievement of black and white children in reading and math are found as early as kindergarten. Recognizing these facts and the important role of early childhood experiences in school readiness, many school districts, nonprofit organizations, and other groups have been focusing on providing all students—particularly those from disadvantaged backgrounds—with access to quality early childhood learning experiences. Head Start was the first of many initiatives with this aim. We must note that there is an ongoing debate between researchers regarding whether Head Start produces lasting benefits, or whether its benefits erode by the time children reach third grade, a phenomenon commonly referred to as "fade-out."

Although there seems to be no definitive answer to the question at this time, our appraisal of the research so far finds the results to be mixed to slightly supportive of Head Start benefits. Additional research in the future will enable us to determine how well all these programs are succeeding in eradicating black–white achievement differences among the youngest students.

Meanwhile, let's go back to exploring the facts that are before us regarding the realities of the achievement gap. In addition to the gap that exists entering kindergarten and then grows over the school year, the data also show that the small achievement gaps between white and black children in kindergarten continue to widen as these students progress through the grades. This pattern is evident not only in overall reading and math proficiency scores but also in the data for specific skill areas. For example, 82 percent of white fifth graders demonstrate an understanding of the concept of place value in math, compared to just 52 percent of black fifth graders. Clearly, then, ensuring that all children enter school equally "ready to learn" appears to be extremely important—but this

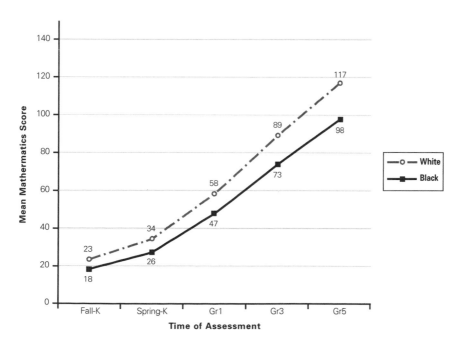

FIGURE 2.4. *Average mathematics scores for white and black children.* Source: U.S. Department of Education, National Center for Education Statistics, Early Childhood Longitudinal Study Data, Kindergarten Class of 1998–99.

alone is not enough. We must also tackle the problems that are causing black students' performance to slip even further as they progress through our education system.

The Pipeline: K–12 Education

Thus far, we have seen that small achievement gaps exist in reading and math when children begin their formal schooling. What happens after that? Data from the National Assessment of Educational Progress (NAEP) enable us to further explore how achievement gaps in reading and math evolve as students move through the grades. NAEP, funded by the U.S. Department of Education, assesses national samples of students in reading, math, and other subjects. Results are reported in terms of average proficiency scores (using a 500-point scale) as well as in terms of the percentages of students reaching successive levels of proficiency (i.e., basic, proficient, and advanced).

READING PROFICIENCY

First, let us look at the trend results for reading, as seen in Figure 2.5. According to NAEP findings:[6]

Grade 4

- The average reading proficiency of white fourth graders rose from 224 in 1992 to 231 in 2007, representing a gain of 7 points over the fifteen-year period.

- The average reading proficiency of black fourth graders declined between 1992 and 1994, then wavered for several years before rising to 203 in 2007, for an overall gain of 11 points over the entire fifteen-year period.

- The black–white achievement gap in fourth-grade reading narrowed slightly by 6 points, between 2000 (34 points) and 2007 (28 points).

Grade 8

- The average reading proficiency of white eighth graders increased slightly between 1992 and 2002, from 267 to 272, then dropped by one point to 271 in the 2005 assessment.

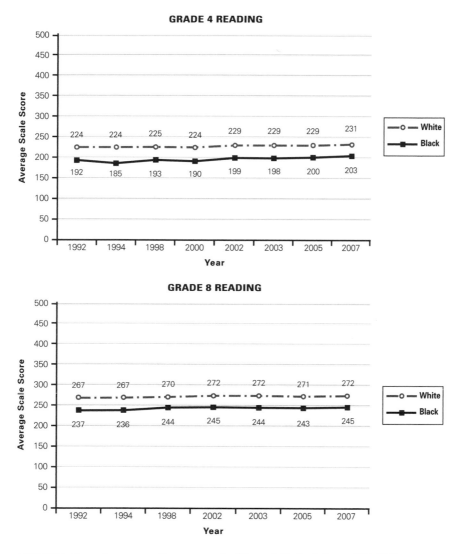

FIGURE 2.5. *Average reading scores of white and black students, 1992–2007.* Source: U.S. Department of Education, National Center for Education Statistics, National Assessment of Educational Progress (NAEP). http://nationsreportcard.gov.

▸ The average reading proficiency of black eighth graders rose from 237 in 1992 to 245 in 2002, then remained relatively steady at 245, until 2007.

▸ Although the black–white achievement gap appears to have diminished slightly in eighth-grade reading between 1992 (when

it was 30 points) and 2007 (27 points), the difference is not statistically significant.

Average assessment results are helpful for making broad generaliza-
tions, but they fail to capture underlying patterns and trends. For example, the average scores of a group may go up because greater numbers of
students at the low end of the performance spectrum are making
progress, or because more students are reaching the higher levels of proficiency. Therefore, it is important to dissect the NAEP results to study
changes over time in the percentages of white and black students who
have performed at various levels of reading proficiency. For simplicity's
sake, we will focus here on two thresholds: the percentage of students
performing at or above the *basic level* of reading proficiency (defined by
NAEP as "partial mastery of prerequisite knowledge and skills that are
fundamental for proficient work at a given grade") and the percentage
performing at or above the *proficient level* (defined as "solid academic performance").[7]

- In fourth grade, 46 percent of black students performed at or
  above the basic level of reading proficiency in 2007; this was an
  increase from 35 percent in 2000 (see Figure 2.6). Over the same
  time period, the percentage of white students performing at or
  above the basic level increased from 70 percent to 78 percent.

- Though gains were made between 2000 and 2007, only 14 percent of black fourth graders were proficient readers in 2007, compared with 43 percent of their white peers.

- Thus, what we see from these data is that the gains made by black
  students have been incremental, and relatively few are reaching
  the level of reading defined as "proficient."

- In eight grade, 55 percent of black students performed at or above
  the basic level of reading proficiency in 2007, reflecting no
  change since 2002. Over the same time period, the percentage of
  white students in this category also remained unchanged at 84
  percent.

- Only 13 percent of black eighth graders, compared with 40 percent of their white peers, were proficient readers in 2007.

GRADE 4 READING

		Black Students	White Students	*Gap*
2000	Basic level	35	70	*35*
2007	Basic level	46	78	*32*
2007	Proficient level	14	43	*29*

GRADE 8 READING

		Black Students	White Students	*Gap*
2002	Basic level	55	84	*29*
2007	Basic level	55	84	*29*
2007	Proficient level	13	40	*27*

FIGURE 2.6. Percentage of white and black students performing at each level of reading proficiency, 2000–2007.

MATHEMATICS PROFICIENCY

What about performance in mathematics? According to the most recent assessment data from NAEP, shown in Figure 2.7:[8]

> In fourth grade, the average math proficiency of white students increased from 220 in 1990 to 248 in 2007—a gain of 28 points. Over the same time period, the average proficiency of black students climbed from 188 to 222, an increase of 34 points.

> As a result of these trends, the 26-point math achievement gap between white and black fourth graders in 2007 was smaller than in any prior assessment year.

> In eighth grade, the average math proficiency of white students increased by 21 points between 1990 and 2007, from 270 to 291. Over the same period, the average math proficiency of black eighth graders rose by 23 points, from 237 to 260.

> As a result of these changes, the 31-point achievement gap between white and black eighth graders was smaller in 2007 than in 2005 (34 points) but was not significantly different from the 33-point gap in 1990.

Once again, this global view is helpful, but we want to know what patterns underlie the averages. What percentages of white and black students

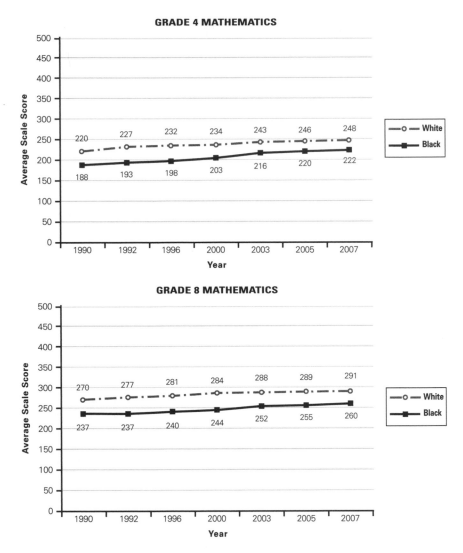

FIGURE 2.7. *Average math scores of white and black students, 1990–2007. Source: U.S. Department of Education, National Center for Education Statistics, National Assessment of Educational Progress (NAEP). http://nationsreportcard.gov.*

are reaching various levels of math proficiency? Here, as shown in Figure 2.8, we find that:

▶ In fourth grade, 64 percent of black students performed at or above the basic level of math proficiency in 2007—significantly higher than the 36 percent who did so in 2000. Among white students, 91 percent performed at or above the basic level in 2007 (up from 78 percent in 2000).

‣ Only 15 percent of black fourth graders performed at or above the proficient level in math in 2007, compared to roughly half (51 percent) of white fourth graders.

‣ In eighth grade, almost half (47 percent) of black students performed at or above the basic level of math proficiency in 2007, up from 31 percent in 2000. Among white students, 82 percent performed at this level in 2007 (up from 76 percent in 2000).

‣ Just 11 percent of black eighth graders performed at NAEP's proficient level in math in 2007, compared with 42 percent of their white peers.

GRADE 4 MATHEMATICS

		Black Students	White Students	Gap
2000	Basic level	36	78	42
2007	Basic level	64	91	27
2007	Proficient level	15	51	36

GRADE 8 MATHEMATICS

		Black Students	White Students	Gap
2000	Basic level	31	76	45
2007	Basic level	47	82	35
2007	Proficient level	11	42	31

FIGURE 2.8. *Percentage of white and black students performing at each level of math proficiency, 2000–2007.*

It is easy to lose the story line in all of these data. To summarize, black students in grades four and eight have made strides in reading and math over the years since NAEP began its assessment program. The black–white achievement gaps have been reduced in some areas. Despite the progress, however, severe performance disparities persist. Black students are far less likely than their white peers to be proficient in reading and math—the backbone of success in school and in life.

Interestingly, state- and district-level NAEP data show that black students do better in some states than others and in some districts than others. As a result, the size of the gap varies from place to place. For example, in 2007, the black–white achievement gap in fourth-grade reading (again on the 500-point NAEP scale) was 17 points in Arizona, but 33 points in Pennsylvania. Among eighth graders, the size of the gap ranged from 7 points in Hawaii to 38 points in Wisconsin.

Similarly, data from the 2007 NAEP Trial Urban District Assessment (TUDA)—a special NAEP study conducted in large urban school districts—show black–white achievement gaps in fourth-grade reading ranging from a low of 23 points in Cleveland and 25 points in Boston to 67 points in Washington, D.C. In fourth-grade math, gaps ranged from 22 points in New York City to 54 points in Washington, D.C.[9]

Nationally, and in many states and districts, the gap has become smaller over time due to the greater gains made by black students relative to white peers. *But in no place is the achievement gap anywhere close to zero.* In fact, we must bear in mind that, on average, the reading and math proficiency of eighth-grade black students in this country is much closer to that of white *fourth graders* than it is to that of white eighth graders.

Furthermore, these data are only for the students who are staying in school. Dropouts, who are disproportionately likely to be minority—as we see in the following section—tend to have even more limited skills. Brutal facts indeed.

High School Graduation Rates

Now that we have examined the achievement gap as students progress through K–12 education, the logical next question is, how many graduate? As it turns out, answering this question is more complicated than one might imagine. In the past, states calculated their graduation rates in different ways. The resulting rates were not only not comparable to one another; they were also largely meaningless, since states tended to calculate the rates according to whichever method would present the most advantageous picture.

In 2000, the Black Alliance for Educational Options (BAEO) commissioned researcher Jay Greene of the Manhattan Institute to conduct a pioneering study of the nation's low graduation rates, particularly among students of color. As Greene remarked at the time, "Unless we have reliable information about graduation rates we cannot begin to consider the severity of problems or make comparisons about the effectiveness of schools in different areas or for different groups of students."[10]

To provide a much more accurate estimate of actual graduation rates than had previously been available, Greene used a simple but elegant method. First, he identified the eighth-grade public school enrollment for each jurisdiction (nation, individual states, and individual districts) and for each subgroup within that jurisdiction during the fall of 1993. Next, Greene obtained the number of regular high school diplomas awarded in the spring of 1998 when those eighth graders should have been graduating from high school. To adjust for mobility (the numbers of students moving into or out of an area), he statistically adjusted the 1993 eighth-grade counts for the student population increase or decrease in that jurisdiction—overall and for each subgroup—between the 1993–94 and 1997–98 school years.

Greene's analysis showed that nationally the high school graduation rate for white students in the class of 1998 was 78 percent. For black students, it was 56 percent. In other words, more than two out of every ten white students and more than four out of every ten black students left high school before graduating. Greene has since repeated the study for subsequent classes of students. For the class of 2002, national graduation rates were 56 percent for black students versus 78 percent for white students—virtually identical to those for the class of 1998.[11]

Like the NAEP research, Greene's studies also show that graduation rates vary widely from state to state for black and white students alike. The states with the highest graduation rates for black students in the class of 2002 were Rhode Island and Oklahoma (70 percent) and Maryland (69 percent). At the other end of the spectrum, the state with the lowest graduation rate for black students was New York (42 percent). In five states, the graduation rate for black students in the class of 2002 was 50 percent or less: Nebraska, Wisconsin, Florida, Georgia, and New York.

Comparing the graduation rates for white and black students within various states provides some sobering contrasts. For example, while the graduation rate for black students in New York, as just noted, was 42 percent, the graduation rate for white students was 81 percent. In other states, the black–white gap in graduation rates was smaller, however. For example, in Maryland, the graduation rate was 81 percent for white students while for their black peers it was 69 percent. Thus, even in the "best" state scenario, the gap in graduation rates between white and black students is still, at 12 percent, unacceptably large.

The Endpoint of K–12: College Readiness

The next segment of the education pipeline, beyond high school, is college. Is there any difference, we want to know, in the percentages of black and white high school graduates who are prepared to continue with their education—and choose to do so?

Greene's research makes it possible not only to compare high school dropout rates but also to compare college readiness rates among white and black students. To be counted as "college ready," students had to meet three criteria: they must graduate from high school, they must have taken certain courses in high school that colleges require for the acquisition of necessary skills, and they must demonstrate basic literacy skills.

We find that for the class of 2002 nationally, 40 percent of white students but only 23 percent of black students were deemed "college ready." As with high school graduation rates, college readiness rates for both racial groups varied significantly from state to state. In only two states (Massachusetts and Rhode Island) were more than one-third of the black students found to be college ready. More brutal facts.

SAT AND ACT SCORES

The two most commonly used college entrance exams are the ACT and the SAT. Data from these programs show that, historically, white students were overrepresented among SAT and ACT test takers and black students were underrepresented. In other words, the percentage of black ACT and SAT test takers was substantially lower than the percentage of black high school students. Over time, though, the numbers of white as well as black students taking these college admissions tests have been rising. According to recent data, while black students represent approximately 16 percent of the public school student population,[12] they represent 13 percent of ACT test takers[13] and 11 percent of SAT test takers.[14]

What about scores on these exams? SAT scores provide one measure of high school students' preparedness for college-level work (see Figure 2.9).

This figure shows that while the average combined SAT score of white students increased by 11 points from 1998 (1054) to 2008 (1065), the average combined score of black students declined by 4 points (from 860 to 856). As a result of these trends, the gap in average SAT composite scores between white and black students increased from 1998 (194 points) to 2008 (209 points).

When we dig further into the historical data, we find that the widening of the SAT score gap between white and black students is part of a longer-term trend. A 1976 study conducted by The College Board found a gap of approximately 240 points (or 20 percent) between the average SAT combined score of black students and that of their white peers. By the late 1980s, the gap was down to 189 points.[15] Since then, however, it has risen fairly steadily, increasing to the current gap of 209 points.

	1998			2008		
	White	Black	*Difference*	White	Black	*Difference*
SAT-Verbal/Reading	526	434	*92*	528	430	*98*
SAT-Math	528	426	*102*	537	426	*111*
SAT-Combined	1054	860	*194*	1065	856	*209*
ACT Composite	22.7	17.9	*4.8*	22.1	16.9	*5.2*

FIGURE 2.9. *Average SAT and ACT scores for white and black students, 1998 and 2008. Sources: College Board, 1998 Profile of College-Bound Seniors, Table 4–1; College Board, College-Bound Seniors, 2008, Table 8; U.S. Department of Education, Digest of Education Statistics, Table 132; ACT, ACT High School Profile, Graduating Class of 2008, Selections from the 2008 National Score Report.*

The average scores of black students on the SAT are not only far below the scores of whites and Asian Americans. They trail the scores of *every other major ethnic group in the United States,* including students of Puerto Rican and Mexican backgrounds—many of whom are not native speakers of English. On the critical reading test in 2008, for example, white students had the highest average score (528 points), followed by Asian or Asian American students (513), Mexican, Mexican American, Puerto Rican, and other Hispanic or Latin American students (scores ranged from 454 to 456), and finally, dead last, black students (430).

On the SAT math exam in 2008, Asian students posted the highest average score (581), followed by white students (537) and students from different Hispanic groups (453 to 463)—while black students once again had the lowest average score (426).[16]

ACT scores, too, vary by race. In the high school graduating class of 2008, black test takers earned an average ACT score of 17, compared with 22 for their white peers—a gap of 5 points; ACT scores are also shown on Figure 2.9.

Of course just because you take these tests does not mean you are college ready. To assess racial/ethnic gaps in college readiness, researchers have compared the percentages of students in various groups who met benchmark scores that they define as representing college readiness. In the 2008 graduating class, more than two-thirds (68 percent) of all students, and 77 percent of white students, met the college readiness benchmark score of 18 on the English portion of the ACT, while only 37 percent of black students did. On the ACT math test, 43 percent of all students and 49 percent of white students, but only 11 percent of black students, met the benchmark score of 22.[17]

College Enrollment, Persistence, and Completion

College enrollment rates have increased over time in response to the rising emphasis placed on higher education, and people have become aware of the benefits associated with a college degree. Not surprisingly, then, between 1972 and 2006, the percentage of students who enrolled in college immediately after graduating from high school climbed from 49 to 66 percent. This figure has remained relatively steady since the late 1990s.

College enrollment rates have risen for white and black students over time, but a gap remains. In 2006, about 69 percent of white students enrolled in college right after high school graduation, marking a substantial increase from the approximately 50 percent who did so in the 1970s. Between 1984 and 1998, the rate of college enrollment rose faster for blacks than for whites, narrowing the gap between the two groups. In 2006, 56 percent of black students enrolled in college immediately after high school; among white students, the corresponding figure was 69 percent.[18]

Once students are enrolled in college, how do they perform? Historical data reveal that the percentage of black Americans earning a college degree has climbed substantially over the years, from just 1 percent in 1940—14 years before the *Brown v. Board of Education* decision was made—to 19 percent in 2006.

Looking more closely at the population of young adults (those between the ages of 25 and 29) is illuminating. As shown in Figure 2.10, only 6.7 percent of young black adults in 1971 had earned a college degree, compared with 18.9 percent of their white peers. A little more than three decades later, in 2003, 17.5 percent of young black adults had earned a college degree, compared to 34.2 percent of their white peers. By 2007, the figures were 19.5 percent vs. 35.5 percent, respectively. Thus,

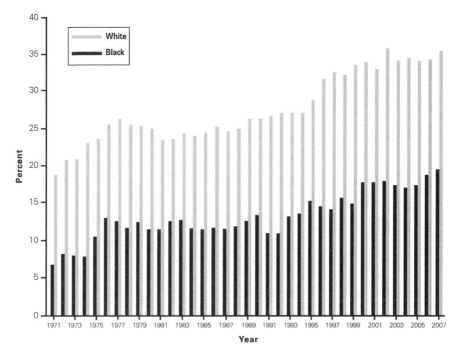

FIGURE 2.10. *Percentage of adults (age 25–29) earning a college degree, by race, 1971–2007.*
Source: U.S. Department of Commerce, Census Bureau, Current Population Survey (CPS), March Supplement, 1971–2007.

we see that young white adults are approximately twice as likely as their black peers to earn a college degree.[19]

A similar pattern is found in the upper echelons of the education system. Though we do not delve into these data here, the black–white achievement gap is also present in data derived from graduate school exams like the Medical College Admissions Test (MCAT), the Graduate Management Admissions Test (GMAT), the Graduate Record Examination (GRE), and the Law School Admissions Test (LSAT).[20] The evidence goes on and on.

Thus, the story is one of good news tempered with bad. To be sure, significant progress has been made in some areas over time. Yet equity in educational achievement remains an elusive goal.

Summary

The data presented in this chapter tell a powerful story about African American educational achievement in this country. Throughout this story, there is one consistent underlying truth: *On academic matters, African*

American students have continuously achieved significantly below their white counterparts, on average. This is the reality of the situation. It cannot be denied. The brutal truth is there in black and white, so to speak. And the truth hurts.

So we must face up to the uncomfortable, distasteful, and deeply distressing reality that, on average, African American students score well below their white peers on just about every scholastic assessment measure in use today. All these statistics shout out the painful fact that there is a black–white achievement gap. The evidence is irrefutable. It's an undeniable truth that we have a serious educational problem in America. The facts can no longer be interpreted in any other way.

Joe Louis, the great boxing champion, is credited with saying, "You can run, but you can't hide." He was referring to an opponent's stated strategy to use quickness and movement to defeat him, but his comment has great relevance to the current status of African American leadership culture and the black–white achievement gap. We can run, but we cannot hide from the facts; and we can be certain that the facts will not hide from us. Discussion of the achievement gap in the education literature, newspaper stories, and education trade journals is beginning to heat up, and in some instances has become so sweeping that its existence is starting to be taken as predestined, even by some African Americans. As state and federal education policies increasingly embrace testing and accountability as a part of their school improvement initiatives, the black–white achievement gap is becoming more and more visible. Yet, despite the gap's wide discussion in the media and education literature, it has triggered little serious discussion in the African American leadership community.

Since there is no longer any question about the existence of a black–white achievement gap, the question becomes, "How shall we respond to this reality?" Shall we simply continue to lament the achievement gap, but do little of consequence to address it, hoping instead, that it will eventually go away on its own? Shall we take it as inevitable, with the view that that's just the way things are, as too many in our society currently seem to be doing? Shall we proceed under the premise that the gap doesn't matter, since it's of little consequence to us? Or shall we press on thinking that solving it is someone else's problem?

No, now is the time to see the gap as what it really is: a major barrier to racial equality and social justice in America that must be confronted and defeated, much in the same manner that past problems that obstructed African American advancement in this country have been confronted and defeated by past African American leaders.

Therefore it is time now for us—African American leaders—to redirect our energies from other, still important, but less destructive problems, and devote them to solving this all-encompassing one.

Of course we are embarrassed about it. Even so, we need to get past the embarrassment because it's not going to go away without our deep and committed involvement. Indeed, it's more than just involvement that is needed, it is dedicated leadership to confront this problem head on that we need; we must spend our energies and resources searching for solutions.

Fortunately, there are a few, far too few, African American leaders who are not ignoring the problem. We salute them and pledge to do all we can to increase their numbers. Unfortunately, these leaders represent the exception rather than the rule.

Now, with these facts in hand—now that we can say for sure that there is a black–white achievement gap in the United States and that in some places it is still growing—let us move forward. We can reflect on these data and begin to answer the many questions that arise from them. Whether or not you agree with the path we propose for closing the achievement gap is a matter of individual choice. But surely we can all *action* agree on this: something momentous must be done. *needed*

CHAPTER 3

"Okay, We Have a Black–White Achievement Gap. So What?"

Disparities in education and training are likely the greatest source of the long-term increase in inequality.
— Ben Bernanke, Federal Reserve Chairman

THE CHAUNCEY Conference Center at the Educational Testing Service (ETS) sits on a charming 370-acre, hilly wonderland conveniently located midway between Philadelphia and Manhattan. In their advertisements, Chauncey officials boldly declare that the center is the kind of place where breakthrough thinking takes place. Their claim would be hard to dispute, as few conference locations can match Chauncey's bucolic charm, guest amenities, and executive accommodations.

It was at this pristine location on a pleasant June 2005 morning that approximately fifty presidents of the historically black colleges and universities (HBCUs) gathered to take part in the 2005 HBCU/ETS Presidents Conference. The conference—founded in 1983 through the leadership of Gregory Anrig, former president of ETS; Donald Stewart, president of Spelman College; and the inimitable Norman Francis, president of Xavier University—stated as its purpose: "to combine resources and expertise to address issues of mutual concern to HBCUs and ETS."

It should come as a surprise to no one that the most pressing issue of mutual concern to HBCUs and ETS in 1983 was the fact that African American students as a group, especially graduates of the HBCUs, were scoring well below white students on the ETS-developed, owned, and managed National Teacher Examination (NTE), and too few were passing. Some states required students to pass the NTE in order to gain certification to teach in their state, and the NTE stood as a massive roadblock to the teaching profession for many HBCU graduates.

The program kicked off right on time with warm welcoming remarks from conference convener Earl S. Richardson, president of Morgan State University. After about ten minutes of informative and challenging remarks, Richardson introduced Kurt M. Landgraf, president and CEO of ETS, who gave a rousing overview of the occasion and a passionate call to action to address the African American underperformance problem. These remarks were followed by the real meat of the conference program—presentations from various experts, education scholars, and ETS researchers and statisticians, most using colorful PowerPoint presentations, all telling the story of specific aspects of African Americans' underperformance on major tests compared to their white peers.

It was during the afternoon session that it became clear that the weight of the African American underperformance on major academic tests was weighing heavily on the HBCU presidents. During one particular question-and-answer session, questions became more emotional. Some presidents offered responses that were clearly defensive. Others questioned the accuracy of the data. Several offered typical, well-worn excuses for the underperformance of African American students. Some blamed the tests, test bias, and so forth. Several presidents seemed to be having difficulty dealing with the blunt realities that were portrayed by the data in many of the presentations.

But it was the sheer frankness of one questioner that fell upon the group like a ton of bricks. A gentleman in the back rose to ask permission to speak. When acknowledged, he said quite unflinchingly something to this effect: "Okay, we have a black–white achievement gap. So what?!"

What kind of question is that? What did he mean by "so what?" Was he suggesting that the black–white achievement gap is of no consequence? Many conference attendees seemed startled by the question. Judging from their facial expressions, they appeared to be grasping for the essence of it. Was his question really a statement expressing the thought that the gap doesn't matter? Or was the question an innocent call for a more fully developed explanation of the consequences of continued African American subpar performance on major academic tests?

In truth, maybe this question about the consequences of the gap had never been quite fully answered. Maybe the reason that there had been so little focus on the closing-the-gap issue is that the "so what" question has not been adequately addressed. What many of us think is quite obvious may, in fact, not be. So, let us interpret this question as one that calls out for help in understanding the consequences of the continued, ever-widening black–white achievement gap.

Because this question deserves a thoughtful and comprehensive answer, we now call upon the African American leadership community to engage in very deep and high-level discussions of this question. It's helpful to broaden the question somewhat so let the question become this: As we approach the end of the first decade of the twenty-first century and look toward a rapidly changing global economic and social infrastructure, what impact will a continued, or ever-widening black–white achievement gap have on African Americans' traditional goals of equality and social justice in this country?

Let us engage the sociologists, psychologists, and economists of our HBCUs, other colleges and universities, and national think tanks in discussions around this question. Let us debate this issue in small gatherings of sorority and fraternity meetings and in large gatherings, including national conferences of the National Association for the Advancement of Colored People (NAACP), the National Urban League (NUL), and the Congressional Black Caucus (CBC). Sure, it will take courage to openly discuss this sensitive subject, but the returns will be of inestimable value in our quest to close the gap.

It's been said that "opinions are like backsides, everybody has one." We too, have an opinion on this matter. We can think of any number of undesirable consequences of a continued black–white achievement gap. But, solely as the starting point for discussion, allow us to suggest three responses to the "so what" question.

– RESPONSE ONE –

The Black–White Achievement Gap Strengthens the "Blacks Are Intellectually Inferior" Stereotype

Of all the various negative consequences of the black–white achievement gap, this—the support it yields for supporters of the "blacks are less well endowed intellectually than whites" argument—is by far the most offensive.

It is a stereotypical burden that African Americans have had to bear since coming to these shores in the early seventeenth century. Some argue that it goes back even further into Biblical days. The idea lives on in the minds of many, notwithstanding the strong statement from the world's largest organization of individuals interested in anthropology, the American Anthropological Association, and the less powerful, yet very clear statement from the American Psychological Association.[1,2] Both declare that there is not much evidence of a link between race and intellect, and what little there is fails to support the genetic hypothesis. *Despite the clear statements by these creditable professional organizations, many ordinary people still believe in black intellectual inferiority.*

Despite the fact that there is still little consensus around how to define the term *intelligence,* and despite the fact that we are not yet sure whether intelligence is a single trait or whether there are multiple intelligences, the stereotype persists. Even though the term *race* is more a social construct than an anthropological identity, there are still those who argue that race and intellect are linked.

Despite our propensity to view people through a racial lens, sorting them into white, black, brown, Asian, or other groups, these distinct divisions do not seem to have a scientific foundation. There are no specific inherited characteristics that all members of one group have that are not found in other groups. In fact, Ian F. Haney Lopez argues that intragroup differences exceed intergroup differences.[3] If truth be told, there may be less variation between groups than within groups. The concept of race just doesn't have a biological underpinning, it is a social construction. Although as a social construction, race has acquired a legal footing, as a biological construct capable of dividing groups up by intelligence potential, the consensus among scientists is that there is just not much scientific support for such a concept.

Don't make the mistake of thinking that the idea that blacks are intellectually inferior genetically is a fringe idea though, supported by a few way-out psychologists, anthropological nerds, far-right academics, and white supremacists. Respected academics and sociologists such as Arthur Jensen of the University of California and Philippe Rushton of the University of Western Ontario advocate the idea that blacks, with respect to intelligence, are inferior to whites. And these two men may represent only the tip of the iceberg. Deep in the minds of many whites—and, if the ideas that are proposed in Sniderman and Piazza's book *The Scar of Race* are to be believed, many blacks—resides a good deal of receptivity to this abhorrent notion.[4]

Most Americans living today have scant, if any, memory of even the pre-1954 educational struggles of African Americans, and of course they have no direct experiences relating to the black experience during the Colonial, Civil War, or post–Civil War days. Although they have access to historical accounts of America's racial struggles, for the most part, their point of view regarding the educational potential of African Americans is based not on the aforementioned days gone by, but on what they have personally seen and experienced. And what have they personally seen and experienced? They have personally seen and/or experienced that *almost without exception, African Americans lag behind every other racial/ethnic group on every academic assessment imaginable.* African Americans doing less well than their white peers is an empirical reality for them. So they can argue that their point of view is based on the empirical evidence they see, hear, and experience daily. Could it be that their point of view is based more on the realities of their world than on racial bigotry? For many, this could be.

Second, there is evidence to suggest that the idea of black intellectual inferiority even resides in the minds of some (maybe even many) African Americans. We cannot identify them as racial bigots, can we? In their book *The Scar of Race,* Sniderman and Piazza report clear evidence that many African Americans are given to many of the same negative characterizations of other African Americans that we often associate with the racially bigoted attitudes of racist whites. Moreover, Sniderman and Piazza suggest that when they found statistically significant differences between the views of African Americans and whites on these matters, African Americans actually had more negative evaluations of other African Americans than whites did.[5]

The point here is a simple one. The continued and widening black–white achievement gap continues to reinforce the stereotype of racial inferiority. This burden weighs more heavily on today's young African American students than all the yesteryears of slavery, creating a vicious circle. The expectation that the gap exists because of inferiority reinforces low expectation, which leads to low achievement, and expands the gap. Further, the deleterious effects of the gap constantly build as it becomes a self-fulfilling prophecy, extending its deleterious effects far into the future and eroding the educational potential of young African Americans of tomorrow.

In his research, Claude Steele, social psychology professor at Stanford University, examined the premise that the stereotype of African Americans' being less academically capable than whites actually creates a level of anxiety sufficient to impair performance when the stereotyped individual feels that his or her performance is under scrutiny.[6]

After conducting a series of experiments, he found that African American students performed less well on a test when the test form required them to indicate their race than when no such identification was required. He also found that African American students made more mistakes and did less well when the experimenter described the test as measuring verbal reasoning ability than when no such description was offered. In contrast, there was no difference in white students' performance regardless of required race identification or what the test was described as measuring. Thus, Steele concluded that when a stereotyped individual is under threat of being stereotyped, the resulting anxiety actually affects performance.

This principle of stereotype threat holds true for any stereotyped group. For example, girls are stereotyped as less capable than boys in math and science. Steele found that when girls are placed under the same threat of being stereotyped, their performance is similarly affected.

Thanks to Steele's research, there is little question that African American students are aware of their stereotypical burden and that they take tests with the idea that they will be stereotyped. The significance here is that the students themselves come to believe the stereotype, and then it becomes true for them. Now our task—the challenge for the African American leadership community—is to do our best to lift this burden by destroying this stereotype and setting our students free to be the best they can be. Dealing with this problem is also critical because letting the stereotype stand lets society at large feel comfortable not doing anything about the problem.

We turn now to our second response to the "so what" question.

– RESPONSE TWO –
The Achievement Gap Slows Down the Accumulation of African American Wealth

It would be difficult to find any aspect of the African American quest for racial equality and social justice in America more disconcerting than the vast and widening income gap between African Americans and their white counterparts. Despite the income success of many high-profile African Americans, in 2004 the African American family income was a little more than half that of a similar white family. Access to wealth is the scaffolding of each person's economic well-being and upward mobility, and neither racial equality nor social justice can ever become a reality as long as there are such wide gaps in income. Clearly, if there is any hope for racial equality and social justice for African Americans, this income gap must be reduced—and some day, we hope, eliminated.

There's little argument that, on average, African Americans earn less than their white peers. This troubling trend is well researched and documented. For example, a 2003 study by Oxford researchers Carneiro, Heckman, and Masterov found that during the 1990s, the wages of African American males were, on average, 25 percent lower than those of white males. Just as troubling, they found that the gap widens as people get older. They also found gaps for women, but these gaps were much smaller.[7] These findings are consistent with those reported by University of Chicago economist Derek Neal and University of Virginia economist William R. Johnson, who in a landmark 1996 study, found that the hourly wages of young African American males were 24 percent lower than those of their white peers and that young African American women earned 17 percent less than white women of the same age.[8]

There's no need for an extensive review of the research on this problem. There is little argument that, on average, African Americans, especially males, are on the wrong end of a vast wage and income gap. We all know the reality of this issue. Instead, let's use our time addressing a more important issue: why does this problem exist? If we answer this question incorrectly, our attempts to solve the problem will go astray. Any effective effort to remedy the problem has to begin with a willingness to accurately understand the problem's root causes.

In general, most attempts to close the income gap assumed that racial discrimination in the labor market is the root cause of the gap. While policies designed to remedy racial discrimination in the workplace have been helpful, racial discrimination still clearly persists in the labor market, just as it persists in almost every other aspect of American life.

But if racial discrimination in employment were the only, or even the most important, cause of the racial gap in earnings, our efforts to close the gap would have produced better results. The very fact that the gap remains so large even after enormous efforts—for example, affirmative action and other such programs based on the assumption that employment discrimination is the root cause of the problem—suggests that other causes should be investigated.

In fact, there are strong reasons to believe that the earnings gap is primarily the product of an academically based skills gap between African American and white youths. In other words, we're looking for racial discrimination in the wrong place. Everyone had assumed employment discrimination was the main problem, when educational disparities appear to be a better explanation for the inequities. Educational disparities short-change African American students. By the time they enter the labor market, this educational discrimination has already ensured that their incomes will be lower for the rest of their lives no matter how they are affected by employment discrimination.

For example, research economists Carneiro, Heckman, and Masterov warn us explicitly that the income gap may be more the result of a skills gap produced by educational discrimination than the result of employment discrimination:

> These gaps are consistent with the claims of pervasive labor-market discrimination against many minorities. However, there is another equally plausible explanation. Minorities may bring less skill and ability to the market. Although there may be discrimination or disparity in the development of these valuable skills, the skills may be rewarded equally across all demographic groups in the labor market.[9]

When we check that theory against the facts, it looks solid. Jencks and Phillips examined the data on income and basic academic skills, and they found that the income gap tracks the educational gap closely:

> We have shown that the disparity in hourly pay between young blacks and whites can largely be traced to a gap in basic skills that predates their entry into the labor market. Black teenagers lag well behind their white counterparts in reading and mathematics, and this skill deficit explains most of the racial differences in wage outcomes among young adults.[10]

These claims are controversial, of course. But rather than get involved in mudslinging debates, it's better to look at the big picture. Taking the basic facts and doing some back-of-the-envelope calculations is highly instructive.

The average yearly household income of African American high school dropouts over the age of twenty-five is $22,795. For high school graduates, the average income is $34,614. That means they make an additional $11,819 every year compared to dropouts. For those with some college experience but no degree, the average income is $46,960—a difference of $12,346 over high school graduates who never entered college. And for those with a bachelor's degree or higher, the average income is $75,901— an amazing $28,941 higher than those with some college but no degree.[11]

Clearly, employers reward African Americans who bring educational achievement to the table. As we said, this doesn't mean there's no such thing as employment discrimination. African Americans do make less than whites—white dropouts over twenty-five make an average household income of $32,648, white high school graduates make an average of $49,909, whites with some college make an average of $60,998, and whites with a bachelor's degree or higher make an average of $103,746. That reflects a lot of complicated realities, and no doubt discrimination is part of that picture.

But does it mean that no one should ask "so what?" about the racial achievement gap in schools? The data are clear: when African American students have higher educational attainment, employers are willing to pay them more. It matters that white dropouts have household incomes $9,853 higher than African American dropouts, but it also matters—we would argue that it matters more—that African American high school graduates make $11,819 more than African American dropouts. Allowing such a huge African American dropout rate is costing us big money.

How big? There are just over 14 million African American households headed by persons over the age of twenty-five in the United States. Suppose the African American high school graduation rate was just five percentage points higher than it is, so that 5 percent of those households were earning at the high school graduate level instead of the dropout level. With that change alone, African American households would be earning $8.5 billion more every year than they are now.

Raise the college enrollment rate five points, so that 5 percent of households move from the *high school graduate* category to the *some college* category, and African American income goes up another $8.9 billion every year. Move 5 percent from some college to having bachelor's degrees, and we make a staggering $20.8 billion more every year. Put all three of those categories together, and you get $38.2 billion.

Is an extra $38.2 billion every year considered to be real money? The total yearly income of those 14 million African American households is $623.2 billion. That means a five percentage point improvement in high school graduation, college enrollment, and college graduation rates would increase household income by about 6 percent. Think of it this way: if you receive a cost of living increase to keep your salary equal with the rate of inflation, and then you get an additional 6 percent raise on top of that, you'd probably agree that you're doing pretty well. More than likely, so would African American households.

If that's not enough to impress you, remember that a five-point improvement in education levels ought to be a very modest goal. Let's suppose we were to pour the same financial resources into fighting educational shortcomings that we have been devoting to fighting employment discrimination. There are several school reform strategies that have been proven to yield good results, so those efforts wouldn't be wasted. Over the course of several generations, it's reasonable to think we might have improved things by ten percentage points instead of only five. So double all the numbers in the preceding paragraphs: $17 billion more income every year for the dropouts who would be high school graduates, $17.8 billion for the high school graduates who would enroll in college, and $41.6 billion for the college students who would graduate with bachelor's degrees—for a total of $76.4 billion, or about 12 percent of total African American yearly income.

That alone wouldn't totally eliminate the income gap, but it would eradicate a huge chunk of it. Education cannot be our only concern, but it has to be one of our top concerns. Any leader who shrugs his or her shoulders at educational disparities is, at the least, irresponsible. Consider again the question, "So what?" Well one of the answers is that we are currently leaving the huge potential for improved African American wealth just lying on the table.

Even these income numbers don't tell the whole story because they only consider people who are working. Better education doesn't just mean more money for those who have jobs. It also means more people will have jobs in the first place.

Only 54 percent of African American high school dropouts over the age of twenty-five are in the labor force, which is defined as people who are either working or looking for work. The other 46 percent don't have jobs and have stopped looking for them. This includes many people who have legitimate reasons not to find jobs such as retirees and stay-at-home parents. Obviously, their absence from the labor force does not present a problem. Nobody would argue with parents who want to stay at home to raise their children; nor would they make senior citizens look for jobs if they don't want them. But that 46 percent also includes millions of people who should have jobs but don't and who have given up looking for employment. By contrast, among African American high school graduates, 74 percent are in the labor force. For those with some college, its 79 percent, and for those with bachelor's degrees or higher it's 88 percent.[12]

In addition to bringing people into the labor force, education makes it easier for those who are looking for a job to find one. Remember, the labor force includes both people who have jobs and people who don't have jobs but are looking for them. It makes a big difference how many African Americans are in the former category and how many are in the latter category. Well, among those who are in the labor force, 87 percent of African American dropouts are employed, compared to 92 percent of high school graduates, 93 percent of those with some college, and 97 percent of those with bachelor's degrees.[13] So education not only brings African Americans into the labor force, it puts them into jobs.

If you do the math for the expansion of the labor force and then for higher employment rates, it works out that if 5 percent of the African American dropouts were high school graduates instead, about 175,000 more of them would be employed. If 5 percent more high school graduates enrolled in college, an additional 45,000 would be employed. And if 5 percent went from having some college to having bachelor's degrees, yet another 86,000 would be employed, for a total of about 306,000 people. Double those numbers for a 10 percent improvement and you get over half a million more African Americans working at jobs instead of being on government unemployment assistance.[14]

Let's turn now to our third response to the "so what" question.

– RESPONSE THREE –

The Achievement Gap Leads to More African Americans Without Health Insurance, in Prison, and Dying Early

Yearly income isn't the only life outcome that's affected by education level. There are all kinds of other ways in which people with higher educational achievement end up with better lives—and conversely, ways in which the racial achievement gap in schools leads to permanent inequality between African Americans and whites for the rest of their lives. The three most important issues are health insurance, incarceration rates, and life expectancy.

HEALTH INSURANCE

With our health care system, it's becoming more difficult for people to get health insurance. Low-income people in general, and disproportionately large numbers of African Americans are bearing the brunt of that problem. The education gap is a big part of the reason. People who enter the job market with higher educational achievement are more likely to land jobs that offer health insurance. As long as African Americans are being underserved in school, they will be underserved by the health care system as well. The racial achievement gap is literally making African Americans sick.

Among African Americans age eighteen and older who have never been to college, 28 percent will go without health insurance at some point during the year. For those who have enrolled in college but never finished, that drops to 21 percent and for those who have a bachelor's degree or higher, it drops much further, to 12 percent.[15]

There are just under 26 million African Americans over the age of eighteen. Thus, a five percentage point improvement in college enrollment rates would mean about 99,000 fewer African Americans going without health insurance, and a five percentage point improvement in college graduation rates would mean another 106,000 fewer, or a total of just over 205,000. Double those numbers for a ten percentage point improvement, and nearly 411,000 African Americans would not lack health insurance.

Thanks to our society's programs that provide for the less fortunate, there is no substantial difference between the percentage of African American high school dropouts and high school graduates who go without health insurance at some point during the year—the rate for dropouts is 27 percent and for graduates it is 28 percent. But closing the racial achievement gap would still make a big difference in social equity for African Americans in this area. Why? Because it makes a major difference to the social standing of a person whether he or she gets health insurance through a job or though a government social program. This is about more than just health insurance; it's about whether our neighbors see us as people who contribute to society or people who live off other people's contributions. In total, over 7 million African Americans over age eighteen are on government health insurance, and it's widely known that African Americans are disproportionately represented on the welfare and Medicaid rolls. As long as that's the case, we won't be equal members of society.

A full 52 percent of adult African American high school dropouts get their health insurance from the government, while the same is true for only 29 percent of high school graduates. Some of these are government employees, but most of them, especially dropouts, are on Medicaid—the major government program providing health care to the poor—and similar social programs. If 5 percent of African Americans went from being dropouts to being high school graduates, there would be about 300,000 fewer African Americans on government health insurance—and again, double that to almost 600,000 for a 10 percent improvement in education level.

INCARCERATION

It's no secret that African American males are much more likely to wind up in prison than males of other races. No doubt there are a lot of factors contributing to this reality, but the importance of education is often overlooked. There is a strong relationship between educational attainment and the chances of being incarcerated. As long as our schools continue to turn out generation after generation of African American dropouts with no skills, we will continue to put generation after generation of African Americans into prison disproportionately as compared to whites. We can never achieve racial equality and social justice under those conditions.

Economist Brian Gottlob calculates from census data that 4 percent of African American males who drop out of high school will be incarcerated at some point during their lives. By comparison, only 2.4 percent of high school graduates and fewer than 1 percent of those with bachelor's degrees will be incarcerated.[16] So dropouts are almost twice as likely as high school graduates to go to prison, and those who never go to college are more than three times as likely as those who graduate from college to be imprisoned.

There are about 360,000 African American males in each high school class, including the ones who drop out and the ones who graduate.[17] If 5 percent more of these students were graduates instead of dropouts, 317 fewer of their class would go to prison at some point in their lives. If another 5 percent went from not enrolling in college to getting a bachelor's degree, an additional 288 would be kept out of prison. For a 10 percent improvement, double those numbers to a total of 1,209 fewer African Americans in prison each year.

Those numbers may seem small, but remember two things: First, these numbers are for each yearly class of students, so they would compound quickly over time. Second, those who go to prison once are highly likely to do so again, so the number of crimes and imprisonments is greater than these numbers suggest.

EARLY DEATH

Low income, lack of health care, higher crime rates, and lots of other factors connected to education combine to shorten the lives of African Americans. To put it bluntly, the black-white achievement gap kills—and so does the indifference of those who could be doing something about it, but aren't.

Unfortunately, the U.S. Department of Health and Human Services doesn't release data on mortality broken down by both race and education. However, we can look at the relationship between mortality and education in the general population and then apply it to the African American population. The relationship between education and mortality is probably even stronger among African Americans, given their lower education attainments, than among the general population. That being the case, this method most likely will underestimate the true impact of the racial education gap on African American mortality.

In the general population, the yearly mortality rate for high school dropouts between the ages of twenty-five and sixty-four is 190 percent of the mortality rate for the entire population in that age bracket (650 deaths per 100,000 people each year, compared to 342). The rate for high school graduates with no college experience is about 140 percent of the general rate (478 to 342). By contrast, the mortality rate for those with at least some college is significantly lower than the general rate (206 to 342).[18]

To apply this to African Americans, let's start with the African American mortality rate for persons between the ages of twenty-five and sixty-four, which is 574.5 deaths per 100,000 people each year.[19] Applying the proportions above, this gives us an estimated mortality rate of 1,091 for African American dropouts, 802 for African American high school graduates with no college, and 346 for African Americans with at least some college.

There are more than 19 million African Americans in that age bracket.[20] If 5 percent were high school graduates instead of dropouts, there would be just under 2,800 fewer deaths each year. And a 5 percent improvement in college enrollment would mean just under 4,400 fewer deaths, for a total of about 7,100. We can double that to 14,200 for 10 percent improvements in high school graduation and college enrollment.

Summary

The sum and substance of the "so what" issue is that, at the very least, closing the black–white achievement gap provides the foundation for accomplishing three extremely important outcomes:

- Eliminating the black-intellectual-inferiority stereotype

- Accelerating the accumulation of wealth for African Americans

- Reducing African American incarceration rates, extending insurance coverage for African Americans, and increasing the African American life span

All this provides strong support for the proposition that there is no civil rights strategy on the horizon that offers African Americans a higher leverage opportunity for movement toward our traditional twin goals of racial equality and social justice in this country than closing the black–white achievement gap. And that is the answer to the "so what" question. Put bluntly, the black–white achievement gap is retarding our progress toward racial equality and social justice in America. That's what!

CHAPTER 4

In Search of Explanations

There are virtually no racial or social class differences in mental ability among infants before their first birthday, and a few social class indicators are able to explain the small differences that do exist.

—Achievement Gap Initiative at Harvard

FINDING EFFECTIVE solutions to the achievement gap problem requires a deep and clear understanding of the gap's causes. Therefore, our next step is to carefully examine the common explanations for the black–white achievement gap and to form a point of view as to why we think it exists.

Common Explanations for the Black–White Achievement Gap

N.B.

There is no universally accepted answer to the question of what are the causes of the black–white achievement gap. Explanations differ widely along ideological, racial, and even political lines. Of the many explanations that have been offered, some are the result of meticulous analysis and thoughtful study. Others spring from ideological—or some might even say prejudiced—positions. But one thing is for sure: these opinions and beliefs are deeply held. The explanations commonly offered to explain the gap stem from sociocultural, socioeconomic, pedagogical, and genetic basis. Because race, commonly used to "classify" human beings, is a social construction with no biological justification, the genetic explanation is viewed by most creditable scientists to be 100 percent incorrect. (The other theories offer more nuanced discussions.)

Even so, it's important to note here that these explanations, though deeply held, are just theories, although many people stick to one, claiming it to be the sole explanation. Reality has a way of always being more complicated than people's ideologies. The truth of the matter, no doubt, is that there is no single explanation.

Let us explore some of the most common explanations for the black–white achievement gap. We have chosen to organize them into five general, and sometimes overlapping, clusters. The first three clusters draw their titles from the writings of the outspoken social commentator Mano Singham, whose seminal article, "The Canary in the Mine," is often quoted by psychologists and education scholars when referring to the achievement gap.[1] We went on to add another two groupings. Although we use Singham's titles for the first three clusters, it's important to note that the views and ideologies listed under those titles are held by many people.

EXPLANATION ONE: SOCIOECONOMIC DISPARITIES

they don't dismiss this.

Many commonly held explanations for the black–white achievement gap have as their foundation socioeconomic disparities between the two ethnic groups. Essentially, the argument is that the gap is caused by the long history of economic disparities between the two communities, tracing back to slavery. Those who favor this explanation refer to the history of oppression that blacks have had to endure. They point to such factors as blacks being legally prohibited from learning to read during slavery, being forced to attend poor schools, being restricted to the constitutionally supported separate-but-equal laws, being required to work in the fields when white children were in school, and other such conditions. They buttress their argument by emphasizing the research that clearly supports the fact that educational achievement correlates more strongly with economic status than with any other single variable—which, indeed, it does.

Supporters of the socioeconomic disparities theory believe that the black–white achievement gap is actually caused by class and race factors. They argue that class and race are intimately connected and that factors associated with class create disparities in school and beyond.[2] Regarding class, they point out the differences between the parenting behaviors of lower-class, middle-class, and professional parents; racial discrimination suffered by blacks; housing conditions; and other socioeconomic factors as predictors of achievement.

We are convinced that there is no question that socioeconomic factors correlate highly with academic performance. Researchers have shown that there are differences (on average) in parenting skills between parents of low socioeconomic status and those who hold professional positions. We know also that the degree to which parents read to their children, and the amount and quality of dialogue between parent and child are powerful determinants of the quality of cognitive development a child will experience. Betty Hart and Todd Risley, two senior scientists with the Schiefelbusch Institute for Life Span Studies at the University of Kansas, studied the difference in the quality of parent–child dialogue between professional families, working class families, and welfare families. They found that language development in young children was overwhelmingly correlated with socioeconomic status. Studying families with infants between one and two years old for two and a half years, they reported their findings in their compelling book *Meaningful Differences in the Everyday Experience of Young American Children.*[3]

- By age three a child from a welfare family could have heard 32 million fewer words than a child from a professional family.

- By age three a child from a professional family could have an observed cumulative vocabulary of 1100 words.

- By age three a child from a working class family could have an observed cumulative vocabulary of 750 words.

- By age three a child from a welfare family could have an observed cumulative vocabulary of 500 words.

- On average, children from professional families heard a higher ratio of encouragement to discouragement than their working class or welfare counterparts.

Richard Rothstein and others who argue that class and socioeconomic factors impact a child's cognitive development are factually correct. While we do not argue with their facts, we do take issue with how the facts are presented, interpreted, and used. Careful reading of Rothstein's *Class and Schools: Using Social, Economic, and Educational*

Reform to Close the Black–White Achievement Gap leaves us with the sense that he sees the black–white achievement gap as indelible.[4]

His presentation reminds us of the biblical passage where Jesus says, "The poor you will always have with you."[5] To Rothstein and others who give the impression that there is no need to try to close the black–white achievement gap until we have first solved the long litany of socioeconomic factors, or that as long as these socioeconomic factors exist, we will have a black–white achievement gap in its current magnitude we say, "Let us off this train!"

In fact, we believe that this attitude is in itself a cause of the gap. The problem with this line of reasoning is that it absolves schools, teachers, and school leaders by saying that the school is not to be held accountable for student achievement because socioeconomic factors are the real causes of disadvantaged children's poor academic performance. How else should one interpret the phrase "Even the best schools can't close the race achievement gap" displayed on the cover of an *American School Board Journal* as the subtitle of a Rothstein article titled "Class and the Classroom."[6] Imagine a teacher reading and believing this statement. This belief takes the wind out of the sails of teachers confronting the challenge of closing the gap.

What impact will that statement have on the teacher's effort when faced with a child whose learning presents a challenge? The last paragraph of the article includes a startling sentence: "Improving lower-class children's learning requires ameliorating the social and economic conditions of their lives." Does that mean that we cannot improve lower-class children's learning until we fix the social and economic conditions of their lives?

This kind of thinking is not a part of the solution. It is a cause of the problem. We argue that this statement should be stood on its head. We should instead be improving lower-class children's learning; it would go a long way toward ameliorating the social and economic conditions of their lives.

There is the story of the grandmother with an eighth-grade education who had ten children and raised them in a two-room apartment, but she instilled in them a belief in education and sent them all to Catholic school (which was cheaper then). Nine of those kids went to college and they all were reasonably successful. This isn't a unique story. Doesn't it prove that socioeconomic status is in no way a barrier to success? Don't the many stories like this disprove the theory? Low socioeconomic status presents challenges, but it doesn't preclude economic nor academic success.

Most Americans know of many people who have risen up from extreme poverty and been successful. There are many stories of these "up from the bootstraps" folks. The idea that you can't succeed coming from poverty is absurd and most folks know it's absurd.

EXPLANATION TWO: SOCIOPATHOLOGICAL CULTURE

Those who advocate that sociopathological culture explains the gap believe that there is something inherent in the culture of African Americans that militates against academic achievement. The list of social ills that many believe are at the root of the poor academic performance of African Americans includes:

- Unstable families

- Poor parenting skills

- Lack of drive and ambition

- Negative peer pressure

- Poor choice of role models

- High levels of teen pregnancies, drugs, and crime

- Lower parental involvement in children's education

Those who hold conservative ideological views favor sociopathological explanations for the black–white achievement gap. From their perspective, the solution to the achievement gap lies within the control of African Americans themselves. To put it bluntly, their thinking is that African Americans should stop whining and complaining and pull themselves up by their own bootstraps.

In support of this idea there is research showing that home and family variables have a strong impact on children's cognitive development.[7] A child's achievement in school appears to be closely tied to the extent to which the child's family is able to create a home environment that encourages learning, communicates high expectations for their children's achievement and future careers, and involves itself in the child's education at school and in the community. So clearly, negative sociopathological factors do contribute to the difficulties that many African American children experience in school. However, we refute this as a comprehensive explanation for the black–white achievement gap.

Growing up in an environment surrounded by adverse conditions obviously challenges a child's expectations for success. More damaging, however, is the tendency of teachers and other educators to focus on the negative environment of children's background rather than on the strengths that the children have. This view grows out of the massive amount of research supporting the conclusion that teacher expectations have powerful influence on student learning.[8]

The fact that many African American children do succeed academically in spite of the challenges presented by societal conditions weakens the sociopathological explanation. There are many examples of individual success stories of African Americans whose resiliency carried them through negative institutional and community circumstances. Furthermore, there are isolated instances of schools in inner-city neighborhoods where success is schoolwide. While it is no doubt imperative that we work to reduce the negative sociopathological factors that impact on children, these factors do not fully explain the achievement gap. Nor can we wait until they are fixed before we work to achieve high academic performance from children whose life circumstances subject them to these undesirable conditions. In every state there are schools serving children from sociopathological cultural environments which are causing their students to achieve high standards. While we agree that sociopathological factors are barriers to high achievement, they can, in large measure, be overcome by great schools.

EXPLANATION THREE: GENETICS

This brings us to genetic explanations for the achievement gap. The thinking here, very simply, is that the gaps in black and white academic achievement, as well as other educational achievement differences between black and white students, result not from economics, culture, scholastic opportunity, or environmental factors, but from a simple act of nature: blacks are intellectually inferior to whites. They argue that genetics simply did not endow blacks with enough cerebral horsepower to compete academically with whites.

By logical extension, then, there are no solutions to the achievement gap with this explanation. You can't change nature. Therefore, regarding the black–white achievement gap, the advice is to get over it and focus on learning to live with educational disparities by designing strategies to minimize their impact on social, economic, and human conditions.

The controversy over race and intelligence can be traced all the way back to French psychologist Alfred Binet, who is credited with developing the first intelligence test in the early twentieth century.[9] Debate on the subject has ensued since then, and Murray and Herrnstein threw fuel on the fire when their book *The Bell Curve* was published.

Responding to the controversy initiated by *The Bell Curve,* the American Anthropological Association (AAA) made its position on the matter clear by adopting a "Statement on 'Race' and Intelligence" in December 1994:[10]

> The American Anthropological Association is deeply concerned by recent public discussions, which imply that intelligence is biologically determined by race. Repeatedly challenged by scientists, nevertheless these ideas continue to be advanced. Such discussions distract public and scholarly attention from and diminish support for the collective challenge to ensure equal opportunities for all people, regardless of ethnicity of phenotypic variation.

> Earlier AAA resolutions against racism (1961, 1969, 1971, and 1972) have spoken to this concern. The AAA further resolves:

> WHEREAS, all human beings are members of one species, *Homo sapiens,* and

> WHEREAS, differentiating species into biologically defined "races" has proven meaningless and unscientific as a way of explaining variations (whether in intelligence or other traits),

> THEREFORE, the American Anthropological Association urges the academy, our political leaders, and our communities to affirm without distraction by mistaken claims of racially determined intelligence, the common stake in assuring equal opportunity, in respecting diversity and in securing a harmonious quality of life for all people.

The American Psychological Association's response was similar. It stated, "Regarding genetic causes, they noted that there is not much direct evidence on this point, but what little there is fails to support the genetic hypothesis."[11]

Although mainstream anthropologists and psychologists seem to offer little support for genetic explanations of the achievement gap, the notion still remains deeply implanted in the minds of a large part of the American (and perhaps even the world) population. Despite the lack of scientific support, many people find it hard to reject ideas like those under the genetic explanations in the face of continued disparities in performance between black and white students.

For us, this raises one critical question: what are the prospects for true racial equality when a large portion of the American population harbors thoughts like those classified under the genetic explanations category? The prospects, in our opinion, are bleak. And this is why we believe that the black–white achievement gap is a major barrier—perhaps even *the* major barrier—to true racial harmony in this country.

EXPLANATION FOUR: BLACK IDENTITY

The late John Ogbu, an eminent professor of anthropology at the University of California, Berkeley, was interested in a broad array of factors that he believed explained low performance among African American students.[12] Chief among these were forces within the African American community itself. Within this category of explanations, Ogbu lists three possibilities:

- Black folk theories of effort and reward

- Black belief that school learning is "acting white"

- Black relational adaptations

The first of Ogbu's three possibilities—black folk theories of effort and reward—involves the view that blacks have developed a folk theory which postulates that hard work does not pay. It is the opposite of "effort optimism," which is the belief that rewards are linked to the amount of effort put into a task.

His second of three possibilities—"acting white"—involves Ogbu's view that African Americans have developed an "oppositional culture" that equates school standard English and school success with white culture and language. The idea that doing well in school is "acting white" involves African American students intentionally doing less well than they could do in order not to be seen by their African American peers as standing apart from their black identity.

For his third possibility, Ogbu uses the phase "relational adaptations" to characterize the ways African Americans have adapted to white society.

In an explosive 1986 *Urban Review* article, Signithia Fordham and John Ogbu assert: "Apparently, Black children's general perception that academic pursuit is 'acting white' is learned in the Black community. The ideology of the community in regard to the cultural meaning of schooling is, therefore, implicated and needs to be reexamined." [13]

Using different terminology, other scholars and social thinkers have voiced similar views. John McWhorter, author of *Losing the Race: Self Sabotage in Black America,* is one of them. He boldly declares that "a culturally embedded wariness of scholarly endeavor is the primary cause of the alarmingly persistent achievement gap between black students and most others." [14] He calls this phenomenon "anti-intellectualism" and asserts that this is not simply an inner-city phenomenon but one that "permeates the whole of black culture, all the way up the social class." [15]

McWhorter minces no words, proclaiming, "A cult of Anti-intellectualism infects black America." This anti-intellectualism, he proposes, "is inherited from whites having denied education to blacks for centuries, and has been concentrated by the Separatist trend, which in rejecting the 'white,' cannot but help to cast school and books as suspicious and alien, not to be embraced by the authentically 'black' person." [16]

Notwithstanding his explanation that the cult of anti-intellectualism actually is a part of our slave legacy, McWhorter's charge raised the hackles of many in the African American leadership community. Many black scholars and old-line civil rights workers would slam back and say that he is just another right-wing pundit playing the "blame the victim" game.

Yet in his keynote address before the 2004 Democratic National Convention, Senator Barack Obama gave the idea currency when he said, "Go into any inner-city neighborhood, and folks will tell you that government alone can't teach kids to learn. They know that parents have to teach, that children can't achieve unless we raise their expectations and turn off the television sets and eradicate the slander that says a black youth with a book is acting white." [17]

Obama's remarks set off a tidal wave of pro-and-con discussions and scholarly work about "acting white." Education and other scholarly heavyweights staked out their positions as to whether or not there actually is an acting-white phenomenon that impedes African American students' academic performance in school.

Harvard University's Roland G. Fryer, Jr., along with his colleague Paul Torelli, entered the dispute on the side of the "oh, yes it is" community when they published a paper, "An Empirical Analysis of 'Acting White.'"[18] Using data from the National Longitudinal Study of Adolescent Health, Fryer and Torelli examined the relationship between popularity and academic achievement among white and black students. The results of their carefully constructed study supported several intriguing conclusions. Among them were that "acting white" is more likely to happen in public schools and among children from low-education families, that it is nonexistent in predominantly black schools, and that, for blacks, higher achievement is associated with modestly higher popularity until a grade-point average of 3.5 is reached, when the slope turns negative.

And the argument goes on. For us, Fryer and Torelli's conclusions carry considerable weight because their empirical analysis was based on data from the only national dataset that includes measures of within school friendship networks as well as measures of parental characteristics and academic achievement.

There have also been studies that show that "acting white" is not an influential factor in African American underperformance. But these studies use self-reported student data from the National Educational Longitudinal Study (NELS), which is inherently less reliable. It is well known that these data, though very useful, offer opportunities for students to stretch the truth and select responses that offer the best opportunities to make themselves look good.

If you think about it, the whole acting white phenomenon really boils down to peer pressure. Few will disagree that peer pressure, positive or negative, is one of the most influential factors that shape adolescent behavior. With respect to the black–white achievement gap, the important question for us is: are there cultural forces in the African American community that act against adolescent intellectual advancement? In other words, for African American students, is there a conflict between academic achievement and the black identity?

We know of no research that definitively answers this question. Informed opinions vary along Afro-centric, cultural, economic, social, and even political lines. Even so, and fully recognizing that others may disagree, based many years in public education, our reading of the literature, and our own experience with schoolchildren in our communities, it is clear that there are indeed powerful cultural forces in the

African American community that work against adolescent academic achievement. A conflict between academic achievement and the black identity *does* exist in the African American community and constitutes one of the major explanations for the black–white achievement gap. This is not the only reason for the gap, to be sure, but it is one of the most important reasons.

a partial explanation

Anyone who denies the existence of a real and active acting white phenomenon that works against the academic achievement of African American students would have a hard time convincing Judy Mathews (a pseudonym), an upper middle class African American woman who was raising a daughter as a single parent. When Judy's daughter was in middle school in a predominantly white environment, many of the black kids would tease her and tell her she was "acting white." They talked about the length of her hair, how her hair was fixed, how she dressed, how she spoke and carried herself. She would often come home from school a nervous wreck, complaining to her mother about being sad and without friends at school. Helping her daughter cope with this phenomenon required enormous effort from Judy. She eventually came up with a strategy that helped. She sat down with her daughter in front of a chart board and told her that they were going to make a list of the behaviors that her African American schoolmates considered "acting white." With her daughter doing the writing on the chart board, they listed such behaviors as dressing appropriately for school, studying hard, handing homework in on time, making good grades, using standard English, coming to class on time, wearing a neat hairdo, and the like. Then they turned to listing the behaviors considered to be "acting black." Listed under this heading were such behaviors as being late for class, not getting good grades, not doing homework, speaking incorrect English, dressing down, trash talking, and being the class clown. Then Judy asked her daughter to list behaviors that she considered to be "acting ignorant." It turned out that many of the "acting ignorant" items were the same behaviors that had been listed under the "acting black" heading. After some extended discussions she was able to help her daughter come to the conclusion that acting ignorant was not race-based at all, it was just acting ignorant. Although Judy's daughter still had to deal with some teasing from some of the black kids, she was better able to cope with it.

When her daughter reached high school she found the acting white phenomenon alive and well there also. But there she had the advantage of other coping tools. Judy and her daughter were active in their local Jack and Jill club. There were a considerable number of students in her high school who, along with their parents, were active Jack and Jillers. Jack and Jill clubs of America is an organization that was founded in Philadelphia in 1938 by a group of prominent black families. The organization conducts monthly meetings with their children to expose them to various educational, social, and civic activities. Many of these kids are in majority white environments throughout the week and these monthly meetings provide opportunities for them to interact with other black children from similar social and economic backgrounds. When the high school kids accused Judy's daughter and other Jack and Jillers of acting white, they would simply say "no, we're acting like Jack and Jillers," or "Jack and Jillers don't do this, or don't do that." The Jack and Jill support system worked so well that some African American parents who were not members of the organization began to inquire about membership. Moreover, the Jack and Jill support system had an impact on non–Jack and Jill students also, as some of them began to feel embarrassed about their poor behavior.

There are many lessons to be learned from Judy's experience with the "acting white" phenomenon. First, up close and personal parental support is needed to help kids cope with the phenomenon. Second, the involvement of parenting organizations like Jack and Jill is an important asset in children's lives. Third, in many instances the strong influence of a determined parent can outweigh pressure that peers could have on children. And finally, kids who are without the kind of support Judy provided her daughter are at a decided disadvantage.

Jason Osborne of the University of Oklahoma offers a related explanation for the underperformance of black students relative to their white peers. Like Claude Steele, Osborne argues that the underperformance of disadvantaged and stereotyped groups (including women, when it comes to disciplines traditionally considered to be male territory) is due to the stereotype-threat phenomenon. Stereotype threat is a fear that one's behavior will confirm a stereotype which has been ascribed to the group to which one belongs. Most students experience a certain amount of anxiety when faced with taking a test that has relevance to their well-being.

In Osborne's research, the data showed that students who belong to groups with negative intellectual stereotypes experience anxiety not only about the potential for personal embarrassment and failure but also the potential for confirming the negative group stereotype.[19] Not surprisingly, this added anxiety further erodes their performance potential, fueling the vicious cycle of underperformance. In the case of African Americans, who are patently aware that they are members of a stereotyped group thought to be intellectually inferior to whites, the test represents not only a personal risk but also a risk for the entire group.

There is mounting empirical evidence that adds to Osborne's assertion that disadvantaged minorities do, in fact, face higher levels of test anxiety when faced with a test known to be, or even thought to be, a measure of their intellectual or academic capability.[20] This theory clearly offers some insight into what is going on.

authors believe this p is the primary reason.

EXPLANATION FIVE: EDUCATIONAL DEPRIVATION

The final explanation for the gap is that it is caused by educational deprivation. Although educational deprivation is defined in different ways, for our purposes we consider educational deprivation to exist when a child is deprived of fundamentals essential to sound cognitive development, most especially, high expectations and great teaching.

Those who hold such beliefs do not necessarily discount the validity of earlier arguments, with the exception of the genetic argument. They just do not view these explanations as powerful *causes* of the gap. Instead, they believe that the other explanations merely represent problems that must be taken into account when designing effective educational practices. They believe that effective educational practices can overcome these problems and that it shouldn't matter what a child's economic circumstances are, what their first language is, and what the educational level of their parents is, or when they came across the border. They really believe that all children can learn when provided with the appropriate pedagogical support.

The essential elements of the educational deprivation explanation are vividly described by educator, psychologist, author, and major contributor to the strategy that won *Brown v. Board of Education* in 1954, Kenneth Clark. He places responsibility for the massive academic failure of ghetto schoolchildren directly with teachers and administrations of ghetto schools. To him, every one of the assumptions associated with the terms "cultural deprivation and cultural difference" is "primarily an alibi for educational neglect, and in no way a reflection of the nature of the educational process." He believes that a key component of the deprivation that afflicts ghetto children is that generally their teachers do not expect them to learn; the teachers think of their function as being one simply of custodial care and discipline. He concludes that the motivational problems of these children will be solved when teachers can be motivated to teach effectively—that is, to set high standards of scholastic performance and to provide good instruction, combined with emotional acceptance and support.[21]

Clark quite clearly disagreed with the other aforementioned explanations. He did not hesitate to insist that the achievement gap is a phenomenon that can be overcome by great teaching.

The argument that great teaching can go a long way toward overcoming children's low economic status has vast support. More recently, alumni of Teach for America (TFA) have reportedly espoused similar views. TFA, an independent nonprofit organization whose mission is to "enlist our nation's most promising future leaders" in the "movement to eliminate educational inequality," accomplishes its mission by building a national corps of outstanding recent college graduates—of all academic majors and career interests—who commit two years to teach in urban and rural public schools in our nation's lowest-income communities and become lifelong leaders for expanding educational opportunity.[22]

A 2005 survey of the TFA corps provides insight into the views of its members regarding the causes of student underperformance. Three findings speak directly to the issue of education deprivation as an explanation for the achievement gap:[23]

1. Educators have the power to close the achievement gap. Corps members emphasize the potential of both teachers and principals to change academic outcomes of students in spite of all the external challenges.

2. Expectations of students—from teachers, schools, parents, the general public, and students themselves—are both a powerful tool and a powerful obstacle. Corps members see low expectations as a significant cause of the achievement gap. They believe that expanding a common belief in the potential of low-income students and students of color is key to closing the gap. Indeed, their experience as teachers has strengthened their belief in their students' ability to meet high expectations.

3. The general public has an inaccurate understanding of issues regarding the achievement gap. Corps members express concern that the public misplaces blame for the gap on students and their families. They also believe that much of the public is simply unaware of the existence of this gap or of the realities of poverty and segregation.

Another source of support for the great teaching argument can be found in the Education Trust, a Washington D.C.–based independent nonprofit organization. It is another strong source of support for the view that educational deprivations are a primary cause of the achievement gap. One of the Education Trust's tenets is: "All children will learn at high levels when they are taught to high levels."[24] And consider its mission statement, which commits this independent nonprofit education organization to working "for the high academic achievement of all students at all levels, pre-kindergarten through college, and forever closing the achievement gaps that separate low-income students and students of color from other youth."[25]

Among the Education Trust's many contributions to educational equity is its work in improving teacher quality. Its leaders point out that in the effort to close the achievement gap, teachers matter most. During testimony before the Commission on No Child Left Behind, Russlynn Ali, Director of Education Trust West, reminded the commission that "the most effective teachers can teach even the most disadvantaged students up to high standards, but a couple of ineffective teachers in a row can hobble a student's education for years to come."[26]

Summary

There is a quagmire of conflicting views to explain the black–white achievement gap. Which view one favors can depend on many different variables, not the least of which are racial allegiances and political ideology.

But the whole issue boils down to whether or not one believes all children can learn. Maybe not all at the same pace, certainly not with the same degree of effort, and maybe not to the same degree of depth— but the degree to which one believes that all children can learn seems to be the determinant of which explanation for the gap's existence one finds most compelling. Based on years of personal witness to the work of committed teachers in "break the mold" schools, we believe the answer is absolutely yes, and this is why we are firm and unabashed proponents of the educational deprivation theory—the primary cause of the African American–white achievement gap is that low-achieving students have been deprived of the educational essentials which support learning to high levels.

We believe that all children can learn at high levels when they are taught at high levels. Our explanation for the black–white achievement gap is that the children on the negative side of the gap suffer from educational deprivation. They have not been taught at high levels. Being taught to high levels means educational support from factors outside of the school. It involves the support and commitment from the entire education triad—home, school, and community.

Perhaps, after reflecting about why the gap exists, we should turn to a new question: why does the gap persist?

It persists because it has been allowed to. It persists because it's a problem that nobody owns. It persists because we, who should be the rightful owners of the problem, have yet to identify it as a problem worthy of our full attention. It persists because, failing to recognize its importance to the advancement of African Americans toward the twin goals of racial equality and social justice in America, we—the African American leadership community—have our heads in the sand.

CHAPTER 5

The Origins of the Problem

If man is without education . . . he lives within the narrow, dark and grimy walls
of ignorance. He is a poor prisoner without hope. The little light that he gets
comes to him as through dark corridors and grated windows. . . . To deny educa-
tion to any people is one of the greatest crimes against human nature.

—Frederick Douglass, 1894

TOO OFTEN, the black–white achievement gap is discussed as if it
has no history or, at the very least, as if its history is inconsequential.
Much can be learned about today's problems by reviewing the history
of African American educational opportunities, as a deep and thorough understanding of the origins of the black–white achievement gap
is an absolute prerequisite for solving this intractable problem once
and for all.

In delving into history, it is important to keep in mind the admoni-
tions of author, journalist, educator, and "Father of Black History," Carter
G. Woodson, who advises in *The Mis-Education of the Negro*:

> To point out merely the defects as they appear today will be of lit-
> tle benefit to the present and future generations. These things
> must be viewed in their historic setting. The conditions of today
> have been determined by what has taken place in the past, and in
> a careful study of this history we may see more clearly the great
> theatre of events in which the Negro has played a part.[1]

Woodson's words underscore the significance of history. The question is: How far back should we go?

Most educators and scholars trace the origin of the black–white achievement gap to the point of its discovery by the U.S. Army in 1917, when the first large-scale mental-testing program revealed that white soldiers achieved substantially higher scores than Negro soldiers.[2] Admittedly, knowing when the gap was discovered is useful. But simple logic indicates that the problem must have existed prior to its discovery, so let's go farther back.

Those looking to lay blame for the black–white achievement gap outside of the African American community typically argue that it is a product of slavery. Without a doubt, no other aspect of this nation's history has had a more powerful impact on our national character, our government structure, or our historical and current racial beliefs and relationships than slavery. Therefore, slavery and its siblings, racial discrimination and prejudice, must be considered when trying to understand the black–white achievement gap. But starting with the aftermath of slavery does not provide a full enough grasp of history to make available a full understanding of this complex phenomenon. For a full understanding we must go back even further, before Emancipation, to the colonial and antebellum periods. In other words, we must concern ourselves with the entire history of the Negro experience in America.

Until recently, few Americans were knowledgeable about this history because—until recently—it has been largely omitted from the official history of the development of this country. In short, American history did not include African American history. Only after the feisty scholarly work of African American scholars like W. E. B. Du Bois and Carter G. Woodson—which then inspired a new generation of scholars, most notably, John Hope Franklin, the James B. Duke Professor Emeritus of History, and Professor of Legal History in the Law School at Duke University—did the true story of the African American experience in America even begin to emerge.

The Charter Generation—the First African Americans

The exact date of the Negro's entrance into the new world of Colonial America is uncertain. Ivan Van Sertima presents a compelling case that Africans arrived in the Americas before Columbus.[3] Likewise, several other scholars offer views of the Negro's introduction into the Americas during or before the fifteenth century. But the first definitive evidence establishes the beginning of the Negro experience in America as August 1619 when a Dutch ship carrying twenty Africans and one hundred English women dropped anchor off the coast of the British Colony of Jamestown, Virginia. The Dutch traders exchanged the Africans for food and the women for the amount of tobacco that would cover the cost of their passage from England. Although the exact status of the Africans is not certain, it is clear that they were not willing passengers, but were held in some form of bondage. The fact that the Dutch were able to trade them for goods suggests that they owned them. In fact, most historians agree that these twenty Africans arrived as indentured servants.

Notice the term *servants*—not slaves. The institution of slavery as we think of it today was as yet undeveloped in British Colonial America in 1619. In fact, the word *slave* didn't become a part of the Colonial lexicon until about the mid 1660s.

Furthermore, as difficult as it might be to believe today, the concept of black and white as racial designations was also unfamiliar in British Colonial America.[4] As Lerone Bennett, Jr., points out in *The Shaping of Black America*, the fundamental division in that society was between servants and masters, and there were blacks and whites in both those categories. All those who traded years of servitude for passage to the New World or for special benefits in the New World were viewed as a single class. No matter whether they were black, white, or Native American, they worked together, lived together, drank together, made love together, and in general, agonized together over the underclass status they had in common.

When blacks arrived in Jamestown in 1619, the practice of using forced labor had already been well established on the backs of Native Americans and whites. Blacks, as latecomers, were simply inserted into the existing system. As Bennett describes it, "When the first blacks landed in Jamestown, they found . . . most of the white population living in the shadow of chains." Writing from Virginia in that year, John Pory said that "our principal wealth consisteth in servants."[5]

Side by side with poor European whites who had agreed to a period of indentured servitude in exchange for passage to America, Africans worked as field laborers growing rice, sugar cane, tobacco, and cotton, or as dockworkers, craftsmen's helpers, unskilled factory workers, shipbuilders' helpers, or household servants. Some African indentured servants, like their white counterparts, earned their freedom by working out the term of their agreement, which was usually four to seven years. As many as a fifth to a quarter of the first generation of Africans on these shores was said to have gained their freedom in this manner.[6]

The story of Anthony Johnson is illustrative. Although there is some dispute among historians about the date of his arrival in Virginia, most believe that he landed in Virginia in 1622, served his indentured period, and became an owner of indentured servants himself. He was granted 250 acres of land for what were known as head rights. The colonial authority would give a landowner fifty acres of land for each worker that they imported so they could establish a successful farming business.[7] The Anthony Johnson story supports the position that the status of Africans who arrived in Virginia during 1619 and the 1620s was that of indentured servants, much the same as other indentured servants arriving from Europe.

But if the conditions for Africans arriving in Jamestown in 1619 were similar to those for non-African bondsmen, this situation quickly changed. Africans who were able to gain their freedom from their indentured status soon discovered that their legal and social status was indeterminate. Many scholars believe that because Africans' skin color distinguished them from the other settlers, and their culture, language, and customs were strange to the European settlers, colonists began to associate dark skin color with racial inferiority. At some point in these early days, treatment of Negroes began to change as the length and terms of their servitude became longer and sentences meted out to the Africans who came before the colonial justice system became much more severe and involved longer periods of imprisonment than that for whites who committed the same crimes.

In 1640, a notable event illustrative of the changing status of Africans took place. A Negro named John Punch and two white men attempted to escape their bondage. When they were caught and brought to trial, the men were given decidedly different sentences, even though the crime they had committed was identical. The two white escapees were sentenced to an additional year of servitude, while Punch's servitude was extended until the end of his natural life. This sentence, in effect, converted Punch from an indentured servant into a chattel slave.[8] Since there appears to be no evidence that any white servant had ever received such a punishment in any of the English colonies, one could reasonably argue that John Punch became the first official slave in British Colonial America.

Although the exact turning point when Negro slavery officially began in British Colonial America is unclear, most scholars generally concur that it happened during the mid-1600s. In 1640, Maryland became the first colony to legalize slavery; Massachusetts legalized it the following year.[9]

The line of differential treatment between Negroes and non-Negroes became progressively more pronounced over the next century. Why did this occur? What fundamental shift led to the situation where Negroes were defined as inferior and whites as superior? Bennett proposes that "the race problem in America was a deliberate invention of men who systematically separated blacks and whites in order to make money."[10]

As the number of colonists grew, wealthy and powerful landowners began to amass multiple tracts of land into large plantations that were too large for them to farm alone. They required abundant, cheap labor. However, the supply of European indentured servants was inadequate to meet their needs; furthermore, there was growing unrest among these servants. So, wealthy white landowners looked to slavery as the answer to their labor needs. In short, these men chose deliberately, for reasons of convenience and economics and fueled by prejudice, to enslave Negro men and women.

Slavery did not come into being as a quickly installed social system. Rather, the roots of racist slavery in British Colonial America grew gradually, but continuously, until the enslavement of Negroes in British Colonial America became institutionalized throughout society and was perceived as a normal way of life by white British Colonial Americans. Because colonial planters and the merchant aristocracy controlled most of the wealth of the colonies, they also constituted the legislative bodies and thus were able to use their authority to codify the colonial slave system they desired. Borrowing again from Bennett:

> Statutes were designed to instill a sense of superiority in whites and a sense of worthlessness in blacks. They were designed to create stereotypes and insidious images. The language of these statutes ("abominable mixture," "barbarous," "savage") was instructive; it designated, pointed out, authorized, and it was a legal requirement, in many cases, for parsons and politicians to read the language at public meetings and church services.[11]

And so it began. Slavery in North America was not designed by nature, but by man—by white aristocrats who used their statutes and a wide array of other devious tactics to define, maintain, and support this racist institution.

Slavery and the Slave Experience

Webster's Dictionary defines a slave as "a person who is held in bondage to another; one who is wholly subject to the will of another; one who is held as a chattel; one who has no freedom of action, but whose person and services are wholly under the control of another." This definition is broad enough to encompass the changing nature of slavery in the Americas over time, for it did change dramatically, from the point when Negroes first arrived in British Colonial America until their emancipation roughly 250 years later. Over the course of that time, slavery evolved from a loosely structured system of contracted indentured status for a specific (and limited) period to an ironclad system of chattel slavery that encompassed not only the period of the slave's natural life but, in many cases, also that of his or her offspring. Starting in the mid-1600s, Colonial America gradually began converting itself from a society with slaves to—by the early 1700s—a slave society based on race.

The actual conditions for individual enslaved persons varied considerably, depending on many factors. Among these were the personalities of the individual slave owners, the time period in history, and the region where the slave lived. Some slave owners treated their slaves benevolently, but others were outright brutal. Generally speaking, slavery was more harsh in the South than in the North and more harsh in rural than in urban areas. The crops worked by the slave, the size of the farm, the number of slaves owned, and other factors also played a part in determining the enslaving conditions. Thus, there was no single slave experience, no single slave condition. But regardless of the particulars, all these slaves had a few things in common: they were not free, they were stripped of their human dignity, and they were Negroes.

THE PECULIARITY OF THE PECULIAR INSTITUTION

American slavery is often referred to as the "peculiar institution." The phrase seems to have originated with Thomas Jefferson. But what does it mean? Slavery itself is not unusual or rare. In fact, the practice is almost as old as human society itself. For example, the Code of Hammurabi, c.1800 B.C.E., referred to the appropriate treatment of slaves. Slavery is mentioned in the Bible. The histories of ancient Rome and Greece, the Middle East, China, the West Indies, medieval Europe, the Mediterranean, and Africa are replete with examples of various forms of human bondage, involuntary servitude, and serfdom. Slavery has existed in one form or another in almost every human society, on every continent in our world.[12]

In many of these historical examples, one finds evidence of slave holders enslaving people who represented different religions, nationalities, ethnicities, or races. It is highly unusual, however, historically speaking, for an entire ethnic group to be enslaved for more than a couple of generations, as Negroes were. This, combined with the racial justification of white superiority and black inferiority, is what makes American slavery such a peculiar institution. The racist underpinnings of American slavery made the institution extremely powerful and extended its reach far beyond the economic fabric of colonial society, where it began, and deep into the social, psychological, and educational fabric of following generations. Branding Negro slaves as racially and intellectually inferior concomitantly branded all Negroes—even those who were free—as racially inferior. Consequently, the enslavement of some Negroes based on the principle of their perceived racial inferiority in effect enslaved all Negroes. Retarding the educational development of Negroes is one of the peculiar institution's most devastating legacies.

Enslavement of the Mind

When people read or think about the horrors of slavery in America, they almost always focus on the physical bondage of the slaves, the imprisonment of their bodies and the horrific physical abuse that they endured. Less thought is given to the mental, emotional, and intellectual bondage that slaves suffered. Social and psychological oppression was absolutely central to slavery, however. To maintain their control over the slave population, owners continually sought to suppress and denigrate the slaves' sense of self-worth. They often used tactics to create in the minds of slaves a genuine feeling of inferiority and an acceptance of their barbaric or subhuman status relative to whites.

Consider the following statement made by a delegate to the Virginia Legislature in 1832.

We have as far as possible closed every avenue by which light may enter slaves' minds. If we could extinguish the capacity to see the light our work would be completed; they (the slaves) will then be on a level with the beasts of the field.[13]

In his powerful book *Oppression and Social Intervention: Essays on the Human Condition and the Problems of Change,* author Ira Goldenberg keenly observed that the owners' goal was to have their slaves wholly adopt a sense of inferiority.[14] In particular, owners wanted slaves to believe that "their African ancestry had tainted them, that their color was a badge of degradation."[15] This steady erosion of self-worth—the process of forcing people "either subtly or with obvious malice to finally succumb to the insidious process that continually undermines hope and subverts the desire to become"—is the hallmark of oppression.[16]

The oppressive tactics of Colonial America caught the attention of French historian Alexis de Tocqueville during his travels in the United States. "The only means by which the ancients maintained slavery were fetters and death," he wrote. "[But] the Americans of the South of the Union have discovered more intellectual securities for the duration of their power. They have employed their despotism and their violence against the human mind."[17]

Indeed, slave owners gave a great deal of attention to the process of conditioning slaves' minds for a lifetime of slavery. Slave owners knew that the effectiveness of their indoctrination efforts would largely determine the success they would have with their slaves. Generally, each slave's indoctrination encompassed at least five areas: strict and immediate discipline, a sense of his own inferiority and of whites' superiority, an unwavering belief in the master's superior power, acceptance of the master's standards, and a deep sense of his own helplessness and dependence.

Speaking about the effectiveness of this kind of mind control, Carter G. Woodson is noted for the following statement:

If you can control a man's thinking you do not have to worry about his action. When you determine what a man shall think you do not have to concern yourself about what he will do. If you make a man feel that he is inferior, you do not have to compel him to accept an inferior status, for he will seek it himself. If you make a man think he is justly an outcast, you do not have to order him to the back door. He will go without being told; and if there is no back door, his very nature will demand one.[18]

ENFORCED ILLITERACY

Most people have heard the phrase "knowledge is power." Slave owners certainly understood this concept. And since their goal was to render slaves powerless and portray themselves as all powerful, prohibiting slaves from gaining knowledge was critically important. Recognizing that slaves' ignorance was a valuable control mechanism, many slave owners strictly enforced illiteracy.

This is central to our understanding of the present black–white achievement gap. It is a historical fact that many (perhaps even most) slaveholders deliberately imposed ignorance as an enslavement tool and, as such, vigorously enforced tactics designed to prevent slaves from learning to read and write. These tactics were not random; they were well thought out and carefully executed. Slave owners enacted laws that imposed harsh legal penalties on slaves who tried to learn to read or write, as well as anyone who was caught teaching them to do so. They also prohibited the employment of slaves in services that involved writing.

In 1740, South Carolina became the first state to adopt a law prohibiting persons from teaching slaves to write:

SOUTH CAROLINA PROHIBITS
THE TEACHING OF SLAVES TO WRITE, 1740

. . . [W]hereas the having of slaves taught to write, or suffering them to be employed in writing, may be attended with great inconveniences, Be it therefore enacted the authority aforesaid, That all and every person or persons whatsoever, who shall hereafter teach, or cause any slave or slaves to be taught, to write, or shall use or employ any slave as a scribe in any manner of writing whatsoever, hereafter taught to write, every such person and persons, shall, for every such offence, forfeit the sum of one hundred pounds current money.

—*David J. McCord,* "The Statutes at Large of South Carolina, VII"[19]

Other states followed in rapid succession, until Kentucky and Kansas were the only Southern states *not* to have adopted such laws. Penalties for a slave caught learning to read or write ranged from severe lashing to physical mutilation. Whites, too, could be punished with fines or even jail time for violating these laws.

As Draconian as these laws were, they did not completely prevent all slaves from attaining some degree of literacy. Slave owners managed their slaves with different levels of cruelty. In fact, some slave owners defied the laws and taught their slaves to read and write. Although the extraordinarily literate abolitionist and journalist Frederick Douglass is a notable exception, illiteracy among slaves was the rule. As a former slave named Georgia Baker would poignantly recall decades later to author Peter Irons: "None of us niggers never knowed nothin' 'bout readin' and writin'. Dere warn't no school for niggers den, and I ain't never been to school a day in my life. Niggers was more skeered of newspapers dan dey is of snake now, and us never knowed what a Bible was dem days."[20]

The African American Struggle for Educational Equality

The institution of slavery in the Americas continued to gain momentum as the seventeenth century rolled into the eighteenth. But by the mid-1700s, voices of dissent were being more widely heard. The early abolitionists' arguments against slavery centered on three guiding beliefs. The first was that Negroes should be educated so that they could read the Bible and become Christians. The second, advocated mostly by Quakers, was that all people should be free. The third was that slavery was out of character for a country based on individual freedom and that Negroes should have the right to become educated so that they could take their place as citizens of a free country.[21]

John Woolman, an influential Quaker, captured the growing view that "liberty is the right of all men and that slaves, being fellow creatures of their masters, had a right to be elevated."[22] Baptists and Methodists also began to express support for the Quakers' position. In fact, in 1748, the Methodist Episcopal Church boldly declared: "We view it as contrary to the golden law of God and the prophets, and the unalienable rights of mankind, as well as every principle of the Revolution, to hold in deepest abasement, in a more abject slavery than is perhaps to be found in any part of the world, except in America, so many souls that are capable of the image of God."[23]

As the teaching of Negroes became more widely accepted in the mid-1700s, more and more "benevolent persons volunteered to instruct them, and some schools maintained for the education of white students were opened to those of African blood."[24] As they seized the educational opportunities they were finally being given, some Negroes began to pursue academics, thus soundly refuting the prevailing notions of their mental inferiority.[25]

As leaders like John Adams, Henry Clay, Nathaniel Appleton, and Benjamin Franklin were thinking deeply about the kind of nation they wanted to build, they drew on the writings of Locke, Milton, Coke, Blackstone, and other libertarian philosophers. The new American leaders were drawn to concepts such as individual liberty, government deriving its power from the consent of the governed, religious and political equality, and the rights of man.

When the colonies agreed to establish their freedom from the British Crown, the Declaration of Independence that was drafted stated that all men are created equal. Although the Declaration of Independence as we know it is silent on the practice of slavery, the first draft did in fact contain language about slavery. However, the Declaration's references to slavery had to be removed in order of get everyone to agree to sign it. The agreement to remove the language about slavery from the Declaration of Independence has been referred to as "the chief moral compromise of the Founding era."[26] The problem was that this idea of "all men are created equal" directly conflicted with the institution of slavery. How could a young nation affirm the rights of man while maintaining the peculiar institution of slavery? The paradox was simply captured by the Tory Samuel Johnson when he asked, "How is it that we hear the loudest yelps for liberty among the drivers of Negroes?"[27] Of course, the Founding Fathers had no answer to this question.

It soon became clear that the young nation was interested in freedom and equality, but not for all. To solve their dilemma, it seems to us that the colonial leaders rationalized their actions in the following way: The Constitution holds that all men are created equal. In the United States, Negroes are purchased and sold as property, and are therefore not men. Since they are not men, they have no right under the Constitution to be treated as equal.

This line of reasoning—all men are created equal, but Negroes are not—enabled the young nation to continue to perpetuate the myth of

the Negro's inhumanity and inferiority, with all its damaging consequences. This was not the belief shared by all the Founding Fathers.
Adams and Jefferson, in their letters of later years, talk about how the
slavery issue was going to have to be solved by future generations and
that they would not have been able to declare or win independence
without the Southern states.

Difficult Days

If the 1700s were a time of expanded learning opportunities for Negroes
(at least in the Northern states), the dreams of progress began to turn into
a nightmare by the last two decades of the eighteenth century. The years
extending from the late 1700s through the Civil War were perhaps the
darkest times in the long trek toward equality. While slaves were increasingly bent on freedom, the worldwide industrial revolution, powered by
inventions like spinning and weaving machines and the cotton gin, had
made the American South more dependent than ever before on slave
labor. This new technology expanded the market for cotton thereby causing the rapid growth of large cotton plantations, which required large
numbers of slaves to tend the crops. This development put the forces of
freedom and human equality and slave labor on a collision course.

When Toussaint L'Ouverture's revolutionary efforts succeeded in free-
ing slaves in Haiti, thousands of refugees from that country streamed into
the American colonies, and the stories of revolutionary success they
brought with them fueled American slaves' hunger for freedom.
Insurrections like the 1800 Gabriel Prosser slave uprising in Virginia, the
Denmark Vesey slave revolt in South Carolina in 1822, and the 1831 Nat
Turner rebellion in Southampton County, Virginia, spread panic among
whites. Frightened, they reacted aggressively to the threat of rebellion;
and as they cracked down, the progress made during the previous years
came to a screeching halt.

The story of David Walker is an interesting case from this era. Born in
1796 in North Carolina, Walker was the son of a slave father and a free
mother, and so by law was free. As a child, he witnessed the violence and
terror of slavery firsthand—including an episode where a son was forced to
whip his mother to death—and it inflamed his strong antislavery feelings.
After traveling widely, Walker settled in Boston, where he began to publish
strong antislavery pieces in the first Negro newspaper, *Freedom's Journal*.

In 1829, he published a pamphlet known as *Walker's Appeal to the Coloured Citizens of the World*. In strong and emotional language, he called on Negro men and women to rise up and fight their oppressors. Even today, *Walker's Appeal* is considered by some to be among the most powerful anti-slavery documents ever written. Distributed throughout the South, *Walker's Appeal* inspired Negroes—and scared slaveholders. Slaveholders were so worried that they offered $10,000 to anyone who would capture Walker and bring him to the South, and they warned of severe consequences for any slave caught with a copy of *Walker's Appeal*. Continued efforts to prevent slaves from learning to read or write were clearly driven by the fear that information such as the kind published in *Walker's Appeal* would reach the slaves. Walker died in Boston just months after the publication of his pamphlet's third edition. His sudden death at the young age of forty-five, combined with the large bounty on his head, caused some to think that he was poisoned. However, this was never proven.[28]

The Civil War Period and Its Aftermath

By the mid-1800s, war between the North and South seemed to be inevitable. The North, with its booming factories and rapidly rising immigrant population, no longer needed slavery. The South, on the other hand—with its heavy reliance on agriculture—was utterly determined to protect this race-bound institution that was so vital to its economic livelihood. These rising tensions spiraled into the Civil War. As President Lincoln told Congress on July 4, 1861, this was not simply a war for the sake of maintaining the Union, it was "a people's contest . . . a struggle for maintaining in the world that form and substance of government whose leading object is to elevate the condition of men."[29]

The war lasted four painful years, and its lasting impact was profound. As the late historian and writer Shelby Foote observed:

Any understanding of this nation has to be based, and I mean really based, on an understanding of the Civil War. It defined us. The Revolution did what it did. Our involvement with the European wars, beginning with the First World War, did what it did. But the Civil War defined what we are, and it opened to us what we became, good and bad things. And it is very necessary, if you are going to understand the American character in the twentieth century, to learn about this enormous catastrophe of the nineteenth century. It was the crossroads of our being, and it was a hell of a crossroads.[30]

Once the Civil War ended in 1865, Congress faced the daunting challenges of putting a divided nation back together as well as providing for the newly freed slaves. In pursuit of these enormous tasks, Congress passed three Reconstruction Acts designed to provide the framework for readmitting the South into the Union and defining, protecting, and facilitating the rights of the newly freed citizens.

The Reconstruction period, which extended from the end of the Civil War until approximately 1877, was one of the most important periods in American history for the elevation of Negro educational attainment and civil rights. Among the Reconstruction's legal victories for Negroes were the Thirteenth (abolishing slavery), Fourteenth (establishing equal protection and citizenship), and Fifteenth (granting all citizens the right to vote) Amendments and the Civil Rights Act of 1866. At the same time these legal barriers to racial equality were being dismantled, educational opportunities were exploding—and freedmen rushed to take advantage of them. Acting on their belief that education, so long denied them, provided the path to mental freedom, former slaves of every age flocked into schools and exhibited a fervent appetite for learning.

The newly established Freedman's Bureau created an astonishing 4,300 schools during this period, including the historically black colleges and universities (HBCU) such as Clark University, Atlanta University, Fisk University, Hampton Institute, and Howard University, many of which are still flourishing today.

Who was behind these expanded educational opportunities? It was not just the federal government. As Eric Anderson and Alfred Moss, Jr., make clear in their intriguing book *Dangerous Donations*, philanthropists from the North also played a very powerful role in the education of Negroes in the South following the Civil War. Initially, northern philanthropy was "primarily motivated by religion and distributed through Protestant denominations seeking to 'elevate the freedmen.'"[31] Later, the work of these missionary societies was overtaken by secular foundations, such as the Peabody Fund, the Slater Fund, and others. Anderson and Moss provide a thought-provoking analysis of the ways in which these donors' priorities and investments changed over time and of the delicate interactions between philanthropists' goals on the one hand and the entrenched system of Southern race relations on the other. They provided interesting insight into the different motives underpinning the philanthropy of the various foundations, funds, and societies providing funds for the educational development of Negroes primarily, but not exclusively, in the South. Whether the newly freed Negroes should be provided a classical education, which equipped them for social and political equality as supported by W. E. B. Du Bois; or a mostly agricultural education, which equipped them for economic independence as supported by Booker T. Washington; or religious education, as supported by certain churches, formed major decision points for various philanthropies.

RACIAL TERRORISM

Although the Thirteenth, Fourteenth, and Fifteenth Amendments had given Negroes certain protections, the Southern leadership found other ways to accomplish their nefarious goals. One was lynching, which terrorized Negroes from the 1890s through much of the first half of the twentieth century.

Racial terrorism, through organizations like the Ku Klux Klan, represented a major way Southern whites expressed their determinations to maintain the racial upper hand. Racial terrorism and violence was the major tactic of the Ku Klux Klan. The Klan was founded by Confederate Army veterans in 1865, but was officially abolished by the Ku Klux Klan Act of 1871. It resurfaced as a formal fraternal organization around 1915 and grew to a strength of nearly 5 million members by the mid 1920s. The Klan suffered a setback in 2008 when an all-white jury ordered the Ku Klux Klan of America's leader, the "Grand Wizard," and two of his former lieutenants to pay Jordan Gruver 2.5 million dollars. Gruver, with the help of the Southern Poverty Law Center, had sued the Klan for a beating he suffered at the hands of the Klan. Gruver's successful suit against the Klan dealt them a serious blow, putting much of their property at risk, but few believe they were dealt a fatal blow.

THE BLACK CODES AND JIM CROW LAWS

Even defeat in the Civil War failed to deter Southern whites' determination to control Negro life. The abolition of slavery required that they find other ways to maintain control over Negroes. Through the enactment of codes designed to regulate such civil rights as freedom of movement, freedom of speech, marriage, ownership of property, and which occupations would be available to Negroes, Southern legislatures aimed to control virtually every aspect of Negro life. Although the Black Codes were different in every state, they were similar in the kinds of restrictions imposed on Negroes. For example, every Southern state had codes controlling the kinds of jobs available to Negroes, as well as codes designed to subject Negroes to arrest and to be charged with vagrancy if they were unemployed.

Although the Black Codes are mostly associated with actions taken by Southern states during the period immediately after the Civil War, some such laws can actually be traced back to the early nineteenth century and even found in several Northern states. The federal government eventually ended the Black Codes through the efforts and actions of the Congressional Radical Republicans who pushed through the Civil Rights Act of 1866 and the Reconstruction Acts of 1867 and 1868.

Not surprisingly, Southern whites were highly threatened by the Reconstruction's rapid expansion of policies and programs providing opportunities for Negroes to gain social equity and economic parity. By the 1890s, the gains made during the period of Reconstruction were beginning to fade as whites reasserted their power and reestablished their culture of white supremacy, especially in the Southern states. There was still racism in the North, though it was not institutionalized in the same way as in the South. In the South many of the old leaders from the Confederate regime regained power throughout the South and resumed their agenda of disenfranchising Negroes. One of their tactics designed to reestablish white supremacy was the enactment of the Jim Crow laws to reestablish their control over Negroes.

The Black Codes of 1860s and the Jim Crow laws of the late 1800s are similar, but are not the same. The Black Codes were enacted during the middle 1860s as attempts by white Southerners to maintain their pre–Civil War way of life by inhibiting the freedom of ex-slaves. The Jim Crow laws were enacted after the Reconstruction period and were primarily designed to establish and maintain segregation between the races in public facilities like public transportation, public schools, public restrooms and the like. White-controlled state legislatures throughout the South passed laws that robbed Negroes of their basic rights and created a dual society based on race that claimed to be "separate but equal." These laws prohibited freed slaves from exercising the basic rights they had been granted during Reconstruction such as voting, serving on juries, carrying weapons, and working in certain occupations. "Separate but equal" was the key Jim Crow strategy, which extended even to the United States military. In many Southern states, race-based laws imposed strict racial segregation that lasted well into the late 1960s, and in some places, even into the 1970s.

With respect to Negro educational opportunities, a signal event during the early part of this period was the *Plessy v. Ferguson* case of 1896, in which the U.S. Supreme Court ruled that racial segregation was legal under our Constitution. This ruling doomed four generations of Negroes to a system of racial segregation in the South and in some western regions of the United States.

Although strict racial segregation denied Negroes equal opportunities in social and economic matters, it caused the greatest damage in terms of educational opportunities. Negro children were required to attend schools in deteriorated buildings and use out-of-date books. They were taught by teachers who were paid significantly less than their white peers and offered poor to nonexistent cocurricular activities. In the South and even in some other agricultural communities, Negro schoolchildren were assigned to split school sessions to give them time to pick cotton.

The Black Codes, Jim Crow laws, and other tactics used by white Southerners to disenfranchise Negroes forced many freedmen in the South to resort to sharecropping, as it was the only option available to support themselves and their families. Sharecropping, an agreement between a landowner and his tenant to exchange crops for the use of land, benefited the owner but often placed the tenant in a vortex of debt. The end result was an economic system and a power structure that were remarkably similar to the antebellum slave regime in the South.

The Turning of the Tide

The tide finally began to turn in the 1950s. The period extending from 1951 to 1970 is sometimes referred to as the second Reconstruction. More often it is referred to as the modern Civil Rights movement. Clearly, it marked a period when Negroes—who by this time preferred to be called blacks (many insisting on "Blacks" with a capital letter)—were fed up and were not going to take it anymore. It was as if they had just read a copy of *Walker's Appeal* and were again roused to action.

Blacks expressed their refusal to accept racial segregation and Jim Crowism by organizing marches, participating in sit-ins at "whites only" lunch counters, filing suit for admission to schools that refused them admission on the basis of their race, and in general, demanding their rights as citizens as protected by the Fourteenth Amendment. Like the proverbial straw house in the windstorm, the legal support for the South's system of segregation fell before the legal assault of the Civil Rights movement.

The most notable victory among many of this era was the *Brown v. Board of Education* decision of 1954, which threw out *Plessy v. Ferguson* and declared that school segregation based on race was unconstitutional. Even then, the Supreme Court's vague "with all deliberate speed" language retarded strict compliance with the decision for another twenty years. Some would argue that even now we are not in strict compliance with *Brown v. Board of Education*.

By this time, four generations of black Americans had endured a highly rigid system of segregation and racial oppression that severely retarded educational development of Negroes. African Americans throughout the nation cheered *Brown v. Board of Education,* feeling that it finally represented new opportunities and new beginnings for black people in the United States of America. But it soon became clear that the path to educational parity would be longer and more difficult than most blacks had imagined.

The Central Question

This brings us to the present day and to the central question of this chapter: to what extent does the legacy of the Negroes' historic educational experiences during slavery, racial segregation, racial discrimination, and Jim Crowism account for the current gap in academic performance between white and black students? Put differently, should we blame the achievement gap as it exists today on our educational history coupled with continued racial discrimination, or on our contemporary educational commitment and actions? Or is something else responsible for the current educational status of African Americans?

Some, like political scholar Manning Marable, firmly believe that "the fundamental problem of American democracy in the twenty-first century is the problem of 'structural racism': the deep patterns of socioeconomic inequality and accumulated disadvantage that are coded by race, and constantly justified in public discourse by both racist stereotypes and white indifference."[32] Those who subscribe to this reasoning—the fundamental problem even today is structural racism—would no doubt feel that today's black–white achievement gap results, in great part, from our legacy of slavery and subsequent racism.

Some suggest that even President George W. Bush found some agreement with this point of view—at least in principle. As evidence, they point to his remarks in July 2003, when he referred to slavery as "one of the greatest crimes of history" and opined, "many of the issues that still trouble us today have roots in the bitter experience of other times."[33] Could he have meant for the black–white achievement gap to be included as one of issues?

George Mason University's Walter Williams is among those who vehemently disagree with the idea that historical experience and structural racism is to blame, countering with, "This vestige-of-slavery argument, as an explanation for the pathology seen in some black neighborhoods, is simply nonsense when you think about it."[34] Williams supports his position by citing statistics that show that African American social and cultural pathologies are more severe now than they were in the early part of the twentieth century, when racism and racial discrimination were clearly much more pronounced.

Similarly, as Sniderman and Piazza assert in their book *The Scar of Race*:

> Bigotry provides a temptingly simple cause for a complex problem; it underlines the moral appeal of working to overcome the legacy of slavery and discrimination by fixing attention on the evil originally responsible for it. And not least, it fixes the responsibility for the persistence of the problem on "them"—on the out-and-out bigots—in the process of diverting attention from us.[35]

Citing survey statistics, Sniderman and Piazza show that whites are now far less likely than in the past to hold racist attitudes toward African Americans, making repeated claims of racism as an explanation for the African American disadvantage largely debatable. The 2008 election of Barack Obama as President of the United States seems to provide a strong argument in support of the Sniderman and Piazza's survey finding that over time bigotry has given ground. While the turnout in support of

President Obama's election was massive in the African American community, everyone knew that he would need strong support from within the white community to win. Even so, most had lingering doubts that enough whites would actually vote for Obama to elect him President of the United States. There was wide spread discussion of the Bradley effect, referring to the Mayor Bradley 1982 race for Governor of California where he was well ahead in the polls even up to election day, but lost the race. The Bradley effect describes what is thought to be the tendency of some whites to tell pollsters and others that they are either undecided or that they support the African American candidate when in fact their real intention is to vote against the black candidate. President Obama's election dashes cold water on the idea of a Bradley effect and adds credence to the Sniderman and Piazza findings.

▶ ▶ ▶

When you consider these two extremes—that the black–white achievement gap is the product of the African American history of slavery and discrimination, and the counterposition that the current gap cannot be justified by the African Americans' history of slavery and discrimination—where does that leave us in our quest to understand the cause of the achievement gap? As is almost always the case, the real answer does not lie at the extremes, but rather somewhere in between. On the one hand, the present day black–white achievement gap most certainly has roots in the African American experience along the historical continuum, beginning with slavery and continuing through the Black Codes, racial discrimination, and legally imposed separate but (un)equal educational opportunities. One cannot simply ignore this history and the lasting effects that it continues to have.

However, by the mid-1970s after *Brown v. Board of Education* was handed down and its implementation codified in the many desegregation consent decrees, discrimination in general—and unequal educational opportunities in particular—were considerably diminished, and as such became less potent barriers to African American educational progress. In fact, it can be argued that after the mid 1970s, racism and racial discrimination, though still barriers to African American educational progress, were no longer the *primary* barriers (note the word "primary") preventing African American students from achieving at high levels. This is not to say that with respect to educational opportunities, everything was peaches and cream for African American students after the mid 70s, because clearly many race-based problems remained. Racism and discrimination still existed well after the mid 1970s and exist even today. But if the question is, do racism and discrimination remain the primary impediments—the greatest obstacles—to African American educational opportunities after the mid 1970s, a fair answer would have to be that whereas they remain as impediments, they are no longer the primary impediments to educational progress of African American students.

cf
p. 95

This short review of the African American educational experience makes it unarguably clear that with respect to educational attainment, African American students have experienced a deliberate and debilitating opportunity gap, when compared to the educational opportunities of white students. The educational restrictions imposed by slavery and educational limitations resulting from the Jim Crow laws and a racist social system were real, and they had real educational effects on African Americans' educational progress. Separate but (un)equal African American schools and school districts where the buildings were inferior, textbooks outdated, and teacher quality poor cannot be ignored. During this period too many African American children simply did not have access to high-quality schools—and this is unfortunately still the case. To believe that the current black–white achievement gap is not in some way influenced by these historical factors is simply beyond unreasonable.

On the other hand, however, while history is important, it is not destiny. We need to stop seeing slavery and its legacy as an explanation for the current dismal academic performance of African American students in this country. The title of Stephan and Abigail Thernstrom's book *No Excuses* says it all.[36] The realities of slavery cannot be dismissed, but neither should they be used to justify the continued existence of the achievement gap. Separate but (un)equal educational opportunities and racial discrimination are historical facts. They are an indelible part of the African American experience. History is history, and it cannot be changed. But history is what has been, not what will be. To believe that because the black–white achievement gap is a historical fact, it is therefore inevitable, is fatalistic thinking and we must reject it. It is always possible for committed people, working together towards common goals, to change the current trajectory of history in service of a better future. History is filled with remarkable examples of this. The civil rights struggle is among those that come immediately to mind.

African Americans are not the only people who have had to overcome racial discrimination, prejudice, and even human bondage on their journey to racial equality and social justice in America. There are numerous racial and ethnic groups which have overcome their turbulent histories and excelled despite the odds being stacked against them. In fact, this is more the rule than the exception. Consider the plight of the Chinese who had to overcome stinging stereotypes, economic discrimination, and social ostracism; still they achieved. Or consider the plight of West Indian Americans who carry the same marks of Africa that African Americans do, yet they have achieved an outstanding record of accomplishments, especially in the field of education.

Though assimilation has been a major challenge for African Americans, particularly given their different skin color, consider how many African Americans have overcome the racial barriers put before them. From the earliest days of British Colonial America, African Americans have succeeded in every conceivable field. Even at the height of slavery in America, they could be found among the rich and even the very rich; they were represented in all professions, among the craftsmen, intellectuals, merchants, and the clergy. Clearly, these were exceptions to the norm, but they were there. Though they had to surmount unbelievable odds, torturous challenges, and life-threatening events, African Americans always overcame. And through their efforts, the road to success has become less rocky and more accessible for their successors.

Even today, as we look at African Americans' academic performance, we can identify pockets of excellence throughout the country, in every state, in most cities, in rural and urban circumstances, and in rich and poor circumstances. The examples of high academic achievement by African Americans are voluminous. There are schools where no difference in achievement exists between students from various racial and ethnic groups or various socioeconomic groups.

Clearly, the achievement gap can be closed. There is nothing wrong with African American children's DNA. They can learn. But in too many places, they are not learning—and too often, their underperformance is blamed on a racist system left over from slavery. This sends the wrong signal to our students and teachers, giving them excuses for failing to achieve.

In a recent interview for PBS's show, *African in America, Part 4*, historian James Horton, a distinguished professor at George Washington University, made an interesting distinction, stating:

> The problem of race in America at the end of the twentieth century is not the problem of slavery. If it had been the problem of slavery, it'd have been over in 1865. But as a Christian nation, as a nation that saw itself as a Christian nation, as a nation that was itself built on the principles of freedom, we had to tell ourselves that there was something about the slave that justified slavery. It is that justification of slavery that we are still trying to deal with, more than 100 years after the abolition of slavery.[37]

Consider this quote carefully. Horton's point is that we suffer now not from the vestiges of slavery, but from the lingering vestiges of the "justification" of slavery. This idea makes a lot of sense when you consider how slave owners sought to dehumanize Negroes by using legal statutes, publications, assemblies, churches, and every conceivable tactic to convince the colonists and the Negroes themselves that the people of Africa were barbarians, incapable of civilized living, and deserving of enslavement. Horton is on to something. It is the justification of slavery that we are still trying to deal with. The stereotype of the Negro as subhuman, as inferior to whites, was reinforced by every legal and societal means available for more than 200 years. This is what made the peculiar institution peculiar. This is what set it apart from other historical episodes of slavery. This is what still lingers—it is the cause of the racial stigma that remains.[38] There is even evidence that some of the negative stereotypes of African Americans have found residency in certain African American thinking.

Returning to Sniderman and Piazza, we note among their surprising findings, that African Americans surveyed consistently expressed more negative views of other African Americans than whites do. Among the most damning of these characterizations is that a large percentage of African Americans surveyed indicated that they felt that African Americans were more aggressive or violent, boastful, complaining, lazy, and irresponsible than whites. In other words, when asked whether African Americans as a group exhibit socially undesirable characteristics, African Americans expressed a more negative evaluation of other African Americans than whites did.[39] If Sniderman and Piazza's findings are correct, it means that a large number of African Americans have bought into many of the negative stereotypes that we thought existed mainly in the minds of whites. Given this reality, it isn't much of a stretch to think that many African Americans are holders of the "blacks are intellectually inferior" stereotype as well. One of our main concerns about the black–white achievement gap is its support for this stereotype.

Defining Racial Stigma

What is a racial stigma exactly? In his book *The Anatomy of Racial Inequality*, Brown University professor Glenn Loury offers an excellent definition:

> An awareness of the racial "otherness" of blacks is embedded in the social consciousness of the American nation owing to the historical fact of slavery and its aftermath. This inherited stigma even today exerts an inhibiting effect on the extent to which African Americans can realize their full human potential.[40]

Loury goes on to propose that racial stigma, rather than racial discrimination, provides the best explanation for "the causes of African American disadvantage."[41] Can we conclude that racial stigma is a cause of the African American academic disadvantage? Can racial stigma be both a cause and a result of the black–white achievement gap? If so, it means that in seeking to close the black–white achievement gap, we must grapple with the lasting stigma associated with the negative racial stereotype of African Americans.

Stereotypes are not changed by changing laws or receiving reparations. Nor are they changed by actions that reinforce them. The black–white achievement gap is reinforcing an already deeply embedded racial stereotype of African American inferiority in the minds of both whites and blacks, as well as others. Howard and Hammond called our attention to this matter as early as 1985 in their *New Republic* article "Rumors of Inferiority."[42]

The stereotype is a major barrier impeding the African American journey to racial equality and social justice. The best way to change the stereotype of African American intellectual inferiority is to close the black–white achievement gap and prove the stereotype wrong. This is not a new idea. It has already been tried successfully in other aspects of American society. It's what we did to the stereotype that African Americans couldn't play baseball in the major leagues, or couldn't run the distance races in track and win, or couldn't be a head basketball coach in the NBA, or couldn't be a quarterback in the NFL, or couldn't lead Fortune 500 companies, or be Supreme Court judges. All these stereotypes have been shattered. The time has come now to shatter the most important and significant one of all: the stereotype that African Americans cannot achieve academic parity with whites.

This requires a fundamental shift in everyone's thinking. It requires that we give up the long-held assumption that the legacy of slavery and continued racial discrimination prevent African Americans from facing and dealing with the central problems they are facing today. Corrective actions based on this false assumption will never succeed since those who hold this view are searching for answers in the wrong places.

Instead, we must adopt the assumption that it is the stereotype of racial inferiority—created by a slave-holding society to justify slavery in the face of the seemingly contradictory ideals of freedom and equality—that is the primary impediment to racial equality in today's society. In other words, racial stigma is the main challenge facing us. Because the black–white achievement gap continues to reinforce and perpetuate this stigma, the best solution is to dispel it through high levels of performance, as we have done in so many cases, so many times.

Summary

This short review of African American history leaves us with the undeniable conclusion that African Americans have experienced an educational opportunity gap. Not only does a review of history show that African Americans' educational opportunities have been much more limited than that of their white counterparts, equally importantly, it shows that during the colonial and pre–Civil War years, there were periods and places where African Americans were legally prohibited from learning to read—and with even greater long-term negative effects, there were also periods and places where African Americans were deliberately taught to devalue education.

Therefore, the important history lesson is that that the black–white achievement gap has indeed been influenced by a black–white opportunity gap. Even so, this educational history cannot be accepted as justification for the contemporary academic performance of African American students relative to their white peers. Our historical educational shortcomings represent a history that we must overcome. Just as the other barriers that impeded African American progress were confronted and defeated, the black–white achievement gap must, likewise, be confronted and defeated. To achieve this goal, the leadership of authentic African American leaders will be required. *That* is the history lesson we must learn.

CHAPTER 6

Yes, We Can Close the Achievement Gap!

I shall always be a flower girl to Professor Higgins, because he always treats me as a flower girl, and always will; but I know I can be a lady to you, because you always treat me as a lady, and always will.

— Eliza Doolittle, from George Bernard Shaw's *Pygmalion*

CAN WE CLOSE the black–white achievement gap? Yes, we can close the gap. But it will require substantial modifications of our thinking, level of commitment, and behavior. Change, the strategy around which President Obama built a successful presidential campaign, is the key strategy that will be required in order to close the gap.

The element that will need to change first is how we view the problem. Currently, the achievement gap is viewed as a problem of student academics. Of course student academics is involved, but for the purposes of closing the gap, we will make more progress if we see it as a leadership problem. At present, what the achievement gap problem needs is authentic African American leadership. This does not mean that the academic elements of the problem are to be ignored. It means that the academic elements of the problem are to be managed within a leadership program committed to closing the gap. It means that a committed leadership structure must take charge of the achievement problem and attend to all its elements including, but not limited to, the academic ones. A first leadership challenge would be internalizing and promoting the idea that, yes, we can close the achievement gap.

The Power of Believing We Can Close the Gap

Educators have been aware of the black–white achievement gap now for nearly a century. During that time, with varying levels of commitment, schools have thrown any number of remedies at the problem. Unfortunately, many of these attempts were based on assumptions and guesswork, rather than comprehensive and definitive research, so these efforts largely amounted to spit and duct tape. Even when there have been isolated spots of success and more thoughtful and well-supported initiatives, the cold hard fact of the matter is that the gap persists. In the face of the gap's stubbornness, many have come to the gloomy premise that maybe it can never be closed.

Consider for example a recent study by Felicity A. Crawford, a member of Boston's Wheelock College faculty. Her research focused on how widely held societal viewpoints shape teachers' beliefs and attitudes and drive their everyday practice.[1] The title of her work says it all. She dubbed her study "Why Bother? They Are Not Capable of This Level of Work." The message was clear: if teachers don't believe the gap can be closed, they will not teach well. The logical extension of her finding is also clear: if African American leaders don't believe the gap can be closed, they will not take action. Unfortunately, the fact that closing the gap has yet to be a meaningful priority among African American leaders suggests a lack of confidence in African American students. It is our position that it should be _the_ burning issue of our time! There is an overarching principle, that _what you believe influences what you do._ This is not new news, of course— and it holds true for all of us, not just teachers. With respect to closing the black–white achievement gap, it's absolutely essential that there be a committed, caring, and determined leadership that believes deeply that the gap can be closed. It's essential because our success depends on the intensity of our efforts, and that intensity in turn depends on what we believe about the possibility of closing the gap.

Communicating to students is another big issue. This is true because of a different, but related, principle: _our expectations of people and their expectations of themselves are the key factors in how well they_ *perform.* Thus, if students look up to African American leaders who in turn have low expectations of them, those students will internalize those negative expectations and react accordingly. The good news is that the opposite is true as well. Students who look up to people who hold high expectations of them will respond by trying to live up to those high expectations.

The idea that a student's performance is influenced by their view of what is expected of them is a form of self-fulfilling prophecy; it is referred to in the professional education community as the Pygmalion effect. The Pygmalion effect drew its name from George Bernard Shaw's play *Pygmalion,* which tells a story of a professor who wins a bet that he can teach a poor flower girl to speak and behave like an upper-class lady simply by treating her as though she is an upper-class lady. The operational principle of the Pygmalion effect is that students internalize the expectations of their superiors, and when they view the expectations as positive, they demonstrate a tendency to succeed. Likewise, when students view the expectations of their superiors as negative, they tend to be influenced toward failure.[2]

The sum and substance of this matter is that the necessary first step in the journey to closing the black–white achievement gap is truly believing that it can be closed. As a starting point, each person involved in activities designed to close the gap—whether educator, parent, or community leader—needs to explore his or her own beliefs about the black–white achievement gap—why it exists, whether it represents the natural order of things, or whether it is a phenomenon in need of our attention and action. Where one stands on this matter, matters—it matters a lot.

Closing the gap may take a generation or more. It will certainly require enormous effort and involve vast shifts in attitudes and behavior about how responsibility for student learning must be apportioned among the home, the community, and the school. Closing the achievement gap will require that the problem rise to national attention on the level with our mid-twentieth century commitment to school desegregation. But close the gap we can! And we must.

How do we know that the gap can be closed? There are six foundational reasons. We hope that after careful consideration, you will agree with us.

- REASON ONE -
We Have Observed Many Underperforming Black Students Become High-Performing Students

During our combined ninety years of experience in public education, we've seen failing black students become successful students. We are not talking about one or two students here, but many. Perhaps this is not statistical proof, but collectively, these students show that children who many would consider lost causes can learn and even excel. In short there is no genetic factor that prevents black students from performing well in school. If it were genetic, teachers would not be able to take underperforming black students and turn them into stars. And while it doesn't happen often enough, it does happen.

These academic turnarounds seem to happen for those who have the good fortune to land in the classroom of a committed teacher who simply will not accept failure. That means that a student's school performance is, in part, based on the luck of the draw, whether he or she is lucky enough to be assigned to a great teacher.

It's not always a great teacher, however. Sometimes it's the football coach, a band teacher, or an art or choral director who ignites a student's passion for learning. It seems that a student's commitment to success in an extracurricular activity can fire an interest in excelling in academic pursuits as well. This is especially true when coaches and other leaders require that a student maintain grades to participate in the activity.

When you dig below the surface, there is one key to these against-the-odds turnarounds—an adult with high expectations who took the time to connect to the student. That adult can be a teacher, coach, parent, religious leader, or community leader. Sometimes students have turned around their academic performance after realizing how tired and worn down their mothers were coming home every day after working two jobs to support their family. Regardless of the quality of the adult's role in the child's life, it adds credence to the adage that the most important determinant of the success or failure of a young person is the extent to which the young person has a caring adult in his or her life.

When a child makes an academic turnaround, nothing about the student's DNA changes. There was no sudden brain-power surge. And their socioeconomic status for the most part did not change. What changed was the student's motivation, attitude, interest, dedication, and commitment. That tells us that if we can figure out how to cause this kind of change in the lives of more students, it will be possible to make a serious dent in the black–white achievement gap.

– REASON TWO –

The Black–White Achievement Gap Is Changeable

The National Assessment of Educational Progress (NAEP), often referred to as the Nation's Report Card, provides the best longitudinal source of student test data that our nation has to offer. NAEP data showed a significant narrowing of the black–white achievement gap during the 1970s and the 1980s. The causes of this narrowing, why improvement slowed and, in some cases, stopped after the late 1980s was and continues to be the subject of much academic discussion. But the main point is that the gap is not now and never has been frozen in place. The fact that it narrowed is proof that it is malleable, and this malleability supports the belief that it can be closed.

– REASON THREE –

During the Early Years of Groups Coming into Mainstream Contemporary Western Society, Lagging Test Scores Are Normal

In the history of ethnic and minority groups entering the United States, many groups lagged behind in education during their early years in this country. America's history is replete with stories of immigrant groups that initially scored low on tests compared to well-established, mainstream groups. A review of immigrant history will also show that although many of these groups initially scored low on tests, they demonstrated significant improvement over time and, in some cases, even excelled when compared with mainstream groups. One has only to read Thomas Sowell's great book *Race and Culture* to gain insight into this phenomenon.[3]

Although African Americans came to this country in 1619, they existed in a state of enslavement until 1865. Even after 1865, a condition of less than freedom existed for African Americans well into the middle 1970s, some would argue even longer. To make African Americans' entry into this country as a free ethnic group analogous with that of other immigrants, we would argue that the appropriate entry date for African Americans should be April 1954, when the Supreme Court handed down its decision in *Brown v. Board of Education*. Under that scenario, African Americans have been in this country as a free ethnic group for less than a century.

Given the fluidity of test scores, it would be reckless to conclude, from viewing such a small slice of history, that a group's test scores represent something fixed in nature. History simply doesn't support this type of reasoning.

As we go forward, we would be well advised to accept the admonition of Thomas Sowell when he states that:

> The point here is that there have always been gaps between the development of one people and another, even if their relative positions did not remain the same permanently, and even if their genes had nothing to do with it.[4]

> That history and its painful consequences are undeniable. But, in a world where whole nations have in effect raised their IQs by 20 points in one generation, it is time for black "leaders" and white "friends" to stop trying to discredit the tests and get on with the job of improving the skills that the tests measure.[5]

In short, it is not unusual for a new demographic group to score lower than mainstream groups on academic tests when they first arrive in this country. If we look at African Americans as having arrived here in the 1950s, then perhaps the gap is neither so old nor so intractable as it might seem.

– REASON FOUR –
Some Federal Education Policy Has Produced Significant Narrowing of the Black–White Achievement Gap

Since the turn of the century there has been a gradual yet steady narrowing of the black–white achievement gap owing primarily to improvement in the math and reading performance of African American and other minority students. It's reasonable to attribute much of this improved math and reading performance to the accountability movement, emanating from the 1991 Education Summit called by President George Herbert Walker Bush, and embedded into national policy through President Bill Clinton's Improving America's Schools Act (IASA) of 1994.

Although the accountability movement as federal policy had its birth in 1994, it matured in 2002 when President George W. Bush signed the No Child Left Behind Act (NCLB) of 2001 into law. On the cover of the NCLB bill enacted by Congress are these words: "An Act to Close the Achievement Gap with Accountability, Flexibility, and Choice." The NCLB literally changed the culture of public education in the United States, and in concert with other factors, caused improvement primarily in math and to a lesser extent reading, especially for minority populations.

One of the most striking changes resulting from NCLB is the require-ment that schools test students in grades three through eight annually against standards set by their state and report the data for each separate subgroup with a substantial enrollment in the school. This meant that schools with a substantial enrollment of African American, Hispanic, white, low-income, and/or Limited English Proficiency (LEP) students could no longer simply report the average performance for all students in the school, allowing for some subgroups' low performance to be ignored within the overall average. This new law made each subgroup's perform-ance highly visible on its own. Other important elements of NCLB were:

- A requirement for highly qualified teachers in all core subjects

- A strong focus on reading and math

- A requirement for schools to report their annual progress against annual goals set by their state

- A requirement for districts to allow students the freedom to enroll in other public schools if their school fails to meet its yearly progress goal for two consecutive years

- A requirement for districts to provide supplemental education services for students enrolled in schools that fail to achieve their annual progress goals for three consecutive years

The Center on Education Policy's data showed that student achieve-ment in math and reading rose, and that the black–white achievement *really?*

gap has narrowed since NCLB was passed. The gains were stronger in K–8 than in 9–12.

Between 2001 and 2006, public schools in Chicago narrowed the academic achievement gap by 27 percent. After conducting a study of 125,000 teachers in Illinois, the Illinois Education Research Council at Southern Illinois University credited the NCLB for the improvement in the caliber of teachers entering work in the Chicago Public Schools.[6]

Although scholars can continue to debate how to apportion credit for the student performance improvements during the period between 1990 and 2006, data showing modest gap closings are sufficient to conclude that federal policy has had a modestly positive impact on student academic performance. This is especially true during the period beginning with the 1989 Education Summit of President George Herbert Walker Bush, continuing through President Clinton's 1994 enactment of the Improving America School Act, and continuing through the No Child Left Behind years of President George W. Bush. Would even better and stronger federal policy further narrow the gap between blacks and whites?

State policies, especially those dealing with educational choice, such as charter school and voucher initiatives, have made positive contributions to improved student performance as well, thereby making strides toward closing the black–white achievement gap. Although the research on charter schools shows mixed results, it has made clear that some charter schools and voucher programs have consistently shown positive student outcomes not only for students attending these programs, but for students left in the traditional schools as well.[7] In a number of cases where charter schools or voucher programs attracted students away from traditional public schools, the public schools responded with educational improvements designed to make their schools more competitive so as to reduce the likelihood of their students being attracted away. Such efforts at improved school operations in traditional schools are examples of how competition from charter schools or voucher programs benefits students who remain in the traditional public school as well as those who choose to leave for the charter or voucher program.

Because there is considerable evidence that state and federal education policies have helped shrink the black–white achievement gap, it seems likely that even better and more effectively implemented state and federal policies can only enhance the potential for closing the black–white achievement gap.

– REASON FIVE –
There Are Great Schools That Are Closing the Gap Even Now

Undoubtedly, the most powerful case that the black–white achievement gap can be closed can be made by looking at the schools that are succeeding in closing the gap with their students. More often than not, these schools are charter schools that are freed from the bureaucratic morass, political control, and stagnation that is typical in many traditional schools and school districts. However, one can occasionally encounter great schools among the traditional public schools, usually headed by a courageous principal who is not afraid to swim upstream, a principal who has assembled, by hook or crook, a great faculty. Within the confines of this book, our words can't begin to do these schools justice. To fully appreciate the full majesty of these schools, one must experience the school first-hand and become immersed in the vibrant educational culture. Nonetheless, allow us to describe four such schools where many great things are happening and the black–white gaps are becoming relics of the past. What follows are brief descriptions of four such schools so the reader can get a feel for the operation of great schools and gain confidence that the gap really can be closed

SEED PUBLIC CHARTER SCHOOL

In 1998, the Seed Foundation opened the SEED Public Charter School of Washington, D.C., with the bold mission of preparing disadvantaged children academically and socially for success in college and in life. SEED adopted a strategy for achieving its mission by providing an intense college preparatory boarding education for the children of Washington, D.C., whose circumstances would otherwise have diminished their chances for a quality education. Through its boarding school strategy, SEED provides students with twenty-four-hour supervision, life-skills training, and after-school support. The SEED charter school accepts students by lottery for grades seven through twelve. Students are not tested for admission and usually enter several grade levels below their age group. Approximately 85 percent of SEED's students are eligible for the federal free and reduced-price lunch program. Most are from single-parent households, with the majority coming from families with no college education. About three-quarters of the students would be without after-school supervision if they were not enrolled in a SEED school, and a majority of the students come from the most depressed areas of Washington, D.C. SEED's enrollment is 98 percent African American and 2 percent Hispanic.

What do you think the expected performance level of a school with such an enrollment would be? You might be surprised to learn that with the exception of two public magnet schools, SEED students outscored all District of Columbia Public Schools (DCPS) schools on the Scholastic Aptitude Test (SAT), and that 100 percent of SEED's first graduating class (2004) was accepted to college.

YES PREP PUBLIC SCHOOLS

YES Prep Public Schools is a system of five state-chartered public schools operating in Houston, Texas, that serve low-income students in grades six through twelve. YES Prep is the vision of founder Chris Barbic, a Teach for America alumnus who taught for two years at the Houston Independent School District's Rusk Elementary School, where the YES concept was born. The strategies to prepare students for college graduation include a rigorous college prep academic model that includes parents and student contracts to comply with the YES culture and standards, an intensive summer school program, Saturday classes, introductory classes to college life, a longer school day, student support services that include access to faculty twenty-four hours a day, seven days a week; social services and student advisory group sessions; and acceptance by a four-year college as a requirement for high school graduation.

Eighty percent of YES students are economically disadvantaged, 95 percent are Hispanic or African American, 88 percent are first-generation college bound, and most students enter YES one grade level behind in math and science.

Yet despite the enormous challenges to achieving its mission of "increasing the number of low-income Houstonians who graduate from a four-year college prepared to compete in the global marketplace and committed to improving disadvantaged communities," YES is spectacularly successful. In 2007, for the second consecutive year, *Newsweek* ranked YES as one of the 100 best high schools in the nation. For seven consecutive years all YES Prep seniors have been accepted into four-year colleges, 90 percent of YES Prep graduates have graduated from college or are still enrolled; and in 2008, Children at Risk, a Houston nonprofit organization, ranked YES as the number-one high school in the Houston area. As you would expect, judging from the high graduation rates, both from high school and college, the achievement gap at YES has shown significant narrowing.

KNOWLEDGE IS POWER PROGRAM (KIPP)

Knowledge Is Power Program (KIPP) is a national network of public charter schools established by two Teach for America alumni—Mike Feinberg and Dave Levin—who, after finishing their two-year fifth-grade teaching assignments at Houston Independent School District's Garcia Elementary School, launched their own school. KIPP schools operate on a set of core principles that are called the five pillars: High Expectations, Choice and Commitment, More Time, Power to Lead, and Focus on Results. KIPP's commitment to the five pillars is unyielding. Starting in Houston with a single school in 1994, Levin moved to New York the following year and opened KIPP's second school. As of this writing, KIPP serves approximately 20,000 students enrolled in eighty-two schools in nineteen states and the District of Columbia.

KIPP's enrollment is approximately 90 percent African American and Hispanic, and 80 percent of the students are eligible for the federal free and reduced-price meals program. KIPP accepts students without regard to their prior academic record, conduct, or socioeconomic background. A visitor to KIPP school can expect to hear people say: "Work hard, be nice," "There are no shortcuts," and "Great teaching and more of it"— all designed to establish a school culture of hard work, unity, discipline, and great pedagogy. In additional to the attention paid to a strong school culture which supports great student performance, KIPP's school day is longer than that of the traditional public schools. They start earlier and they last longer; KIPP students attend school a half day on Saturdays; parents of KIPP students are required to participate in their children's educational activities, and KIPP teachers undergo special training.

KIPP student performance is outstanding. The 2008 KIPP Report Card tells the story:[8]

> ‣ Many students begin KIPP in the fifth grade at least one grade level—and in many cases two or more—behind their peers in reading and math. After four years at KIPP, 100 percent of KIPP eighth-grade classes outperformed their district averages in both mathematics and reading/English language arts, based on state tests.

‣ The average KIPP student who stays with KIPP for four years starts fifth grade at the 41st percentile in mathematics and the 31st percentile in reading. After four years at KIPP, these same students are performing at the 80th percentile in math and the 58th percentile in reading, based on national norm-referenced tests.

‣ Less than 20 percent of low-income students go to college nationwide. Nationally, more than 85 percent of KIPP students from the original two KIPP Academies are matriculating to college.

MABEL WESLEY ELEMENTARY SCHOOL

In the 1990s, Mabel Wesley Elementary School was one of the Houston Independent School District's elementary schools. It served Houston's Acres Homes community, a predominantly black community, made up of low-income and working class families on the city's north side. Wesley Elementary, with its pristine landscaping, neatly maintained flower beds, and clean walkways and floors, gave the appearance of an island paradise in a sea of drug-infested, boarded-up vacant buildings with uncut lawns. Almost 100 percent of Wesley's students qualified for the federal free and reduced-price lunch program as well as federal Title I education funds made available through the enactment of the Elementary and Secondary Education Act of 1965 as a part of President Lyndon B. Johnson's "War on Poverty." Ninety-nine percent of its students were African American. But in the district's ranking of schools based on their students' performance on the state required tests, Wesley was often among the top performers. This was a situation that attracted national attention, causing people to wonder about the secret behind Wesley's success. But to those close to the situation, there was little mystery. The secret was its principal, Thaddeus Lott, a no-nonsense, "damn-the-torpedoes," whatever-it-takes educator who accepted nothing but excellence.

He used his own modified version of the Direct Instructional System for Teaching and Remediation (DISTAR). It's a commercial arithmetic and reading program of SRA/McGraw-Hill. Direct Instruction, the program's teaching model, is a method of teaching which is based on rigorously developed, highly scripted content and constant and fast-paced interaction between teacher and students. His kindergarten through second-grade reading strategies involved a heavy dose of phonetics, memory exercises, extra reading, and daily assessments, a much more intense program than that found in most other schools. All of Wesley's teachers had high expectations of students and the conviction that all children could learn if taught well. Unlike teacher training at many schools, staff development at Wesley was carefully tailored to ensure that staff learned how to teach Wesley's specific curriculum, which was selected based on its proven results.

Lott's teachers were selected on the basis of their high-energy ability, willingness to go the extra mile, high expectations of students, and willingness to learn to teach the Thaddeus Lott way. Whereas in many school districts, teachers are assigned to schools by the district's central office, Lott defied this practice and insisted on personally selecting his teachers. Excellent student discipline was the expectation; and both parents and students understood and accepted the rules for student conduct and effort. To get a feel for Lott's zest for high academic achievement for his students, just consider how he described himself to Melanie Markley, a reporter for the *Houston Chronicle*. He said, "I'm obsessed. I feel the same way about education that religious people feel about salvation."[9]

Bottom line: students at Wesley Elementary were virtually all African American, nearly all poor, mostly from the same poverty-burdened environment. Few had parents with much formal education, yet they achieved. Now, one can argue that Wesley represents the exception, and that's true. But it doesn't have to be. Following Wesley's model, other schools can become exceptional as well, even to the extent that the exception becomes the ordinary.

A postscript: Thaddeus Lott retired in 2002. Wesley Elementary, without Lott's leadership, has unfortunately lost the high academic achievement that was so common during his tenure at the school.

▶ ▶ ▶

There you have it: four examples of schools that we have personally visited and found to have achieved superb student outcomes despite students' low socioeconomic status, low parent educational attainment, prior school failures, or unsupportive community environment. No doubt there are many other such schools. In fact, fifteen such schools are described in Karin Chenoweth's book appropriately entitled *"It's Being Done": Academic Success in Unexpected Schools*.[10] To assure that the schools described in her book were the kinds of schools usually associated with low academic performance and were not significantly different from other traditional public schools in terms of resources and admission criteria, she only considered schools that met the following seven-point selection criteria:

- A significant population of children living in poverty and/or a significant population of children of color.

- Either very high rates of achievement or a very rapid improvement trajectory.

- Relatively small gaps in student achievement in comparison with achievement gaps statewide.

- At least two years' worth of data.

- In the case of high schools, high graduation rates that are higher than state average promoting power index (a measure that compares the number of seniors enrolled in a high school to the number of ninth graders enrolled in the high school three years earlier).

- Meeting Adequate Yearly Progress (AYP, a state-developed measure that defines the minimum level of student improvement that the state, the individual schools, and the individual districts within the state, must achieve each year in order to meet requirements of the federal No Child Left Behind legislation).

- Open enrollment for neighborhood children—that is, no magnet schools, no exam schools (schools using exams to determine admission), and no charter schools.

After "spelunking" (her word) through the data on state report cards and spending two years visiting schools, Chenoweth identified the following schools as examples of schools where the question "can it be done?" is answered, not with high-sounding platitudes, but by actually doing it:

- Frankford Elementary School, Frankford, Delaware

- University Park Campus School, Worcester, Massachusetts

- Oakland Heights Elementary School, Russellville, Arkansas

- Elmont Memorial Junior-Senior High School, Elmont, New York

- Lincoln Elementary School, Mount Vernon, New York

- Dayton's Bluff Achievement Plus Elementary School, St. Paul, Minnesota

- Centennial Place Elementary School, Atlanta, Georgia

- Lapwai Elementary School, Lapwai, Idaho

- Granger High School, Granger, Washington

- M. Hall Stanton Elementary School, Philadelphia, Pennsylvania

- West Jasper Elementary School, West Jasper, Alabama

- East Millsboro Elementary School, East Millsboro, Delaware

- Capitol View Elementary School, Port Chester, New York

- The Benwood Initiative, Chattanooga, Tennessee

Need more convincing? Read Samuel Casey Carter's book, *No Excuses: Lessons from 21 High-Performing High-Poverty Schools,* where nineteen additional such schools are offered (KIPP and Wesley Elementary School are included in his list of twenty-one schools).[11] These schools stand as confirmation that African American students can indeed achieve. Further, they make inescapably clear that where students are not achieving, we are not doing as much as we need to do in order to provide appropriate learning environments. If the schools described above can cause student learning at high levels notwithstanding the students' "disadvantaged" situation, others can as well.

– REASON SIX –
We Know That Attention to Students' Course Selection Can Help Close the Gap

There is evidence that the gap is heavily influenced by students' high school course selection. For example, we know that students who elect and complete rigorous high school courses, regardless of their ethnicity, perform better on standardized measures than students who take the easy way out by dodging rigorous courses or students who were assigned to less rigorous classes as a result of poor counseling. This point was driven home by a 1998 report entitled *Charting the Right Course: A Report on Urban Student Achievement and Course-Taking by the Council of the Great City Schools* (CGCS), a coalition of the nation's largest urban school systems and ACT, Inc., which administers the ACT assessment. The report was based on a study of the impact of specific course sequences, student ethnicity, and gender, as well as poverty levels of 55,334 high school graduates of CGCS member districts in June 1997.

The most important finding offered major support for the "yes we can" argument when it reported that "when urban high school students complete rigorous courses—even in the poorest school districts—they outperform their inner-city counterparts who do not take those courses and significantly reduce achievement gaps between urban and non-urban students preparing for college."[12] It is undisputed that African American students are underrepresented in Advanced Placement (AP), International Baccalaureate (IB), and other advanced high school course enrollments. It may not be an exaggeration to say that the African American school integration efforts left advanced high school courses quite untouched, and they may now be among the most segregated aspect of American public schools. They are segregated not because of legal prohibitions, but because too few African American students are encouraged to enroll in these courses. The black–white achievement gap is, in part, a function of this fixable situation. Reversing African American student underrepresentation in vigorous high school courses will improve African American performance on standardized assessments, and as a result, narrow the black–white achievement gap.

This is not an argument in support of putting students in courses for which they are not prepared. On the contrary, it is an argument in support of providing all students the kind of counseling that will provide access to advanced courses for those who can benefit from them. Many students fail to enroll in advanced courses simply because they have not been advised about the importance of taking such courses, are not aware of the availability of the courses, or simply lack the encouragement necessary to enroll in challenging courses. Explaining the importance of enrolling in advanced courses and encouraging prepared students to enroll in them is an area where authentic African American leadership can play an important role.

Summary

In past years when voting rights and school desegregation were glaring barriers to social justice and equal rights for the African American community, our African American leaders of the day led the struggle to overcome. Today, the barriers are different. Lagging academic performance of African American children and youth has replaced the old barriers. The need to close the academic achievement gap between African American youth and their white peers has emerged as the civil rights issue of the day. As in the past, African American leaders are called upon to chart the course and to rouse the troops to tackle the issue.

There is no doubt that the achievement gap can be closed. The gap did in fact narrow between the early 1970s and the early 1990s. This lets us know that it is not a fixed phenomenon. Further, today the gap is being closed in various schools and communities around the nation. All across America there are schools—charter schools, private schools, Catholic schools, and even many traditional public schools—where the black–white achievement gap is being closed. In these schools African American youth are excelling academically.

What is it about these schools and communities that enable African American youth to perform as well academically as other youth in those schools? Fortunately, the answer to this question is known—youth in successful schools excel because the right combination of involvement and intervention from school, community, and parents is put into play. A student's academic success rests on three sturdy pillars: effective school operations, sound community values, and positive home educational advocacy.

Reforms in schools moving throughout America and resulting in more effective school operations are visible. Not enough is seen, however, of sound community values and positive home educational advocacy. African American leaders must tackle the difficult matters relating to community values and parental effectiveness. Leadership for change in these areas will only succeed if it comes from within the African American community.

CHAPTER 7

What's Leadership
Got to Do with It?

A real leader faces the music even when he doesn't like the tune.

—Anonymous

THE ACHIEVEMENT GAP between black and white students is enormous in many schools, districts, and communities; it has devastating consequences as students proceed into adulthood. But what's leadership got to do with closing the black–white achievement gap?

Asking this question is tantamount to asking what leadership has to do with America's preeminence in the world, with the success of General Electric, Microsoft, or Wal-Mart, or with the dominance of the New York Yankees. All these questions have the same answer: high-quality leadership makes a difference. Were there other important factors involved in the success of these organizations? Yes, of course, but the core element determining the success of every extraordinary enterprise is high-quality leadership. Leadership matters. Indeed, it matters most, especially in social movements.

What Is Leadership?

Leaders are those who have followers, and they exercise leadership when they influence others to follow them. But dig a little deeper. Rulers have followers, too. What, if anything, is the difference between a ruler and a leader? What is meant by the phrase "leadership position," and is its holder automatically a leader? For example, is holding an elective office, by definition, leadership? Are those selected by the media for their quick wit and their easily quotable one-liners automatically leaders? Are all power wielders leaders?

Consider Osama Bin Laden, Saddam Hussein, and Adolf Hitler. Are they leaders or tyrants? Can a person be both a leader and a tyrant, or are the two terms mutually exclusive? At the other end of the spectrum, are Earl Graves, Wynton Marsalis, Richard Parsons, and Toni Morrison leaders? Must one be African American to be an African American leader? These questions make it clear that pinning down the exact nature of leadership is no simple task.

Although the word "leader" has a long history extending as far back as 1300, the term "leadership" is of more recent vintage. It first emerged in the 1800s in the context of political influence.[1] The term gained traction in the 1980s, attracting the interest of scholars from a wide range of academic fields. Whereas the number of definitions of the word "leadership" hovered around a dozen during the 1800s, the number of such definitions found in books and journals had reached more than 220 by 1991, powered by growing interest from a wide range of scholars.

To complicate the matter further, leadership can be viewed through many lenses. The political science lens focuses on power and influence; the business lens focuses on effectiveness, efficiency, and outcomes; the anthropological lens focuses on cultural influences, symbols, and norms; the historical lens focuses on the influence of key figures during major social movements and significant times; the psychological and sociological lenses focus on individuals and groups as they interact.[2]

The complex notion of leadership is defined in many different ways, usually specific to the field of use or interest. But a common theme that flows through most definitions is the notion that leadership involves the *act of motivating individuals and/or groups to work toward the accomplishment of a predetermined common goal.* Even though this general concept is central to most respectable definitions of leadership, it doesn't help us distinguish between African American leadership and what we wish to designate as "authentic" African American leadership. Our idea of authentic African American leadership requires much more than just motivating others to work toward common goals. It requires consideration of the significances of the leadership goal to the overall mission of furthering African Americans toward racial equality and social justice in America. It also requires consideration of the morality of the tactics and strategies used to accomplish the goal. Using the common theme of motivating others to work toward a common goal as a foundation, let us take the next step and discuss what we mean by *authentic* leadership—more specifically, authentic African American leadership.

What Is Authentic African American Leadership?

In a broad sense, authentic African American leadership describes the kind of leadership that is necessary to make real and lasting progress in closing the black–white achievement gap, and to guide African American progress toward the twin goals of racial equality and social justice. To craft a definition that adequately describes the kind of leadership we seek, we began by studying authentic leaders from history to see the ways in which key leaders used their power and influence on behalf of African American advancement.

Researching the offerings of scholars of leadership and specially African American leadership was also helpful. Ronald W. Walters, Professor of Afro-American Studies and Government and Politics and Senior Fellow at the Academy of Leadership, University of Maryland, along with Robert C. Smith, Professor of Political Science at San Francisco State University,[3] studied the work of many scholars and found that most who defined African American Leadership agreed on two themes, which are paraphrased here:

1. African American leadership involves affecting the attitudes and behavior of African Americans, insofar as social and political goals, methods, or both are concerned.

2. African American leadership is not limited to African Americans but may, and indeed does, include whites.

In crafting a definition of authentic African American leadership, we accept the two themes found by Walters and Smith and add two additional descriptors to round out our definition. The two additional descriptors are:

1. Authentic African American leadership identifies and confronts primary barriers to African American advancement.

2. Authentic African American leadership acts with moral purpose.

Let us consider the latter two criteria more carefully. When we focus on identifying and confronting primary barriers to African American advancement, the word "primary" is pivotal. Authentic African American leaders are able to identify and confront the primary obstacles from among all the myriad barriers that impede the progress of African Americans in this country. They distinguish between big and small issues, important issues and symbolic ones. They discern the issues that cause pain and those that cause discomfort. They identify the real issues—those that have high-leverage possibilities to further African American advancement—and they decide on a course of action to effectively confront them.

A lesson learned in a first-aid course years ago may help illustrate the point. The instructor presented a first-aid situation in which a patient had multiple life-threatening conditions. He was bleeding profusely. He had just been pulled from the water and was on the verge of drowning. He also was showing symptoms of having digested something poisonous. Which condition should be tackled first? The correct answer is to stop the bleeding. If you don't stop the bleeding quickly, the other conditions will not matter. You've got a dead patient.

Authentic African American leadership will, figuratively speaking, identify the bleeding as a primary problem and act quickly to stop it. While others waste their precious time and resources focusing on problems that represent lesser barriers to African American advancement, authentic African American leaders forge ahead with what matters most. This distinction is critically important.

In doing so, as the fourth and final criterion indicates, they act with an authentic moral intent. Acting with moral purpose—that is, with the intention of making a positive difference in the lives of the constituent group—does not foreclose self-interest on the part of authentic leaders. Elliott Sober and David Sloan Wilson, authors of *Unto Others: The Evolution and Psychology of Unselfish Behavior,* make this point when they argue that it is futile to discuss whether people are driven by egoistic (self-centered) or altruistic (unselfish) motives. Both drive all effective leaders. Sober and Wilson call this "motivational pluralism," which is "the view that we have both egoistic and altruistic ultimate desires."[4] This is why we shouldn't expect our leaders to be without self-interest. Most of us have mixed motives—and that's fine.

Nevertheless, acting with moral purpose requires that the major intent of the leader's actions and behavior is to cause positive movement toward the overarching goal of the masses. James MacGregor Burns points out that "moral leadership is not mere preaching, or the uttering of pieties, or the insistence on social conformity. Moral leadership emerges from, and always returns to, the fundamental wants and needs, aspirations, and values of the followers."[5] To that we say, Amen.

The ability to both recognize and confront primary barriers with a firm moral purpose is an essential ingredient of authentic African American leadership. We believe this ability is absolutely vital to embark on the ambitious change agenda that is required for authentic African American progress. By authentic progress we mean progress not just for some individuals or some subgroups but for the African American people as a whole.

In case there are still lingering doubts about the nature of authentic African American leadership, let us explain what we do not mean. Perhaps most important, we do *not* mean that merely holding an elective office necessarily qualifies a person as an authentic African American leader.

We do not wish to imply that elective officeholders are not serving a positive purpose. They may be. But while the number of African American officeholders (e.g., mayors, county officials, school board members, members of Congress, etc.) has catapulted to record heights since the late 1960s, too many in the African American population remain mired in underdevelopment, deep poverty, and hopelessness. If mere office holding correlated with authentic African American leadership, then we would be much closer than we actually are to fully achieving racial equality and social justice in this country.

Proceeding along the same lines, neither does being African American and being a leader in business, arts, academia, medicine, law, the military, science, or politics automatically make one an authentic African American leader. As laudable as these leaders may be, in order for them to meet the threshold, they must, through a strong moral purpose, find ways within their leadership to identify and confront the primary barriers to African American progress. Some do, most do not. Keep in mind the definition we have proposed: *activity by individuals or groups—regardless of ethnicity—which, with moral purpose, affects the attitude and behavior of African Americans, through identifying and confronting major barriers to African American advancement.*

If you accept the premise that leadership is the key determinant of success in international affairs, business, professional sports, and individual school performance, then it should not require too great a leap to conclude that leadership matters in social movements as well. The black–white achievement gap has become so entrenched that it seems to be accepted, even by many African Americans, as inevitable—as an inescapable part of the African American identity. To uproot this point of view, a well-led social movement is urgently needed. Social movements just don't magically happen; they require leadership.

One of the most remarkable social movements in our nation's history is the African American journey from slavery to today's continuing quest for racial equality and social justice. Even those of us who believe that African Americans are still far short of achieving the long-coveted goal of full equality must concede that enormous advances have been made in the 143 years since the enactment of the Thirteenth Amendment.

This progress is largely attributable to high-quality African American leadership. Indeed, authentic African American leaders have been at the forefront of all the great social, economic, educational, legal, and political movements that have been responsible for African Americans' progress to date. With unwavering moral purpose, those remarkable leaders of the past identified the primary barriers to achieving racial equality and social justice in this country. After all, authentic African American leadership is not required for the small or trivial matters that simply bring us discomfort. Great leaders rise to the occasion when they identify primary issues impeding progress toward our goals.

CHAPTER 8

Today's Shortage of Authentic African American Leaders

The first responsibility of a leader is to define reality. The last is to say thank you.
—Max De Pree, *Leadership Is an Art*

AS DU BOIS WROTE in 1903, "The Negro race, like all races, is going to be saved by its exceptional men."[1] And, we would add, its exceptional women. But who are, and where are, the men and women who will rise up and advance racial equality and social justice for African Americans today by confronting the black–white achievement gap?

We deeply respect and admire the leadership of our forefathers. We sing their praises and offer our thanks. Our concern here is not with past leaders, but with contemporary ones. In this chapter, we examine what we believe contemporary African American leadership is and is not focusing on. More specifically, we explore what we see as the general failure of African American leadership and our powerful civil rights organizations to confront the greatest civil rights challenge of our time: eliminating the black–white achievement gap.

The great progress that African Americans have made in America has been powered by the rich legacy of black leadership, dating back to the darkest days of slavery and continuing through the Civil Rights struggles of the late fifties and most of the sixties. Anyone who thinks otherwise could use a good dose of valid black history.

The achievements of African Americans since slavery ended have been nothing short of phenomenal. To be sure, it has been a long, hard struggle. The Black Codes of the first few years after Emancipation, the volatile struggles of Reconstruction, the legalized racial segregation launched in the mid-1890s and extending through 1954, and the organized and state-supported resistance to *Brown v. Board of Education,* which continued well into early 1980s, converted the first 115-plus years after Emancipation into years of something less than freedom.

To think that such achievement could have occurred without authentic Negro and black leadership is ridiculous. Pre-1970 Negro leaders provided the superb leadership that enabled us to be where we are today. How did they do it? First and foremost, they consistently addressed the primary obstacles to African American advancement toward the goals of equality, equity, and social justice.

During the slavery period, African American leaders pursued a variety of actions in pursuit of freedom for slaves. Some of these leaders focused on planning, organizing, and implementing opportunities for slaves to escape their captivity and find freedom in the North, Canada, and other places of safety.

Others chose insurrection as the means to freedom. Still others were abolitionists who filed petitions, raised money, published newspapers, and lobbied lawmakers in favor of freedom for slaves. But regardless of their differing methods, all the authentic leaders of this period clearly understood that slavery was the primary barrier to African American advancement and with great moral purpose they sought to overcome that barrier.

African American leaders during the Reconstruction period (and beyond) following the Civil War faced a wholly different set of circumstances.[2] This was a time of triumph for newly freed Negroes, as the Emancipation Proclamation, the 1866 and 1875 Civil Rights Acts, and the Thirteenth, Fourteenth, and Fifteenth Amendments to the U.S. Constitution provided the promise of new opportunities. Yet it was also a time of tribulation. Former slaves were thrust into freedom with little or no education, few employable skills, and no land or housing to an environment replete with Southern white people who showed deep hostility towards them. Houston Hartsfield Holloway, a freedman of the period, described the situation well when he wrote, "For we colored people did not know how to be free and the white people did not know how to have a free colored person about them."[3]

Recognizing that African Americans during this period were an under-developed people, authentic African American leaders at this time championed development primarily through education. They established schools and colleges and taught adults life skills, as well as political and economic skills. Some also fought in legislative bodies to defeat the Black Codes and to ensure passage of the 1866 Civil Rights Act. Among these leaders were men like Booker T. Washington, W. E. B. Du Bois, Charles Sumner, Thaddeus Stevens, and Carter G. Woodson, and women like Ida B. Wells and Mary McLeod Bethune. The leaders of this era recognized that the lack of Negro human capital development was the primary barrier to racial equality and social justice at the time and tackled it as the key strategy for advancement.

During the Civil Rights era, authentic African American leaders viewed racism and racial discrimination—for example, the "separate but equal" laws of the Old South—as the major barrier to African American advancement. Accordingly, they protested, they preached, and they undertook a variety of legal actions in order to eradicate racial discrimination in an effort to obtain equal opportunities for African Americans. This was done because they correctly identified racism and racial discrimination as the major barriers impeding African American progress toward the goals of racial equality and social justice.

Some would argue that racism and racial discrimination are still the foremost barriers impeding African American progress today. With them, we strongly disagree. While racism still exists, it exists in a vastly different mode from that of past years. Then, racism and discrimination were systemic, as they were embedded in the foundation of our social, economic, legal, and political systems, more so in the South than other parts of the country, but in fact everywhere. Racism and discrimination still exist today, but they exist as sporadic incidents, episodic to our national being.

In fact, we see soundness in the position taken by Harvard sociologist William Julius Wilson in his powerful book *The Declining Significance of Race: Blacks and Changing America,* where he asserts that economic class is now more significant than race in determining well-being in America.[4]

Without a doubt, vestiges of racism and discrimination linger in the United States. These problems unfortunately have not disappeared. But to view them as the primary problem for African Americans today puts blame in the wrong place and, therefore, leads to misguided action. Too often now, racism is used as an excuse for subpar performance or some other failure to achieve. The race card is often played without due cause.

The unfortunate result is that attention is deflected from the real culprits that are plaguing African Americans' progress toward racial equality and social justice in America. In such cases, an inordinate amount of time, money, and passion is spent on secondary issues, leaving the core issues untouched and unresolved.

Failures of Leadership

In the previous chapter, we examined the qualities of authentic African American leadership. Chief among these was a consistent, burning focus on the primary barriers thwarting African American progress.

Race (and by extension, racism) is less a factor now than it was before 1960. It is clearly no longer the primary barrier facing African Americans in this country. So why have African American leadership strategies changed so little? And why is so little attention being paid to what is clearly the primary barrier today, the achievement gap?

Of course, there are episodic bits of African American leadership action here and there that address the achievement gap. There are even scattered genuine attempts at solving the problem at the local level, in churches, community-based organizations, and fraternity and sorority programs; and there are many isolated efforts at the school and school district level, as we discussed in Chapter 6. But this is akin to fighting a bear with a switch. These small efforts are heroic, but utterly insufficient; the black–white achievement gap is a big problem and fighting it with small efforts will lead to a predictable conclusion: the bear is going to win.

The best-organized efforts currently underway that offer the greatest prospects for substantial impact on closing the achievement gap are mostly regional or academic and usually quite apart from the African American leadership community. The Minority Student Achievement Network (MSAN) is an example of such an effort. MSAN is an unprecedented national coalition of multiracial, relatively affluent suburban school districts that have come together specifically to study the disparity in achievement between white students and students of color. It was organized specifically to address issues associated with the achievement gap with fifteen urban-suburban superintendents coming together to form a network dedicated to the academic improvement of all students of color, specifically African American and Latino students.

Another example is the North Central Regional Educational Laboratory (NCREL), one of ten regional educational laboratories that worked to improve student achievement. NCREL stood out because of its long-standing, very high-quality research and publications addressing the achievement gap. Its federal contract ended in 2004 and Learning Point Associates was funded to continue this important work.

The Harvard Achievement Gap Initiative, co-chaired by Harvard professors Ron Ferguson, Dick Murnane, and Charles Ogletree, is an example of academic efforts to aid policymakers, educators, researchers, and parents in addressing the achievement gap.[5] Another fine example for leadership in closing the gap is LevelTen. In operation since 2003, LevelTen is a nonprofit organization aimed at eliminating the nation's achievement gap through innovative academic solutions, effective support initiatives, and mobilized community engagement.[6]

As an advocate for academic achievement for all students at all levels, with special emphasis on closing the achievement gap, the Education Trust is unrivaled. Its advocacy of closing the achievement gap is tenacious and supported by high-quality research and active participation in the education policy arena. Education Trust is an excellent source for information on the achievement gap issue.

Conspicuously absent from the list of organizations with well-developed initiatives that flow from a missionary zeal to close the black–white achievement gap, however, are the very organizations African Americans have traditionally depended upon for leadership—the National Association for the Advancement of Colored People, the National Urban League, and the Congressional Black Caucus, just to name a few.

To date not one of the national traditional civil rights organizations has identified closing the black–white achievement gap as a national priority. While African American leaders representing these organizations meet regularly to discuss issues relevant to the advancement of African Americans, little of their time is spent discussing the African American leadership role in closing the black–white achievement gap.

Consider for example, the NAACP. It was formed "to ensure the political, educational, social, and economic equality of rights of all persons and to eliminate racial hatred and racial discrimination."[7] Yet, indications show it has paid little attention to the black–white achievement gap. In determining where the achievement gap stands in terms of an organizational priority, it seems reasonable to conclude that the issues discussed during their national conventions would provide a rough idea of the organization's main concerns, would it not? The NAACP's 99th annual convention was held in Cincinnati, Ohio, on July 12–17, 2008. Judging from session titles listed on the convention schedule, of approximately ninety-three hours of sessions, including dinners, late-night worship services. and concurrent workshops, a two-hour period was committed to adult education and a similar one to education for youth. According to the schedule, no session time was dedicated to discussion of the achievement gap. No doubt there were references to education in other sessions, but the schedule of session titles leaves little doubt that during the 2008 NAACP National Convention, education in general and the black–white achievement gap in particular were on the organizational back burner, if on the stove at all.

The Congressional Black Caucus Foundation (CBCF) held its 2008 Annual Leadership Conference over a period of four days in September of that year. Serving as a forum for African American members of Congress to share their work and ideas with the community, the conference's theme was "Embracing the Promise, Realizing the Vision."[8]

The 2008 CBCF conference involved over fifty-eight hours of conference programming, including exhibit showcases and a variety of breakout sessions occurring simultaneously throughout each of the four days. Concurrent with the main conference schedule were a series of sessions referred to as Braintrusts. Various CBCF members sponsored Braintrusts to discuss issues they felt to be important. The 2008 schedule listed seventy-six Braintrust sessions involving more than 105 hours of session programming, of which four had titles suggesting a discussion of some aspect of education. Most of the Braintrusts were scheduled for two hours. One Braintrust session, "Addressing Disparities in Education: A Road Map for the Next Four Years," sponsored by eight Congressional members, was scheduled for four hours. Nowhere among the 2008 Braintrust session titles, nor the main conference session titles, is there any specific mention of the black–white achievement gap. But although there were no titles suggesting discussion of the achievement gap, we cannot rule out the possibility that the topic was brought up.

At the 2008 Annual Conference for the National Urban League (NUL), an organization whose mission is "to enable African Americans to secure economic self-reliance, parity, power and civil rights,"[9] was held in Orlando, Florida, July 30–August 2, 2008. Including the various Exhibit Hall and Career Fair sessions, luncheons, breakfasts, and hospitality sessions, the 2008 NUL conference involved more than sixty-two hours of conference programming. None of the session titles suggested that education would be a part of the session discussions. The schedule did show two concurrent sessions, one scheduled for two hours and another of an hour and fifteen minutes, for which no titles were provided; in fairness, we must admit that these may have been on the black–white achievement gap.

The NUL publishes an annual report entitled "The State of Black America," in which it addresses black progress in the critical areas such as homeownership, health, entrepreneurship, and education as well as other areas important to black well-being. The 2008 "State of Black America" is essentially silent on the black–white achievement gap. The 2008 report focused primarily on black women and contains ten essays, one of which, "A Pathway to School Readiness: The Impact of Family on Early Childhood Education," makes a brief reference to the achievement gap, and there is a short discussion of it under a section entitled "Making the Case." The 2009 report carries three essays on education, two of which provide passing references to the black–white achievement gap but in no way present the gap as a critical problem impeding the African American quest for racial equality and social justice. Nor did either report give any indication that closing the gap should become an important objective on the African American agenda.

But overall, like the NAACP and the Congressional Black Caucus Foundation, the NUL does not appear to have identified the black–white achievement gap as an issue deserving much attention.

The inescapable conclusion to be drawn from this discussion is that the black–white achievement gap and its negative impact on the African American struggle for racial equality and social justice has been overlooked by the three aforementioned organizations as a barrier impeding progress toward civil rights in America. The fact that we hold this view, however, should not be interpreted as disrespect for these organizations. Far from it. Each of them has a proud history of contributions to the advancement of African Americans. Each clearly cares deeply about the well-being of African Americans; each is strongly committed to the betterment of African Americans; each is constantly working to advance

African Americans toward our goals of racial equality and social justice in America; and each has our indelible respect. While we consider the limited national conference attention paid to the black–white achievement gap to be evidence of their failure to prioritize the black–white achievement gap as a major barrier to racial equality and social justice in America, we do not want to insinuate that these organizations ignore the education of our black youth. In fact, the NAACP, NUL, and CBC all address raising the academic achievement of black youth through calls for action, sponsored research, and other approaches. While these scattered efforts are helpful, they fall well short of the national prioritization needed to close the gap.

Our point is simple and straightforward. Despite the historical good work of such national organizations, the fact remains that currently, none of the three aforementioned nationally organized African American leadership organizations have committed to a plan to closing the achievement gap.

How can we expect to close the achievement gap and attain our goals when African American leaders with the power and the resources to make a real contribution to closing the gap are not even formally discussing the issue? This situation does not represent a commitment dilemma, for each of the organizations is committed to racial equality and social justice in America. The situation represents a problem-identification dilemma, in that it appears that none of the organizations view the black–white achievement gap as an important civil rights impediment.

The South Carolina Flag Flap

Saturday, July 1, 2000, was a beautiful, sunny day in Columbia, South Carolina. This day was much like any other summer day in that fair Southern capital city, except for one special event. Around lunchtime, people began to gather on the Capitol grounds to see the Confederate flag being taken down.

The South Carolina Legislature had hoisted the Confederate flag above the Capitol more than forty years earlier, in 1962, ostensibly to celebrate the centennial of the Civil War. It was the only state in the nation to do so. Supporters argued that the Confederate flag was a legitimate state symbol honoring Southern heritage and the Confederate Civil War dead. But state and local African American leaders viewed the flag as a symbol

of hate, racism, and white supremacy and as a legitimizing signal for the activities of groups like the Ku Klux Klan. The civil rights movement was underway when the flag was raised and student sit-ins, civil rights marches, and other activities by African American leaders asserting their rights as Americans were widespread. Many viewed the decision to fly the flag above the Capitol as a gesture of protest against the civil rights movement in general and racial integration in particular.

In 1999, local African American leaders called on the NAACP to support their efforts to bring down the Confederate flag once and for all, and the NAACP threw the full weight of its 500,000-member, 2,200-branch organization behind the effort. The issue became a hot topic of discussion across the state and swiftly escalated into an outright war between South Carolina conservatives and African American leaders. The two sides traded jabs, countered each other's punches, and hardened their positions. In the summer of 1999, the NAACP warned that if the Confederate flag were not removed from the state Capitol by January 1, 2000, it would impose a national boycott against South Carolina with the goal of shutting down the state's $15-billion tourism industry.

In a news release, NAACP president Kweisi Mfume said, "We are determined to bring that flag down. It represents one of the most reprehensible aspects of American history, not only for people of African ancestry but for people from every background who know and understand the destructive horrors created by slavery in this country."[10]

On January 1, 2000, however, the flag was still flying above the Capitol building, so the NAACP delivered on its threat. African American leaders from South Carolina, along with state and national NAACP forces, sent out strongly worded news releases announcing the boycott against the South Carolina tourism economy and called on conventioneers, labor unions, major companies, and others planning to travel to South Carolina to cancel their trips to the Palmetto State. The NAACP dispatched patrols to stage protests at highway welcome centers along South Carolina's borders in an effort to encourage motorists to turn back or drive straight through without stopping. And brilliantly linking the "take the flag down" effort with the commemoration of Martin Luther King Jr.'s birthday celebration, flag opponents staged a rally in front of the Capitol that drew 50,000 people.

South Carolina officials and African American leaders tried repeatedly in the early months of 2000 to reach a compromise. One proposal was to

remove the flag from atop the Capitol and place it at or near a monument on the Capitol grounds honoring a fallen Confederate soldier. Confederate flags would also be removed from the South Carolina House and Senate chambers. The Legislature voted to accept this proposal, and so, around noon on July 1, 2000, cadets from a South Carolina military academy ceremoniously lowered the contested Confederate flag from above the Capitol dome and handed it to the state's governor to be placed near the soldier's monument as the new compromise specified.

But the South Carolina NAACP wanted no part of the compromise. According to the state NAACP, the flag's location was too visible.[11] Angrily, they voted to continue the sanctions, and the battle continued. As of this writing, the flag remains on the South Carolina statehouse grounds, in its compromise location. State and national NAACP organizations are still imposing the tourism boycott and holding demonstrations to protest the flag. The state has lost millions of dollars, hurting both white and black South Carolinians alike. Valuable resources and emotional energy have been expended, and much ill will has been generated. Still, the battle goes on.

Majoring in Minors

The South Carolina Confederate flag demonstration and boycott are classic examples of contemporary African American leadership's propensity for what we call "majoring in minors," expending major effort on matters that have only a minor impact on the advancement of African American people. To be sure, the Confederate flag flying above the South Carolina Capitol is offensive. That flag reminds us of the evils of slavery and the legal oppression of our forefathers and foremothers. We would much rather have the flag removed from the Capitol altogether. But at what price?

Earlier, we talked about African American leaders' responsibilities in identifying and confronting the major barriers to African American advancement. Is the Confederate flag a major barrier to African American advancement? Compared to all the other actions and strategies we could spend our resources on, does this issue offer the greatest opportunity for African American development? When and if the flag comes down, we will feel a lot better, but will we be significantly better off? Will the black–white achievement gap be any narrower? Will the high school dropout

rate be reduced? Will the endangered existence of the black male be improved? Will the wage disparity be smaller? Will black neighborhoods be any safer? Will the spread of AIDS, or the teenage pregnancy rate, or black poverty, or infant mortality, or black-on-black crime decline? In sum, is this the best use of our energies and resources?

Clearly, the answer to these questions is no. This is not to say that the Confederate flag issue is unimportant. It is important. Demanding the flag's removal is entirely appropriate. But the flag's significance is largely symbolic. Even if African American leaders are victorious in their attempts to completely vanquish this flag, it will have little impact on advancing the prospects for African Americans in this country. It is this propensity to focus on symbolic issues and posturing rather than deal with the truly big problems that constitutes the major failure of contemporary African American leadership.

It is not our intent here to belittle the NAACP. No organization has done more for African American development. But today's NAACP bears little resemblance to the pre-1960s NAACP, which confronted real issues of major relevance to African American advancement. This once proud organization has taken a wrong turn. The issues it takes on today may be high profile, may help some well-positioned individuals, and they may attract significant national attention; but for the most part, these issues have little bearing on the economic and social well-being of African Americans as a group.

The main point is that there are some big problems out there facing today's African Americans, and the Confederate flag is not one of them. The black–white achievement gap is. Admittedly, confronting the achievement gap doesn't have the glamour of the South Carolina boycott—but it holds major promise for advancing African Americans' development. To repeat the words of Jencks and Phillips, the authors of *The Black-White Test Score Gap*:

> If racial equality is America's goal, reducing the black-white test score gap would probably do more to promote this goal than any other strategy that commands broad political support. Reducing the test score gap is probably both necessary and sufficient for substantially reducing racial inequality in educational attainment and earnings. Changes in education and earnings would in turn help reduce racial differences in crime, health, and family structure, although we do not know how large these effects would be.[12]

"No Dirty Laundry"

To date, most of the activity designed to close the black–white achievement gap takes place in the school. It is well established that a student's academic performance is a function of what happens in the school, in the home, and in the community. To accomplish our goal of closing the gap we must attend to all three areas which contribute to a student's academic performance. What leadership exists for closing the gap exists primarily in the areas of school quality. What about leadership for beyond-school factors? As African American leaders, we have failed in this area too, by neglecting to launch or support any sustained national program of activities to address the student achievement gap through efforts that fall under the dominion of home and community. Who among us believes that matters concerning African American children's home, community, and cultural lives can be addressed by leadership from outside the African American community? No one we've ever heard from.

Senator Daniel Patrick Moynihan would share our view on this. In 1965, Moynihan, under the auspices of the U.S. Department of Labor, released his famous report, *The Negro Family: The Case for National Action.* The report concluded that Negro families were unstable, that the weakened position of Negro males in society raised questions as to their ability to function as the family's authority figure in future generations, and that the low education levels among Negroes, in turn, produce low-income levels that continue the deprivation of opportunities for Negro children.[13] The black leadership community was highly critical of the report and of Moynihan as well, notwithstanding the fact that far from presenting new facts about the black family, the report mostly presented facts about the black condition that had been pointed out before by noted black scholars.

To understand the African American response to the Moynihan report it's necessary to know that deeply embedded in the African American leadership culture is a strong aversion to open discussions of issues which might reflect negatively on the African American community. Discussing unflattering matters critical of black community behavior in public settings is often referred to as "airing our dirty laundry in public," and is a strict no-no in the African American community. Bill Cosby ran into this when, in a 2004 speech on the fiftieth anniversary of the landmark Supreme Court decision *Brown v. Board of Education,* he criticized black

parents for such things as not showing interest in their children's school-work, style of speech and dress, and buying their kids $500 sneakers when they wouldn't spend $200 on "Hooked on Phonics." He received polite applause from the audience, but shock and amazement from the wider black community. The problem was not so much about the content of his remarks, but that he had the audacity to make such remarks in public. Cosby found himself on the receiving end of fire from an upset African American leadership. One of his most outspoken critics was Michael Eric Dyson, the Georgetown University sociologist, who in his book *Is Bill Cosby Right?* described Cosby's remarks as "a vicious attack on the most vulnerable among us."

Another example of the sensitivity about open discussions of matters that might reflect negatively on the African American community is found in the experience Harvard researchers Jeff Howard and Ray Hammond had in finding a publisher for their piece "Rumors of Inferiority: The Hidden Obstacles to Black Success in America." In this powerful piece the authors discussed what they viewed to be a retreat from academic competition by black adults and students, resulting in a widely held stereotype about the intellectual inferiority of African Americans. Interestingly, the piece was finally published in *The New Republic,* after being turned down by three of African America's most respected publications, *Ebony, Black Enterprise,* and *Essence.*

Some time ago, the Harvard Achievement Gap Initiative at Harvard University ran a poll on their web page soliciting the public's view on the impact of media coverage of the achievement gap. Almost a third of those responding (30.07 percent) indicated that they felt that media coverage of the achievement gap was not a good thing—13.29 percent selected *Does more harm than good,* 16.78 percent chose *Stigmatizes and mostly hurts progress,* while 7.69 percent thought it *Makes no difference.* Fortunately, for us at least, a whopping 62.24 percent indicated that they thought that media coverage of the achievement gap was a good thing—12.94 percent chose *Mostly helps progress,* and 49.30 percent picked *Is absolutely necessary for progress.*

Although there clearly is a significant reluctance in its leadership culture to embrace open discussions of negative aspects of the African American community, the Harvard Achievement Gap poll offers reasons for hope. Judging from its poll results, there is majority support for the idea that facing the brutal facts is a necessary condition for progress.

The critical element in the "airing dirty laundry in public" phenomenon is that it is reacting to matters that occur outside of the community of trust. The same kinds of discussions would no doubt encounter less hostility if they occurred in an environment considered to be "inside the community of trust." The relevance here is that closing the achievement gap will require addressing issues that can best be handled by leadership considered from within the community of trust. This does not necessarily mean that providers of such leadership must necessarily be African American. But it does mean that leaders who are African American must have a significant presence in the overall leadership assemblage. Currently, this is the major problem impeding progress toward closing the black–white achievement gap; there is an insufficient presence of authentic African American leadership from within the African American community.

Sitting This One Out—Leadership Disengagement

The African American leadership's failure to lead in the area of the achievement gap is mostly one of omission—neglecting to do that which is urgently needed. There are also glaring leadership failures that must be classified as sins of commission—actions that have been taken but should not have been.

One powerful example of leadership omission can be seen in African American leadership's reaction to the No Child Left Behind Act. Its response to this law, both during its enactment and since, has ranged from indifference to completely oppositional. It is important to also point out that the leadership for NCLB came (and continues to come) from outside the African American community. The law was championed by President Bush, with the assistance of the Congress, especially Chairman John Boehner, Congressman George Miller, and Senators Edward Kennedy, and Judd Gregg—all of whom, incidentally, are white.

In an April 18, 2005, *New York Times* editorial entitled "On the Sidelines of the Most Important Civil Rights Battle Since 'Brown,'" Brent Staples, an editorial writer for the newspaper, reflects on this situation. In the editorial he observed that the once fiercely independent civil rights leadership community, which historically stood as a mighty force for the advancement of the poor, was standing comfortably on the sidelines while the fight to close the achievement gap through NCLB raged on. Staples wrote:

The same civil rights groups that sing hosannas to Brown have been curiously muted—and occasionally even hostile—to No Child Left Behind. But the groups have mainly been missing from the debate, according to Dr. James Comer, the educational reformer and Yale University psychiatrist. "They have been absent," Dr. Comer told me last week. "They need to pay attention to what works. They need to be in the middle of the fight because these are our kids.[14]

In other words, the civil rights leadership community opted for inaction during the struggle to enact what Staples calls, "the best hope for guaranteeing black and Latino children a chance at equal education."[15] Staples went on to explain that the mostly Democratic civil rights community chose to stand aside on the NCLB fight because, among other reasons, they were wary of embracing a law associated with a conservative Republican president. If this is the case, it stands as testimony to an African American leadership culture more committed to party loyalty than to the advancement of African Americans.

How can one make sense of this inaction with respect to NCLB? Let's take it as a given that the civil rights leadership community is interested in building better futures for African American children. Accepting that assumption, three explanations remain:

- African American leadership didn't accept NCLB as helpful in closing the achievement gap.

- They did not view school improvement and school accountability for student performance as a priority.

- They were obligated though party loyalty to oppose any initiative identified with President Bush, notwithstanding its potential to improve African American students' performance.

You can choose from among these three alternatives but there isn't a good answer among the three, as all of them are examples of leadership omission. The fact that strong national African American leadership was missing in support of the efforts of the President and Congress to close the achievement gap through national policy represents a huge missed opportunity for progress not only toward higher academic achievement for African American children but also toward racial equality and social justice.

Let us imagine for a moment that the situation had been different. Imagine that the African American leadership was aggressively support- ive of NCLB and working diligently to ensure its effective implementa- tion. What message do you think the schools would get?

Imagine what would happen if, in speeches by elected African American leaders, the importance of closing the achievement gap con- stantly rang out. Imagine that from the pulpits of the nation's black churches, African American students constantly heard the message that we expect them to succeed in school and that we know they can suc- ceed. Suppose African American students constantly heard from African American leaders that even when the odds are stacked against them, we believe they can overcome, and we expect them to overcome. Suppose that they heard that we understand it is difficult, but that they are made of tough stuff. Imagine what might happen if the major civil rights organizations—the National Association for the Advancement of Colored People, the National Urban League, the Congressional Black Caucus, and the National Association for Equal Opportunity in Higher Education (NAFEO)—made closing the achievement gap a front-burner agenda item, developed plans, adopted strategies, and committed funds to this cause.

The sheer momentum would go a long way toward sending the black– white achievement gap to the trash piles of history where it belongs. But that's all a figment of our imagination. In reality, no such African American leadership exists.

Another example of omission can be found in the absence of any effec- tive national parenting program among the civil rights strategies. Given what we know about the impact of parenting on children's cognitive development and given that the black–white achievement gap is such a major barrier to African American advancement, one would think that African American leadership would place a major emphasis on actively providing national leadership to improve parenting practices in the African American community.

If you thought so, you would be wrong. There are scattered local efforts but nothing on the scale needed to confront the black–white achievement gap. Improving parenting practices of African American parents is simply not enough of a pressing issue for the African American leadership community to rank it as a national civil rights priority. But such a program would offer high-leverage returns for

furtherance of African Americans toward the goals of racial equality and social justice in America.

For example, research presented in the book *Meaningful Differences in the Everyday Experience of Young American Children* by researchers Betty Hart and Todd Risley, discussed in Chapter 4, could form the foundation for a great national program of parenting skill development. From their work we learned that:

 • A child's language skill and vocabulary growth is greatly influenced by the quality and quantity of conversation that takes place between parent and child from the very early years of the child's life.

 • It is next to impossible for experiences in preschool to compensate for educational deprivation that occurs during the child's first three years in homes where parenting skills are poor.

 • Children who hear a higher ratio of encouragement to discouragement have enhanced possibilities of development.

Parents can be taught ways to increase the effectiveness of their relationship with their child so as to improve not only the child's language skills and vocabulary development, but their overall cognitive development. Considering the huge benefits to be gained, the moderate cost that would be incurred, and magnitude of the need, especially given the high level of teen births in the African American community, a national program of effective skills would go a long way toward closing the black–white achievement gap.

Student effort and engagement are also clearly crucial to effective learning, but there's not much evidence of African American leadership in these areas either. Instead, African American leaders give students excuses for underperformance: students can't succeed because their schools are denied appropriate resources, they are poor, or school officials harbor racist attitudes.

If we need an example of what African American leadership could do if it expanded its focus to student engagement and effort, look at the powerful cultural forces powering the success of Vietnamese American students. In the Vietnamese American community, there is a culture of effort, a belief that effort yields success, and a determination to succeed despite whatever odds may be in the way.

Party Trumps Race

When he was Maryland's lieutenant governor, Michael Steele decided to throw his hat in the race for the U.S. Senate seat vacated by Senator Paul Sarbanes, who decided not to seek reelection. If you don't know Steele, an African American, he is a Republican and is now the head of the Republican Party. The attacks came quickly and furiously. That they came quickly was no surprise, as the battle between Republicans and Democrats for control of the Senate was intense. In an evenly divided Senate, any one seat could turn the tide for either party.

Steele expected a hard fight. He knew that the Democrats were not going to let that seat go to a Republican. What he didn't expect were the mean and vicious attacks from the African American members of the Maryland Democratic Party, who pelted him with Oreo cookies, called him an Uncle Tom, and depicted him as a black-faced minstrel on liberal websites. They freely used the same types of racial attacks against Steele that African Americans have been subjected to since Emancipation. When Maryland State Senator Lisa A. Gladden, an African American, was asked about the racism underpinning the attacks against Steele, she replied, "Party trumps race, especially on the national level. If you are bold enough to run, you have to take whatever voters are going to give you. It's democracy, perhaps at its worse, but it is democracy."[16]

The "party trumps race" concept which was so vividly displayed in the Steele senate race is emblematic of the idea current in the African American leadership culture—that racial interest is openly secondary to party interest. While closing the black–white achievement gap will obviously benefit the nation as a whole, it is, or should be, of special interest to the African American community. But under "party trumps race" terms, considering it a priority is only possible if it offers no conflicts with party advantage and interest.

We are not arguing here that African Americans should move in lockstep with any other African American who decides to run for office. But the "party trumps race" principle is now so deeply embedded in the African American leadership culture that it has affected the political struggle to close the black–white achievement gap. In the development of national, state, municipal, and even local (school-board level) education policy, African American leaders are locked in a leadership culture that typically demands allegiance to party before all else.

At least in the area of education, with specific reference to the black–white achievement gap, flipping this principle so that it becomes "race before party" would be a courageous act of authentic African American leadership.

To further illustrate the party trumps race situation, we offer another true story. Some years ago, an African American leader solicited the support of an African American member of the Texas Legislature for a piece of proposed legislation. It was crafted to provide state funds for low-income, high-need, low-performing students that could be used as tuition payments to attend a private school of their choice. One condition was that the private school had to be accredited by the Texas Education Agency, which accredits the state's public schools as well. The two individuals were from different political parties. After careful attention to his friend's appeal, the legislator responded with the comment, "Can't go with you. Even if it would help a few kids, I can't be in a position of helping you guys win a victory."

This statement—can't be in a position of helping you guys win a victory—is a clear manifestation of the party trumps race phenomenon, and a major African American leadership problem. This kind of decision—all too common in contemporary African American leadership culture—is an example of political allegiances superseding the mission of furthering racial equality and social justice.

This kind of decision is one that contemporary African American leaders are faced with on a regular basis. For many, it really is an agonizing decision. For the authentic African American leader, it's an easy decision because the highest priority is the advancement of African Americans. For the authentic leader, those goals cannot be achieved in the face of the devastating black–white achievement gap.

In truth, closing the black–white achievement gap, and other educational issues as well, should not only trump party, but should trump politics as well. Closing the achievement gap would improve our overall national education attainment and strengthen our national economic competitiveness with our international neighbors. The effort to close the gap must transcend party politics. It's not about Republicans and Democrats; it's about kids and their future, and the future of this country. For our national well-being we need good ideas from everyone, and for everyone—and we need commitment from everyone to solve the problem. If we remain in our partisan corners and continue to witness good

initiatives being shot down by the other party because of politics rather than the educational merits of the proposals, we all lose, no matter which party we support.

Mo' Money

The final example of African American leadership failure is an egregious act of commission: aggressively promoting the idea that a lack of resources is the major explanation for African American students' under-performance. To be sure, appropriate resources are necessary to support effective teaching, and there are instances where resources are, in fact, inadequate. There is no question that there are places (states, cities, schools, classrooms) where more funds are needed. But to explain away African American student underachievement as the result of underfund-ing is profoundly misguided and misleading. If greater funding were the solution to address the consistently poor academic performance of African American students, then the system of public schools in Washington, D.C., would be the most successful in America, because it has one of the highest per pupil expenditures in the nation. It is not the most successful; in fact, as we saw in Chapter 1, it is the worst school district by far in terms of the achievement gap.

It has become popular among African American leaders and many oth-ers to claim that the NCLB is an unfunded mandate. But NCLB is neither unfunded nor is it a mandate. States are under no obligation to accept the billions of dollars a year in federal education aid that NCLB offers. States that do not want to be held accountable for improving student achieve-ment or that prefer to do things their own way can simply decline the money. NCLB's core requirement—and the requirement that many African American leaders argue requires the greatest cost—is that after twelve years, children should read and do math at grade level, as defined by the state. Those who argue that NCLB is an unfunded mandate are, by extension, arguing that the school system had no intention, prior to NCLB, of having children read and do math at grade level.

In lamenting the need for more funding for education, African American leaders rarely discuss the record amounts of spending in K–12 public education, much less the unprecedented growth in spending, over the past ten years. Current estimates put spending on K–12 alone, from federal, state, and local sources combined, at more than $525 billion per

year. To put that number in perspective, consider that in the United States, the 2004–05 school year average expenditure per pupil was $9266, which ranks the United States among the world's highest spenders on K–12 education. In fact, according to a report entitled "Comparative Indicators of Education in the United States and Other G-8 Countries: 2006," issued by the Institute of Education Science's National Center For Education Statistics, the 2003 average per pupil expenditure in the United States was $8900, compared to $7700 in Italy; $7200 in France; $6800 in the UK and Japan; and $6500 in Germany. Education, along with health care, is one of the largest public expenditures in the United States.

Moreover, there is no direct relationship between educational expenditure and student performance. There are worlds of examples where educational expenditures are high, while student performance is low. One of the best examples, referred to earlier, is that the average reading score for eighth graders on the National Assessment of Educational Progress' 2003 assessment, which is commonly referred to as the Nation's Report Card, was 261. The average reading score for eighth graders in the District of Columbia was 239, 22 points lower than the national average. Yet, according to the U.S. Census' Public Education Finances 2003 report, the District of Columbia's average per pupil expenditure was $13,328, a figure significantly higher than the per pupil expenditure in any of the fifty states.

This is not an argument that more money is not needed, and it is well understood that it costs more to deliver effective educational services in some locations than in others. The argument here is that whereas the amount of resources available for support of educational services is important, more important is the question of whether the resources available are being put to effective use. In other words, while arguing for more money, there should at least be concern about whether the money available is being used in the best way. Simply to explain away poor student performance in terms of inadequate resources is, in most cases, a misdiagnosis of the problem and one that invariably leads to incorrect approaches to solving the problem.

By constantly broadcasting the message to the public that the reason that African American students aren't performing better is because they're being denied appropriate funding sends out at least two bad messages. First, it gives students a ready excuse for weak achievement: they are not funded adequately to perform well. Second, it sends the message to teachers and administrators that they too are not expected to achieve

high standards because they are underfunded. Furthermore, the constant chorus about underfunding takes attention away from other aspects of the learning process that are critically important. In other words, it masks other, more valid reasons for student underachievement. For these reasons, the underfunding argument frequently touted by African American leadership is not only erroneous but also deeply harmful to the cause of improving black student achievement and eradicating the achievement gap.

Let us underscore an important point. Contemporary African American leaders are not to blame for originating the black–white achievement gap. They inherited this problem. But we are all responsible for perpetuating it through sins of omission (forgoing leadership actions that should be taken) as well as sins of commission (pursuing tangential or overtly harmful actions).

In short, we are failing to use our leadership to effectively address the achievement gap in a serious and committed way, choosing instead to hold fast to political party loyalties, dogma, or symbolic posturing above all else. This must change if we are ever to have any hope of achieving full equality and social justice for all African Americans.

How Did African American Leadership Lose Its Sense of Direction?

How did we get to this point? Given the clarity of purpose and the crystal clear sense of direction that characterized authentic African American leadership through the 1960s, what derailed this train? Somewhere in the process of converting itself from Negro and black leadership to African American leadership, something vital got lost. Negro, and later black, leadership was primarily focused on issues considered important for the furtherance of Negroes and/or blacks toward the goals of racial equality and social justice in America. Its allegiance was almost solely to the Negro or black community, and its tactics were more confrontational. African American leadership is different. It is focused more broadly, its allegiance to a wider constituency, and its tactics more moderate and almost always political.

This change (or as some would call it, this transformation) has attracted the attention of numerous scholars. Although they debate the advantages and disadvantages of this leadership transformation, few dispute that it occurred.

Among the factors identified by Ronald Walters and Robert Smith in *African American Leadership* as contributing to this leadership transformation are population changes, changes in the Negro class structure, the civil rights revolution, the community action program, the ghetto revolts, the black-power movement, and changes in white attitudes toward black people.[17]

Let us concentrate for a moment on the civil rights movement as a factor that contributed to the leadership transformation. As a direct result of the 1965 Voting Rights Act—a core element of the civil rights movement—thousands of black men and women joined the voter rolls, especially in the Southern states. This surge in new black voters powered a rise in newly elected black officials in local, state, regional, and even national elected positions.

When the Joint Center for Political and Economic Studies published its first National Roster of Black Elected Officials in 1968, it listed 1,469 black elected officials in the United States. Its thirtieth-anniversary edition, published in 2000, listed 9,040 black elected officials, a six-fold increase in thirty-two years. This swift rise in the number of black elected officials, along with the other factors listed by Walters and Smith, created a seismic disruption in the black leadership community along three fault lines:

1. Negro and black leadership prior to the civil rights era came primarily from the ministerial community. The surge in newly elected blacks shifted the leadership base from ministers to elected officials.

2. This shift caused a corresponding incorporation, integration, or co-optation of black leadership into the mainstream (some would say "white") political apparatus. The cost to the black elected official joining the institutionalized political system was an erosion of black leadership's capacity to press for an exclusively black agenda. It could be argued, with some justification, that this transformation was good for our society as a whole. Even so, it stranded the African American community somewhat by limiting the adversarial tactics available to mainstream African American leaders.

3. This new institutionalized African American leadership position causes African American leaders to shoulder a dual agenda

serving two masters: one focusing on the needs and loyalties of the black community and the other serving the needs and loyalties of society as a whole, rather than just one group. This juggling act has not only drained intensity from the black leadership community, but has also caused a corresponding strategic and tactical shift from relying primarily on protest to relying primarily on politics.

It's not necessary to calculate the positives or negatives of this Negro to African American leadership transformation. Our interest is in education in general and the black–white achievement gap in particular. The leadership transformation is of interest to us because it has contributed to the intractability of the achievement gap.

Consider the plight of the African American big-city mayor whose city charter calls for two-year terms. Consider also that this mayor has the authority to appoint members to the city school board. The mayor is pressured by the union to appoint school board members who are sympathetic to their issues. Our mayor is in a tight race for reelection, and the union promises to be very helpful. The mayor is very interested in education and realizes that the school system needs major reform, which the union opposes. Can you predict where this story goes? Undoubtedly, you can.

The Mayor will no doubt see his need for reelection as primary. As such, he cannot afford to make an enemy of the union. Although he is genuinely interested in leading the much needed school reform, he will no doubt have to put school reform on the back burner and appoint school board members who are sympathetic to the union.

The Declining Ranks of Authentic African American Leaders

The end result of these myriad forces is that the ranks of authentic African American leaders have been steadily declining. We are by no means alone in this belief. If there is anything original about our position, it is that we link the scarcity of authentic African American leadership to the intractability of the black–white achievement gap.

Consider the following passage from the book *We Have No Leaders* by Robert C. Smith. It echoes our views on the scarcity of contemporary African American leadership.

At a lecture at Prairie View A & M University in 1989, in response to a question asking him to evaluate black leaders, Harold Cruse responded, "What leaders? We have no leaders." The puzzled student questioner responded by listing the familiar names or the heads of the civil rights organizations, members of Congress, and big-city mayors. Cruse, responding with evident irritation, said that those persons were not leaders because they had no plan, no program of action, and no organization to mobilize or lead blacks in a direction that would deal with their communal problems.[18]

Similar views regarding the lack of powerful (or as we would call it, authentic) African American leadership are articulated in other sources, including the following:

- H. Viscount Nelson, *The Rise and Fall of Modern Black Leadership*[19]

- John White, *Black Leadership in America, 1865–1968*[20]

- Earl Ofari Hutchinson, *The Disappearance of Black Leadership*[21]

- Manning Marable, *Black Leadership*[22]

- Ronald W. Walters and Robert C. Smith, *African American Leadership*[23]

- John Brown Childs, *Leadership, Conflict, and Cooperation in Afro-American Social Thought*[24]

Admittedly, the aforementioned scholars and writers have somewhat different perspectives regarding the quality of post–civil rights era African American leadership. But the common theme is that African American leadership is at a crossroads. The literature is flush with scholarly analysis of post–civil rights black leadership. Much of it supports what civil rights activist W. E. B. Du Bois predicted in his brilliant 1952 book *In Battle for Peace,* that class divisions among African Americans would grow as racial discrimination decreased.[25] Du Bois was right again, just as he was correct in predicting that race would be the problem of the twentieth century. Paraphrasing this great scholar, we predict that the problem of the twenty-first century—at

least for African Americans—will be the declining ranks of authentic African American leaders.

The idea that the ranks of authentic African American leaders, authentic as we have defined it, are declining should come as a surprise to few who follow shifts in the social order of America. As racial discrimination and racism in general become less and less robust in America, concomitantly, there becomes a less obvious and apparent need for actions designed to counter them. Even now, it is not uncommon to hear or read material suggesting that class is now becoming a more virulent social divider than race. The frightening element in this circumstance is that the black–white achievement gap is such a strong contributor to class divisions, and because it doesn't exhibit the intense emotions brought about by overt racial discrimination and racism, it often flies under the civil rights radar and cruises on unchallenged.

Let's put this whole matter in the proper perspective. There is nothing wrong with drawing African American leadership from a wider occupation than was true pre-1950s. There is nothing wrong with politicians directing their allegiance more broadly, to society as a whole as opposed to a more limited allegiance to only a racial segment of society. Additionally, there is nothing wrong with leaders relying more on politics than on confrontational tactics as a way to solve contemporary problems. Present-day circumstances may indeed require that contemporary leaders consider broader constituencies, and more political tactics to achieve success in today's more complex world. The big problem we see is that due to this leadership transition, current African American leadership has failed to identify the black–white achievement gap as a primary barrier to the achievement of racial equality and social justice in America. And has, therefore, overlooked closing the gap as a major civil rights strategy—a strategy which, more than any other civil rights strategy available to us at this time, offers high-leverage opportunities for furtherance of the African American cause.

Summary

Let's return to the question that initiated our discussion for this chapter, "What's leadership got to do with it?" Leadership has everything to do with it!

As we've seen, the black–white achievement gap is an extremely complex and multifaceted problem. Therefore, remedying it will require

national social movement

nothing less than a national social movement. National social movements require authentic leadership.

The great authentic African American leaders of the past pursued
many different strategies to achieve black equality and social justice, but
all of the leaders had something important in common. They were all able
to distinguish between big issues and small issues, between important
issues and those that were merely symbolic, between issues causing pain
and discomfort and issues that were truly thwarting black people's
advancement. Prior to 1865, slavery was the primary barrier impeding
Negro progress. Authentic leadership during this period identified slavery
as the problem and confronted it. Following the Reconstruction period
through the mid-1970s, legally supported racial discrimination and
racism were the primary barriers impeding black progress. Authentic
leadership during that time identified racism and discrimination as the
problems and confronted them. After identifying the correct problems,
the authentic leaders of past years were then able to determine which
strategies held the greatest promise to further African Americans'
advancement. In other words, they dedicated themselves unswervingly to
the issues that mattered most.

The point here is that while racism and discrimination are still barriers to African American progress, they are no longer the *primary* barriers.
For African American leadership to be authentic, it must identify the correct targets for action.

The most urgent task for African American leaders today is to do what
their predecessors did and that is to figure out which problem is doing the
most damage and then deal with it directly, completely, and with full commitment and full moral purpose.

The achievement gap can only be closed by contemporary African
American leaders acting together in a concerted way. These leaders are in
a unique position to influence the cultural and social environment in
which education occurs. Current strategies designed to close the achievement gap have focused primarily on the schools and are led primarily by
non-African American leaders. But as we have seen, the black–white
achievement gap is affected by a myriad of factors, many of which lie
beyond the school, including the home and family, as well as sociocultural elements in the community. African American home and family factors can be effectively addressed best by leadership from within the
African American community.

more than schools

In the past, authentic African American leaders used their power as opinion leaders, role models, and advocates to overcome institutional barriers and promote African Americans' advancement. Today's African American leaders must do the same if we are to have any hope of success in eradicating the black–white achievement gap and attaining the goals of full racial equality and social justice that we have sought for so long.

Throughout this book, but especially this chapter, we have decried the eroding ranks of what we have defined as "authentic" African American leadership. Likewise, we have called for the contemporary African American leadership community to use its power to wage war against the most important civil rights issue of our day, the black–white achievement gap. We have made particular note of the need for our leaders to form an *authentic* African American leadership culture, one that will tackle the most important issues impairing the African American struggle in America. As we close this chapter, we want to acknowledge how pleased we are that there appears to be an emerging African American leadership movement toward the kind of leadership authenticity we are calling for. To us, the Reverend Al Sharpton stands as a personification of this emerging authenticity.

On June 11, 2008, Reverend Sharpton and Joel Klein, the chancellor of New York City's public schools, announced the launch of the Education Equality Project. The mission of this group is to "eliminate the racial and ethnic achievement gap in public education by working to create an effective school for every child."[26] Klein and Sharpton have called themselves the "odd couple," acknowledging that typically we do not see a partnership between an activist and a school chief. While Sharpton admits that "I'm sure we won't always agree in the future, . . . both of us are passionate about the fact that the gap is really not being discussed." He continues by saying, "Somehow the fact that black students are not being taught is all right with everybody."[27]

The alignment that Sharpton has made is the type of action that we consider represents authentic African American leadership. Sharpton found an ally who shares his common interest to erase the achievement gap between black and white students, and he has nurtured this relationship because it is in the best interest of the children. With this move, Sharpton has distanced himself from contemporary African American national leadership, which not only fails to address and give an appropriate amount of attention to closing the black–white achievement gap, but

commonly sacrifices the good of the children to avoid crossing political, racial, or traditional boundaries. We encourage other members of the African American leadership community to go against the grain, as Sharpton has done, and take a visible stand against the perpetuation of the black–white achievement gap, and to create alliances based not on political expediency, but on the potential that these alliances offer for improving the education for African American students.

Eliminating the Achievement Gap
What Authentic African American
Leaders Must Do

Education is a troubled area in black communities for numerous reasons, but certainly one of them is that many black children are not truly imbued with the idea that learning is virtually the same as opportunity.

—Shelby Steele, from "Being Black and Feeling Blue,"
in Gilbert T. Sewall's, *The Eighties: A Reader*

THE BLACK–WHITE achievement gap is a complex phenomenon that has powerful tentacles, buried deeply not only in school quality but also in African American home and family life and in African American community sociocultural life. Given the complexity of such a phenomenon and the degree of sensitivity, trust, and understanding required to cause the kind of change needed to close the achievement gap—not just to narrow it—one can appreciate the need for high-quality leadership. Because the changes required to close the achievement gap include fundamental adjustments in beliefs, values, and assumptions, this high-quality leadership must come from inside the African American community. This is not to suggest that leadership from outside the African American is not needed as well. Of course it is needed. But outside leadership without authentic leadership from inside the community cannot succeed. In fact, in earlier chapters we have gone as

far as to contend that the absence of authentic leadership from within the African American community is a major contributing factor to the current achievement gap and its intractability. Such complex and intricate change cannot be accomplished without a strong foundational leadership from within the community of trust. This does not suggest that leadership from beyond the African American community is not important. It is most certainly an important condition—but it is an insufficent one.

So, one may ask, what must African American leaders do to effect the kind of change needed to close the gap? What role can African American leaders play? There are many answers to these questions, for there are many things we, as African American leaders, must and can do to accomplish this goal. But instead of dealing with the universe of actions we need to take, let us direct our attention to six of the most important things authentic African American leaders must do.

– ONE –

Understand the Black–White
Achievement Gap Issue

During a presentation at the New York offices of IBM in 2005, the discussion turned to the lessons IBM had learned about school reform as a result of its many years of philanthropic efforts in public schools. IBM representatives from across the nation acknowledged many lessons learned, but the most compelling was: "You can't change anything without being prepared to understand it. School governance, school finance, and school personnel are issues that must be internalized and understood before—and not while—one is attempting a reform."[1]

The necessity of having a keen understanding of the black–white achievement gap as a prerequisite to trying to eliminate it would seem so obvious as to go without saying. Admittedly, there are individual exceptions, but among the general African American leadership community, the level of deep understanding of the black–white achievement gap and its dire consequences for African American advancement is abysmally low. This is a problem on multiple fronts.

First and foremost, action—which is required to close the gap—springs from dissatisfaction, not from general awareness. Our main premise is that changing the black–white achievement gap will require

action, effective action. Model-Netics, a comprehensive management training and development program developed by Harold Hook, president of Main Event Management Corporation, teaches that effective action always progresses through five critical steps: awareness, understanding, concern, dissatisfaction, and, finally, action. To close the black–white achievement gap, therefore, individuals, leaders, organizations, and cultures must move through these five steps as well. Currently, the present level of dissatisfaction with the existing black–white achievement gap within the African American leadership community is much too low to bring about the level of action needed to address the problem. This is not to say that there is no awareness, understanding, concern, or dissatisfaction about the gap, but the level of concern is not high enough or shared by enough of the leadership to result in the desired action to close the gap. We want to raise the level of dissatisfaction about the black–white achievement gap so that we will finally initiate action to close it.

Whereas the first problem stemming from an insufficient understanding of the black–white achievement gap brings about a lack of action from the African American leadership, the second and equally important problem deals with the fact that insufficient understanding also results in the wrong kind of action. After all, our goal is not action alone; it is effective action. A prerequisite for effective action is a deep understanding of the problem one is trying to resolve. Remember the point of the IBM quotation—you can't change anything unless you understand it deeply.

There is little chance that leaders can provide effective leadership on any issue that they don't understand. In fact, absent such understanding, leaders may not only *not* be helpful (the *omission* problem), but may, in an attempt to be helpful, actually cause harm (the *commission* problem). Absent a deep understanding of the black–white achievement gap, attempted leadership will most likely mislead rather than lead, thereby providing more confusion than clarity. Part of the problem now is that there is so much ineffective activity and senseless chatter in the efforts to close the achievement gap that strategic action is the casualty. Ineffectiveness also comes from completely baseless rhetoric, political posturing, and misguided actions from those who have taken little time to fully understand the issue.

Without a thorough knowledge of the problem, scarce resources, precious time, and irreplaceable emotional energy will be wasted on

ill-conceived initiatives. Too many of our current achievement gap work-shops, presentations, and seminars fail to provide much help precisely because they are based on an insufficient understanding of the problem.

This is not to say that every African American leader must become a sophisticated expert on the black–white achievement gap, but as leaders, they must have a level of understanding above that of simple awareness. This is especially true of issues that have high-leverage potential for affecting the quality of life of African Americans. Constituents have a right to expect that their leaders understand the issues that would have so much impact on their well-being.

So in this case, what can African American leaders do? We make three suggestions.

First, leaders should gain some history and context of the problem by reading books and accessing other high-quality material on the black–white achievement gap. We like Jencks and Phillips' *The Black-White Test Score Gap* and Abigail and Stephan Thernstrom's *No Excuses: Closing the Racial Gap in Learning.* "The Evolution of the Black-White Achievement Gap in Elementary and Middle Schools," by Eric Hanushek and Steven Rivkin provides good foundational information on the gap, as does Ronald Ferguson's video *Racial and Ethnic Disparities in Home Intellectual Lifestyles.*[2] A list of other essential books on the subject is provided in Appendix B. Second, we recommend that leaders with sufficient resources assign a staff member to the task of tracking information on the black–white achievement gap. This person would be dedicated to the task of reading the literature and research, tracking the daily news articles, and providing their principal with the kind of summaries that would keep the principal current and knowledgeable on the subject. A good starting point for the assigned staff member would be to use Google News Alerts and RSS feeder to track news and blog posting that mentions the achievement gap.

Third, we suggest that leaders invite people like Kati Haycock, cur-rently Director of the Education Trust, or some other highly knowl-edgeable person to make a presentation on the achievement gap to leadership organizations under their influence. There is no better instructional activity to learn more about the black–white achievement gap than to hear Haycock's enlightening presentation. Many of her pre-sentations are available on the Education Trust website: http://www2. edtrust.org/ edtrust/.

– TWO –
Accept Leadership Responsibility for Closing the Black–White Achievement Gap

After presenting a powerful critique of the lagging academic performance of African American students and how that performance has a relationship to a sense of inferiority, Jeff Howard, Harvard University social psychologist, and Ray Hammond, physician and minister, chose to close their authoritative article "Rumors of Inferiority" with a commanding admonition: "When economic necessity and the demands of social justice compel us toward social change, those who have the most to gain from change—or the most to lose from its absence—should be responsible for pointing the way."[3]

Howard and Hammond continued with an even more emphatic caveat:

> It is time that blacks recognize our own responsibility. When we react to the rumor of inferiority by avoiding intellectual engagement, and when we allow our children to do so, black people forfeit the opportunity for intellectual development that could extinguish the debate about our capacities, and set the stage for group progress. Blacks must hold ourselves accountable for the resulting waste of talent—and valuable time. Black people have everything to gain—in stature, self-esteem, and problem-solving capability—from a more aggressive and confident approach to intellectual competition. We must assume responsibility for our own performance and development."[4]

There we have it: the answer to the question posed in the chapter's title, what can African American leaders do? First and foremost, we must "be responsible for pointing the way" and secondly, we must "assume responsibility for our own performance and development,"[5] In other words, African Americans must assume responsibility for African American performance and development. But consider the phrase "we must assume responsibility" not in the sense of blame, but with the understanding that we are the only ones who can do it. If we don't do it, it won't get done. We must take it upon ourselves to solve the problem of the black–white achievement gap. We must accept the responsibility of leadership on this issue. We must point the way, and lead our

children out of this morass of academic underperformance. We end this section with the words of author, columnist, and research fellow at Stanford University's Hoover Institution, Shelby Steele:

> In the deepest sense, the long struggle of blacks in America has always been a struggle to retrieve our full humanity. But now the reactive stance we adopted to defend ourselves against oppression binds us to the same racial views that oppressed us in the first place. Snakelike, our defense has turned on us. I think it is now the last barrier to the kind of self-possession that will give us our full humanity, and we must overcome it ourselves.[6]

– THREE –

Develop a Sense of Urgency About Closing the Achievement Gap

In creating change—especially the kind we need to close the black–white achievement gap—John P. Kotter, the Harvard professor noted for his expertise in leading change, and author of the book *A Sense of Urgency*, warns that "if a sense of urgency is not high enough and complacency is not low enough, everything else becomes so much more difficult." With respect to the black–white achievement gap, our current level of urgency can only be described as low, especially among contemporary African American leadership, while the current level of complacency must be considered high—exactly the opposite of what we need in order to close the gap. As a result, an early essential task for leadership is to reverse the urgency-complacency situation. Leadership can start this important task by personally adopting a strong sense of urgency to close the black–white achievement gap and then helping elevate the sense of urgency in others. Absent urgency, we are in for a disaster.

In his book *Political Leadership and Education Failure*, Yale University Professor Emeritus Seymour Sarason tells a story of two different kinds of disasters.[7] He likens the first kind of disaster to those that are easily detected, and the potential problem that could result from the disaster is seen as serious. An example would be a disaster caused by severe weather conditions, such as a great hurricane or a tornado. This kind of disaster happens suddenly, but one still has the advantage of some

warning from the meteorologists indicating that bad weather is imminent. Since one knows how dangerous this kind of weather situation can be, one heeds the warning and takes appropriate precautions, with whatever measures are available

Then there is the second kind of disaster, the kind that silently insinuates itself into one's life. Sarason describes it as "the kind of disaster that never 'comes,' we do not know it is 'here,' we do not label it until its implacable destructiveness becomes visually apparent."[8] This type of disaster—such as a drought, global warming, and the spread of disease—give us warning signs also, but the warnings are quiet, nonthreatening, even innocuous. The advance warning from this kind of disaster leaves the impression that there is no particular need to rush; there is no need for urgency because there is plenty of time to take precautionary actions. People who try to raise the sense of urgency are decried as alarmists. The danger builds up over a long period, revealed only in short glimpses, its full menace not unveiled until it has grown to a point where the impending devastation is too clear to be ignored. And then it's too late to take the necessary precautionary steps. By the time one develops a full appreciation of this kind of disaster, one is already in trouble!

The disastrous consequences to the African American social, economic, and civic well-being of not closing the black–white achievement gap can be likened to Sarason's second kind of disaster. It's a quiet, creeping disaster—one that is running under the radar, its potential danger not yet labeled. It has not awakened the concern of those who have the most to lose. Its danger is seen only in tiny glimpses in almost innocent-looking reports of student achievement, college dropout rates, low African American male enrollment in postsecondary institutions, and the incarceration rate of young African American males. It shows itself in ways that lead us to believe there is plenty of time to fix it, there is no urgency, and we think there is no need to hurry or no reason to get personally involved. There is also the normalization of the whole thing. It happens slowly, so people's attitudes about what is "normal" and what is expected adjust without anyone realizing. If these changes happened suddenly, there would be outrage and intense dissatisfaction.

African American leadership must awaken us from this slumber before we wake up to a real disaster, but leadership must first develop a sense of urgency itself before it can help translate that level of urgency to everyone else.

– FOUR –

Help Constituents Understand the Issue

After leaders have developed a deep understanding of the black–white achievement gap, accepted responsibility to close it, and developed a sense of urgency regarding the need to find a solution for it, the next thing that they must do is to help their constituents understand the issue. For an issue with such high-level impact on the well-being of the African American community, the black–white achievement gap is little understood by the general public. This must change. This change is a necessary condition for the community to progress through the stages of awareness, understanding, concern, and dissatisfaction needed to achieve the intensity for effective action.

Max De Pree, the noted expert on leadership, tells us that the leader's first job is to define reality.[9] Leaders have a responsibility to inform, to provide guidance, to evaluate, to report on the effectiveness of prior initiatives, to suggest future actions, and to—in the words of Hammond and Howard—point the way. In doing so, leaders can help their constituents understand the realities associated with the consequences of continued African American student underperformance in academic matters and the realities of the black–white achievement gap.

Wide-ranging, broad-based communication is essential. Leaders have bully pulpits such as ready media access, large-scale forums for discussions, newsletters, radio and television shows and appearances, and the power to convene meetings and assemblies. Leaders are in positions of authority and have countless opportunities to communicate and be heard by constituents. There are many opportunities to send the message that we have a problem and it is our problem. We have the responsibility, as well as the capability to solve this problem.

Imagine the power of a unified African American leadership voice sending that message. Imagine that message being followed by action, such as high-achieving students featured in the news and offered congratulations at assemblies and programs, fraternities, sororities, and churches. Imagine African American–controlled community and nongovernmental organizations tutoring students who need extra help. Imagine students being told that we know that they can achieve and that we expect them to achieve. Why not a nationally televised Image Awards program for students who achieve academically, similar to what now exists for television, movie, music, and literary personalities?

We offer more specific suggestions in the final chapter as a call to action. Here, we simply ask leaders to help create a culture of academic success, one that values academic effort and achievement.

– FIVE –
Think Education Before Politics

At a time when all across the nation, citizens and education officials are working on decisions regarding the establishment of rigorous academic standards, accountability systems, sound curriculum and textbook decisions, and other means of improving education, it seems a little out of touch to ask that we think education before politics. Because every one of the decisions dealing with the establishment of the aforementioned education practices will be made through a political process, education seems inherently political. In the United States we use politics to determine what is taught, when it is taught, where schools are built, who builds them, how much we pay teachers, and every other big decision underpinning the operation of the U.S. education system. There is simply no way to separate education from politics. So how do we think education before politics?

It may not be necessary to separate education from politics in order to think education before politics. The problem isn't that we make educational decisions through the political system. The problem surfaces when we elevate the political system above the educational *result* that we seek. It's a matter of priorities; which comes first, education or politics? If we keep education as the goal and politics as the means to achieve the goal, education and politics can coexist in harmony. Our problem is that over time, in too many instances, we have allowed politics to become the goal, and education has simply become another battleground. In too many educational decisions the goal becomes the dominance of a particular political ideology, not the accomplishment of the best education circumstance. So the way to think education before politics is to think of them in the right order—education as the goal we are trying to accomplish, and politics as the means by which we make the decision as to which action is best to further our educational interest.

Allow us to make this point by telling a story, a true story.

Like public school districts in the other large cities of our nation, the public school district in our nation's capital has, over time, transformed

from a district with minorities to a district of minorities. Of the 65,099 students enrolled in the District of Columbia Public Schools (DCPS) during the 2003 school year,[10] the ethnic breakdown of the students was 85 percent African American, 9 percent Hispanic, 4 percent white, 1.6 percent Asian/Pacific Islander, and less than 1 percent American Indian/Alaskan Native.[11] Given these numbers, it is quite safe to consider the D.C. public school system to be an African American district.

Few of the nation's education watchers would disagree with *The New York Times'* description of the DCPS as one of America's most dysfunctional public school systems.[12] This characterization was supported by data released by the U.S. Department of Education's Institute of Education Sciences and the National Center for Education Statistics. According to the National Assessment of Educational Progress (NAEP) for 2003, only 7 percent of the district's African American fourth graders were at or above proficiency in reading. At the same time, the district's white fourth graders led the nation's other big cities with a 70 percent proficiency score in fourth-grade reading.[13] This translates into an astounding 63-point achievement gap between the African American and white students in D.C. public schools in 2003. Nationally, the gap in 2003 was 27 points. *The New York Times* summarized the situation in this way:

> Although white children do better here than in any state, the odds appear stacked heavily against the 85 percent of students in public schools who are black. Their reading and math skills are among the poorest of blacks in any city or state, with two in three fourth graders, and more than half the eighth graders, lacking even basic reading skills, according to the national assessment.[14]

Further, according to the College Board website, which publishes national and statewide SAT scores, the average verbal SAT score in D.C. for 2003 was 484, which was 23 points below the national average. This poor showing was overshadowed only by its 2003 math performance of 474, which was 45 points below the national average.[15] Disaggregating the data by ethnicity unfolds an even grimmer picture of the black–white achievement gap. In 2003, the national difference between black and white students' SAT verbal scores was 98 points. For math, that difference was 108 points. In D.C., the black–white verbal gap in 2003 was

223 points, and the math gap was 232 points. When comparing this data to the national averages, D.C.'s black–white achievement gap on the SAT was more than double the national average—a heart-stopping difference. (See Figure 9.1.)

		2003					2003	
		Verbal	Mathematics				Verbal	Mathematics
NATIONAL	Black	431	426	**DISTRICT OF COLUMBIA**		Black	415	400
	White	529	534			White	638	632
	Black–white gap	*98*	*108*			Black–white gap	*223*	*232*

FIGURE 9.1. *Average 2003 SAT Scores for Washington, D.C., and the Nation.* Source: College Board, 2003, http://professionals.collegeboard.com/data-reports-research/sat/archived/2003.

Scores on the NAEP assessments also demonstrated that the DCPS needed improvement. Only 6 percent of the district's eighth graders scored at or above proficiency on the 2003 NAEP math assessment, while only 7 percent of the fourth graders met that goal.[16] The district's fourth- and eighth-grade math performance on the 2003 NAEP earned the DCPS the dubious distinction of being ranked dead last, behind all fifty states.[17] We will simply state that the 2003 NAEP fourth- and eighth-grade reading performance in the DCPS is basically at the same level as the math performance and not burden you further with the gruesome details.

In 2003, the DCPS was hemorrhaging in student enrollment, as parents frantically sought alternative educational opportunities. In the words of *The New York Times,* "In Washington, in addition to those children opting for private schools, many others are flocking to charter schools, which siphoned off about 25 percent of [the district's] children, and $37 million in revenue this year alone."[18] District student enrollment in the fall of 1981 was more than 100,000. By the fall of 2001 it had tumbled to 68,449.[19] As of 2003, student enrollment in the DCPS was 65,099 pupils. District parents were competing desperately to gain access to the limited space available in Washington, D.C.'s private and charter schools. Table 9.2 tells the tale.

By looking at the enrollment data for charter schools authorized by the D.C. Board of Education (BOE) and the D.C. Public Charter School Board, we can see the rapid increase in student enrollment for charter

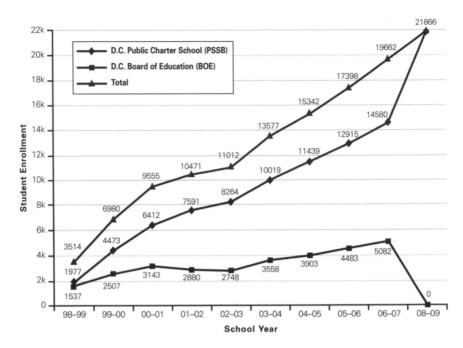

FIGURE 9.2. DC Public Charter School Enrollment 1998–2008. *Source: District of Columbia Public Charter School Board, "PCSB Annual Report 2008: Leading the Transformation," 10, http://www.dcpubliccharter.com/publications/docs/PCSB_AR2008.pdf.*

schools. The enrollment increases in charter schools demonstrates the option of choice that many parents wanted for their children. It is estimated that 25 percent of all D.C. students are enrolled in a charter school.[20] The evidence, using 2003 data, is overwhelming: in 2003, the DCPS did not appear to be serving children well. Even the most supportive DCPS observers would have to agree that in 2003 the district was in need of improvement.

When a school or school district is faced with clear evidence of underperformance, the usual response of its defenders is to claim a lack of financial support. But before the reader jumps to that conclusion, let us examine the facts. Data compiled by the National Center for Education Statistics show that the per pupil expenditure for the 2003–04 school year was $12,959 for the District of Columbia.[21] This amount ranked *second* in the nation, following only New Jersey. It could be argued that if a different data set were used, different results would be achieved. Yes, but even so, we have been able to find no creditable evidence that refutes the argument that the DCPS, during 2003, had one of the highest expenditure levels per student of any of the states. Of course, there are claims common to all public school districts, as well as the DCPS, that within school districts there is significant waste of taxpayers' money. However, in the D.C. public schools, that claim may be justified with evidence seemingly showing that as a district, in 2003, it appeared not to be delivering the kind of educational services needed by children in the nation's capital.

Let us review the facts. In 2003, no more than 10 percent of the students in fourth and eighth grades attending the District of Columbia Public Schools met national standards in reading and math.[22] We know from research that a child not reading at grade level by the third grade has a diminished chance of ever catching up to grade level standards. We know that a student's academic deficits continue to increase if they are not remediated before the student moves on to more challenging schoolwork. We know that as little as one year of such deficits is difficult to overcome even if the child's educational environment is improved the following year. The D.C. public school system is ranked dead last in the nation in student achievement for the fourth and eighth grades by most creditable educational research organizations, but, as indicated earlier, ranked second in per pupil spending by the National Center for Educational Statistics. Finally, out-migration from the public schools in the district is massive and limited more often than not only by the lack of available capacity in the private and charter schools in the area.

Given this set of circumstances and assuming an unquestioned interest in the education of African American students in Washington, D.C., what should be the African American leadership's reaction to a proposal by the U.S. Department of Education that the federal government sponsor a scholarship program offering up to $7,500 to low-income families in Washington, D.C., that could be used to send their children to a private or parochial school of their choice?

For African American leaders in the district, there are three choices:

1. Support the proposed program (referred to as the D.C. Voucher Program) and provide—in the words of *The Washington Times*—"thousands of children currently confined to the atrocious DC public schools an opportunity to escape the failure-plagued system."[23]

2. Fight the proposal and support the continuation of a policy that denies parents the right to choose their children's schools and effectively chain their children to a program whether or not it serves children well.

3. Stand by and do nothing.

Some would argue that another option would be to fix the public schools. Yes, fixing the schools is something that should be considered. But can we tell the students to wait until we fix the schools? How long will it take us to fix the schools? Wouldn't fixing the schools require years while thousands of children would have their lives diminished by subpar educational experiences while waiting for the schools to be fixed? And isn't fixing the schools what we have been trying to do for years? No, fixing the schools is not a fourth option; it's the same option as doing nothing.

Which of the three alternatives would the authentic African American leader choose? Here is a clue. Ask yourself which of the three alternatives offers enhanced educational opportunities for African American students. It would be naive not to understand that there are those who would argue that the answer to the question is alternative two, based solely on the notion that supporting alternative one would be to support vouchers, an absolute no-no in the world of the ideological left. In fact, deciding among the three alternatives is an example of the decision making that distinguishes between authentic African American leadership and simply leadership from those who are African American (not to disparage such leadership—we need this kind of leadership too). Authentic African American leadership requires one to see this decision-making process through the unobstructed lens that reflects the best interests of the children, rather than the lens that reflects political interests. The basic issue here is that the D.C. school system of 2003 was not serving children well. Authentic leadership would be open to change, as the alternative would be to continue the status quo: not serving children well.

Lest the reader leave with the wrong idea, let us state, in the most unambiguous way, that this is not an argument for vouchers. Rather, this is an argument about figuring out which policies and practices are good for African American students and having the courage to support them even when they conflict with one's political agenda.

In the case of the D.C. public schools, one thing seems clear; current policies and practices were not moving African American students toward desired achievement. Clearly, effective change was needed.

So what must African American leaders do? To start, the current situation is not working. It is what got us the current black–white achievement gap, so we must change it. This means new policies, new techniques, and maybe even new people in positions of power in the D.C. education universe. Authentic African American leadership must support policies that change the current situation. And this change must be based on educational needs, not politics. We can't get different results by doing the same things over and over. Authentic African American leaders must identify and support new policies and practices that offer enhanced educational opportunities for African American students, notwithstanding competing political priorities and interests.

You may be wondering how the District of Columbia's political leadership reacted in the situation regarding the scholarship program. Which of the three alternatives did they choose?

You guessed it! Unfortunately, the District's congressional representative chose alternative two and fought passionately alongside the other guardians of the status quo to keep low-income children—mostly African American—imprisoned in schools that were not serving them well. However, you will be interested to learn that then D.C. Mayor Anthony Williams and then City Councilman and Chair of the Council's Education Committee, Kevin Chavous, chose alternative one and were tenacious warriors on behalf of the District's children.

Both former Mayor Williams and former Councilman Chavous are members of the Democratic Party. At considerable political and even personal risk, they made their political careers secondary considerations to actions they believed were in the best interest of the children of the District of Columbia. Councilman Chavous lost his bid for reelection. Many believe that his support for the scholarship program cost him party support, and that was too much for him to overcome. Commenting on the Mayor's support for the scholarship program, *The New York Times* observed, "Mr. Williams [and Councilman Chavous] ignored the ire of fellow Democratic labor unions and advocates of public schools."[24] These two men are examples of authentic African American leaders. They put education before politics.

What is the "so what?" of this situation? We offer this story as an example of a situation where the behavior of some African American leaders not only failed to support educational policy and practice that represented enhanced opportunities for African Americans but also actively fought to retard such opportunities. The story also provides an example where other African American leaders adopted the authentic African American leadership mantle and did the right thing for children. Our answer to the question posed in the title of this chapter—"What must authentic African American leaders do?"—is modeled by Mayor Williams and Councilman Chavous. The answer to the question is clear—put children first and put education before politics.

– SIX –

Pay Close Attention to Local School Board Elections

Few actions would improve school quality more than African American leaders' paying close attention to their local school board elections. There is no point along the education organizational continuum that offers greater opportunities for influencing school quality than the local school board. Among other things, local school boards hire the superintendent, approve district budgets, establish district policies, set salary structures, approve the district curriculum, oversee building and renovation of schools, and provide oversight of school operations. The local school board is a major power and the primary determinant of school district effectiveness. There is simply no other part of a state's K–12 organizational structure that has as much power to influence school quality. The relationship between a district and its governing board is direct. If the school board functions well, you have a well-functioning school district. Likewise, if the school board is dysfunctional, there is a strong probability that the school district will not perform well.

Given this important relationship between local school board quality and the quality of schools, one would think that those who claim to be concerned about the quality and the impact that schools have on children would pay more attention to the process that determines which men and women are elected to serve on their local school board. Regrettably, it just isn't that way.

In the main, school board elections are down-ballot elections—among the issues listed toward the end of the ballot—which almost always generate low voter turnout. It's not unheard of for individuals running for school board seats representing geographical jurisdictions with as many as 50,000 eligible voters to get elected with as few as 5,000 votes. Need evidence? Consider that it was estimated that only 2 percent of New York's voters turned out to vote in the May 18, 1999, New York City school board election.[25] That was 2 percent of the eligible voters, which is an even smaller percentage of the total population. This, admittedly, is an extreme example, but a school board election turnout of between 4 and 10 percent is more the rule than the exception.

Low voter turnout for school board elections can perpetuate a myriad of problems for school quality, but none more detrimental to school quality than the fact that it gives a huge advantage to groups with intact organizational structures, large budgets, and a lot of people to do campaign work, like teacher unions. Low voter turnouts increase the likelihood of such groups being able to swing elections in their direction, and they often do. Such low voter turnout enhances the probability of electing men and women to the school board whose interest in children's education is only tangential to their primary interest, which in many cases is building name recognition to run for other offices, gaining position to influence vendor contracts, positioning themselves to enhance or protect adult constituent interests, or in an all-out effort to lower property taxes and don't much care about the schools at all.

The bottom line is that African American leaders cannot claim to be interested in the education of African American children when they don't do all they can to help ensure that the right men and women, who are running for the right reasons, get elected to our local school boards.

Don McAdams, President and CEO of the Center for the Reform of School Systems, is one of the most knowledgeable school board governance experts in the nation—if not *the* most. He offers some suggestions regarding the qualities of effective school board members. McAdams strongly recommends that an individual running for a school board position should:

▸ Be passionate about public education.

▸ See public education as the foundation for our way of life.

‣ Be an independent thinker.

‣ Be forward-thinking.

‣ Be committed to the success of *all* children.

‣ Be committed to the school district's goals.

‣ See student achievement as the main focus of schools.

‣ Be a lifelong learner.

‣ Be able to collaborate with others.

‣ Be open-minded.

‣ Be knowledgeable in a wide range of areas.

‣ Support school reform rather than the status quo.

‣ Have a thick skin.

Probably the most important thing that authentic African American leaders should require for school board candidates is to determine that they are running for the right reason. And there is only one right reason—a burning desire to help provide a world-class education for all children.

Let us suggest a starting point: pick up the phone and call each member of the school board in your community. Ask each of them, "What is the size of the black–white reading achievement gap for fourth-grade students in the district?" Ask the same question about fourth-grade math. Pick any grade you like (it's best to stay with reading or math), and see if your school board member knows the district's black–white achievement status. If he or she doesn't know the answer to the question, it may mean that he or she hasn't been paying much attention to the achievement gap problem. If that's the case, ask your board member to find out and call you back. What you have just done is sent the signal that you are interested in the black–white achievement gap issue. This little action alone will cause the school board member to pay attention to the matter, which in turn will generate interest on the part of the district's administration and through them, the schools.

Summary

The question of what authentic African American leaders must do in order to provide the kind of leadership that will help close the black–white achievement gap has easy answers. They all boil down to getting effectively involved in closing the gap. Getting involved and getting *effectively* involved are not the same thing. Getting effectively involved requires at a minimum:

- Developing an understanding of the black–white achievement gap issue

- Accepting leadership responsibility for closing the gap

- Acting with a sense of urgency

- Helping constituents understand the issue

- Putting African American children's educational opportunities above political considerations

- Paying close attention to local school board elections

These six actions that African American leaders should take to provide the authentic leadership needed to close the achievement gap does not exhaust the possible ways they can contribute to closing the gap. Each community is different and will no doubt present different issues that need leadership. But no matter the uniqueness of the particular community, the six suggestions offered above should form the foundation upon which effective African American leadership should rest.

CHAPTER 10

The Way Forward

doesn't cost much. ⟶

A Call to Service

an effort to mobilize the entire community.

> *If we can finally succeed in translating the idea of leadership into that of service,*
> *we may soon find it possible to lift the Negro to a higher level. Under leadership we*
> *have come into the ghetto; by service within the ranks we may work our way out*
> *of it. Under leadership we have been constrained to do the biddings of others; by*
> *service we may work out a program in the light of our own circumstances. Under*
> *leadership we have become poverty-stricken; by service we may teach the masses*
> *how to earn a living honestly. Under leadership we have been made to despise our*
> *own possibilities and to develop into parasites; by service we may prove sufficient*
> *unto the task of self-development and contribute our part to modern culture.*
>
> —Carter G. Woodson, *The Mis-Education of the Negro*

IN THE PREVIOUS chapter we presented the notion that there is a certain set of actions that we need from our leaders in order to close the black–white achievement gap. In this chapter however, we contend that while courageous leadership is a necessary condition for closing the gap, it is nonetheless an insufficient condition.

The gap will not be closed just by the actions of those we currently know as leaders. When we talked about leaders in previous chapters, we were referring to national, state, and local elected officials, and those in leadership positions in nongovernmental organizations, faith-based organizations, national, state, and local commissions and committees, civic organizations, and other large state and national social organizations. Although our main focus has been directed to these leaders, the responsibility of closing the gap is not theirs alone. In a real sense, closing this gap requires a determined effort not just from our leaders but from all of us. We cannot escape the responsibility of doing our part in this great undertaking, lest we default on the great legacy left by our forefathers and foremothers. Although closing the black–white achievement gap is critical for all Americans, it is especially critical for those of us who bear the mark of Africa. Earlier, we made the point that our definition of authentic African American leadership included those—black and white—who, with moral conviction, identify and confront the major barriers to black advancement. Notwithstanding this firmly held position, we now direct our call to service directly to those who trace their roots to the fertile soil and lush meadows of Africa.

All the negative realities associated with the black–white achievement gap have an enormous impact on those who are of African ancestry. Therefore, we have a vested interest in its elimination. Each of us has a responsibility to do our part. This means that with respect to closing the black–white achievement gap, leadership and action are required of all of us.

To close the black–white achievement gap, we must initiate a massive, bold, and comprehensive set of actions guided by authentic African American leaders who are committed to removing the barriers to learning. This effort must include a coalition of organizations and agencies working in concert to instill a culture of school success among all African American students. It must be led by those who have the respect of their various communities. Such an approach must be national in scope with a strong grassroots footing.

This is a task that offers opportunities for all to serve. As we go forward, let us revisit the words of an African American leader who provided unquestioned and courageous authentic leadership during the great civil rights movement of the sixties and seventies—Reverend Martin Luther King, Jr. "Everybody can be great . . . because anybody can serve. You don't have to have a college degree to serve. You don't have to make your subject and verb agree to serve. You only need a heart full of grace. A soul generated by love."[1] So let us now focus on what each of us can do to provide leadership in the effort to close the achievement gap.

Framework for Service

As a framework for service dedicated to closing the black–white achievement gap, we are suggesting a bold, wide-ranging, five-level framework for action. This approach involves African Americans in every community and every African American–led organization across the nation tackling the problem at the level that fits them best. It's bold because it assumes the characteristics of past social movements that have changed the character of our nation. It's wide-ranging because it provides everyone with opportunities for action. More important, it's personal because it calls not only for organizational efforts but also personal intervention opportunities, providing direct service to children and parents. It is socially uplifting because it has, as its driving principle, service to others.

Scope of Service

To enhance the probability of our individual actions actually helping to close the achievement gap, it is critical that the actions be carefully focused. Although the gap exists in nearly every academic area, it is unwise to scatter our efforts. Therefore we propose a more narrowly focused strategy, one which would give us the best opportunity to make a critical difference. For that reason, we suggest that our actions center on the following three objectives:

▶ Improving elementary and middle school African American students' performance in reading

▶ Improving elementary and middle school African American students' performance in math

▶ Enhancing African American students' belief in the value of education and their own role in their own success

A big advantage of this individual-service approach is that our work can begin immediately. There is no need to wait for committees, commissions, or research reports to tell us what works in educating African American children. The information is already available. The only thing one needs to get started is the will to do so.

We can all step up to the plate as leaders did during the early days of the civil rights struggle and demonstrate our will to serve now. Instead of marching in the streets, staging sit-ins, or attending mass meetings, we can offer service that provides support for children's learning. This will require gaining a greater insight into the achievement-gap problem and becoming more personally involved in providing service to children and families. There are countless individual-service activities that can be undertaken within our five-level framework that will further our three objectives.

LEVEL ONE: PERSONAL DIRECT SERVICE TO CHILDREN AND PARENTS (SUGGESTIONS FOR INDIVIDUAL ACTION)

- If you have parenting responsibilities, start with your own children. Individuals who are involved in parenting can help close the black–white achievement gap by providing their children with the very best parenting support possible. Great parenting provides children with the foundation they need to achieve in school and succeed in life. For individuals interested in improving their parenting skills, we recommend the *Helping Your Child* brochure series, available from the U.S. Department of Education. This series of brochures provides outstanding suggestions for parents of school-aged and preschool children who are interested in helping their children in the fields of reading, math, science, homework, and/or values. *The Helping Your Child* brochure series can be accessed at http://edpubs.ed.gov/.

- Serve as a mentor to an elementary or middle school child.

- Serve as a tutor in a one-to-one tutoring program.

- Volunteer at a school to read to children.

- Volunteer in organizations such as Big Brothers and Big Sisters to provide one-to-one guidance and encouragement to a child.

- Work with new parents on parenting skills.

- Work with Boys' and Girls' Clubs or similar organizations.

- Help elect high-quality individuals to serve on local school boards.

- Attend local school board meetings and inquire about the achievement gap. In her article "The Achievement Gap: Is Your

School Helping All Students Succeed?," Victoria Thorp offers the following suggestions regarding questions to ask a school principal in order to assess the school's commitment to helping all children reach high standards:[2]

Ask: *How are students achieving in the school now? Are there any groups of students that are scoring below others on standardized tests? If so, what is the school doing to address this challenge?*

Listen for: Exact achievement data for each group of students in the school, specific strategies (curricular programs, interventions, etc.) the school is using to raise the achievement of low-performing students, and concrete, measurable school goals for improving test scores.

Ask: *How do the teachers hold all children to high expectations and measure progress to ensure that all students are learning?*

Listen for: Concrete examples of assessments that teachers use to gauge student learning and ways that teachers analyze this assessment data to make sure all students are on track.

Ask: *How is the school working to close the achievement gap? Are teachers using any new curriculum or instruction? Are they offering extra academic support for students?*

Listen for: Specific actions the school is taking to raise achievement for low-performing students. Potential actions include implementing new teaching strategies that have been proven successful in other schools and providing additional academic support for students, during the school day and after school. Ask how many children take advantage of these resources and how parents are notified about this extra help.

Ask: *Do all students have equal access to the most challenging classes or are lower-achieving students grouped in remedial programs?*

Listen for: Evidence that all students have access to high-level courses and enriched curriculum and the school discourages permanent "ability grouping" and remedial programs. If you're not sure, ask to see the demographics of the students in accelerated courses vs. remedial courses. The goal is not to put students in courses which are beyond their abilities, but to assure that high-level and enriched curriculum courses are available to all students who can benefit from them.

These are great questions, and they can be asked of school board members as well as school principals.

LEVEL TWO: SERVICE THROUGH AFRICAN AMERICAN– LED ORGANIZATIONS

‣ Through organizations such as NAACP, National Urban League, Elks USA, 100 Black Men of America, Inc., National Coalition of 100 Black Women, the Sigma Pi Phi Fraternity, National Council of Negro Women, and various fraternities and sororities, you can do the following:

Gene Marsh.

– Work to make academic achievement a major focus area for the organization.

– Support the development of supplemental educational programs such as Saturday academies, after-school reading clubs, etc.

– Provide job-exploration programs.

– Sponsor orientation programs for teachers, counselors, parents, and other educators.

– Design and implement programs aimed at teaching children reading and math, and the value of education.

– Become engaged in school board elections.

– Require a report on the progress of local students in reading and math as a part of the organization's regular meeting agenda.

– Plan school visits for the organization.

– Appoint a member of the organization who would have the responsibility to keep the membership informed on the academic progress of African American students in the area.

‣ Sponsor parenting skills programs for local parents. The U.S. Department of Education's *Helping Your Child* Series can serve as the basic curriculum. The series can be accessed at http://edpubs.ed.gov/.

‣ Promote service through faith-based organizations.

– Increase the opportunities for children to speak before an audience.

– Advocate for the infusion of instruction in basic reading skills for children in Sunday school and other church- or mosque-related programs.

– Provide pamphlets and other materials that inform members about academic achievement and how it is measured.

– Develop training sessions for new parents. Hold them in members' homes to encourage expanded attendance.

LEVEL THREE: SERVICE THROUGH PUBLIC ORGANIZATIONS, AGENCIES, AND BUSINESSES

‣ Lead activities to help increase general understanding of the black–white achievement gap and its impact on social justice and equality.

‣ Encourage these organizations to monitor matters related to all student progress but especially African American student progress.

‣ Increase awareness of schools and classes that have experienced success in increasing African American student performance.

‣ Advocate for after-school programs and Saturday academies to fill in the learning gaps that some children exhibit.

‣ Facilitate school–community partnerships.

‣ Arrange for reports regarding how your local school system is doing regarding the achievement gap.

‣ Promote the development of scholarship programs or other ways of rewarding/praising/encouraging high-achieving students.

LEVEL FOUR: SERVICE THROUGH HISTORICALLY BLACK COLLEGES AND UNIVERSITIES

‣ Encourage colleges and universities to direct their research capa- *research*
bilities toward understanding the black–white achievement gap
phenomenon.

‣ Sponsor programs, seminars, and discussions on topics relevant
to closing the achievement gap.

‣ Lead the development of effective parenting skills curricula for
use in faith-based and service-oriented organizations.

‣ Work to enhance the quality of the teacher education programs.

‣ Work with local public schools to enhance the quality of their
reading and math pedagogy.

‣ In fields such as social work, sociology, economics, education,
and psychology, direct student projects and readings toward matters associated with the black–white achievement gap.

LEVEL FIVE: SERVICE THROUGH ADVOCACY WITH SCHOOLS AND EDUCATION POLICY MAKERS

‣ Become educated in matters of local, state, and national education
policy and become involved with entities organized to impact
such policy.

‣ Read the literature on education, track education policy coverage
in the news media, and express your views to your local representatives through letters, phone calls, op-ed articles, and com-
ments at appropriate meetings.

Clearly, all these suggestions merely serve as starting points for the
development of comprehensive lists of ideas of actions for service to eliminate the black–white achievement gap. Undoubtedly there are many
other activities that interested individuals and organizations can become
involved in to play a part in this great mission. The key is simple: get
involved, do something, act!

National Action Approach

With respect to our interest in a national approach to this effort, a statement in the strategic plan of the Black Alliance for Educational Options (BAEO) is instructive. It asserts, "History has shown that social movements which positively impact black people have been most effective when the mantle of leadership is borne by a credible black-led organization that has the capacity to work closely with allies of all races and political parties to reach common objectives."[3]

So how shall we go forward? The most tempting recommendation is to call for a national action plan embraced by all African American leaders and their organizations and support groups. Merely calling for a national collaborative will not, as we have seen, solve the problem. Such national collaboratives have taken place before and have realized a mixed record of achievement. Most recently, we witnessed an example of a successful collaborative in Tavis Smiley's *The Covenant with Black America*.[4] During this collaborative, Edmund W. Gordon, Professor of Psychology Emeritus at Yale University, presented a case for a national commitment to improving academic achievement levels in black and other populations that are underrepresented among the high achievers in our society. Gordon's message was a part of a larger set of recommendations on improving the lives of African Americans in areas such as health care, education, criminal and environmental justice, housing, and economics. In *The Covenant with Black America*, Smiley presents explanations on the status, recommendations for action, and examples of success in the various facets of concern; it is a call for community action. The call to action suggested herein differs from that in *The Covenant with Black America* in that its focus is much narrower. Because we feel that education is the core of the African American disadvantage in America, closing the achievement gap offers the high-leverage opportunities to further African American progress in America.

Hugh B. Price, former president of the National Urban League, took a different approach. In his thoughtful book, *Achievement Matters: Getting Your Child the Best Education Possible,* Price addresses parents and outlines actions that each parent should take to improve his or her child's education.[5] This book is also a resource for community mobilization efforts to reduce the achievement gap.

We would be wise to learn from the experiences of those who have approached similar projects before. We have paid close attention to previous efforts to enhance African American educational attainment and we can build on their contributions. We strongly recommend that each leader invest in personal service to the community and lead the way for other African Americans and others to join in serving children. To support and maximize the efforts of individual leaders, we believe that the participation or creation of a national organization will be required.

The logical next step is to assemble groups of thinkers and doers to expand on these ideas and develop concrete plans for further action. We believe that closing the black–white achievement gap ultimately will require a massive social movement not unlike those in the twentieth century that focused on women's liberation, welfare, and civil rights. It will require a coming together of the African American community around the common goal of putting an end to the absurd idea that young African Americans cannot achieve academically as well as other young people.

To launch this effort, it is our intent to call for a national summit involving a small number of leaders from civil rights organizations, advocacy groups, fraternities, sororities, and faith-based organizations who have a demonstrated history of involvement with the issue of the black–white achievement gap. These individuals would serve as a forum for developing plans and strategies to expand the effort to a national membership. The goal must be to forge an agreement to dedicate significant support from each representative toward a national goal of eliminating the black–white achievement gap by 2025.

The summit should address the following five actions:

- Formally adopt a goal of eliminating the black–white achievement gap by 2025.

- Develop a discussion and draft of an action plan, theory of action, and organizational structure.

- Organize a national leadership and resource entity.

- Develop a set of actions that individuals and organizations may adopt to work to close the gap.

- Develop a plan for providing support for the effort.

We are presently in discussion with several nationally respected leaders regarding moving forward with the establishment of the aforementioned summit.

Summary

There is an old adage that simple problems require simple solutions while complex problems require complex solutions. In other words, there are no simple solutions to complex problems. The black–white achievement gap is certainly a complex problem. We can be assured that the achievement gap problem can be eliminated, but its resolution will require that we match its complexity with well-thought-out, energetic, and sustained efforts. For this, we need a strong leadership and involvement from all of us.

CONCLUSION

In a people's rise from oppression to grace, a turning point comes when thinkers, determined to stop the downward slide, get together to study the causes of common problems, think out solutions and organize ways to apply them.

—Ayi Kwei Armah, *Osiris Rising*

ON THE WEBSITE of the Demarest Nature Center in Demarest, New Jersey, the education programs page begins with the sentence *Education is the heart of it all and the hope for the future*.[1] This is the message that we hope can be heard, internalized, and used as a foundation for future action aimed at furtherance of the African American journey—we should say here America's journey—toward the twin goals of racial equality and social justice in America. The journey is imperiled by countless barriers, each of which represents a challenge that must be overcome in order to arrive at an America where racial equality and social justice reign. Although the barriers are many, and although they represent a broad array of problem areas, they all have something in common. They all are impacted, one way or another, by the education attainment of African Americans. And although we can't know for certain exactly what the future will hold, we do know for certain, that whatever it holds, it will be influenced by the quality of education of our people. So, the crux of the matter is, it is true that education is at the heart of it all and the hope for the future.

This is not news to us. We have heard it before. Authentic African American leaders have told us this time and time again. Admonishments about the importance of education have been shouted at us by W. E. B. Du Bois, Mary McLeod Bethune, and countless others. One of clearest and most unforgettable messages about education's importance comes to us from Malcolm X, who put it in clear and unambiguous terms when he said, "Education is the passport to the future, for tomorrow belongs to those who prepare for it today."[2]

Current African American educational status covers a broad array of problem areas and even some areas of accomplishment. There are multiple educational needs in the African American community and working toward remedies in any of the areas is helpful. But the single best indicator of the educational status of African Americans in America, and the problem area with the broadest possible battlefront and highest leverage improvement payoffs possibilities, is closing the black–white achievement gap. Chapter 1 begins with a Jencks and Phillips quote which we will paraphrase here: Closing the black–white achievement gap would probably do more to promote racial equality in the United States than any other strategy now under consideration. Eliminating the test score gap would sharply increase black college graduation rates. It would also reduce racial disparities in men's earnings and would probably eliminate racial disparities in women's earnings. Eliminating the test score gap would also allow selective colleges, professional schools, and employers to phase out racial preferences that have caused so much political trouble over the past generation.

As we work to continue our national efforts to bring America closer to the fulfillment of the vision promised in our Declaration of Independence—*that all men are created equal, that they are endowed by their Creator with certain unalienable Rights, that among these are Life, Liberty, and the pursuit of Happiness*—closing the black–white achievement gap is a priority. To accomplish this task, authentic African American leadership is needed to reawaken the African American thrust for education.

Going Forward

The message is clear: we must take effective actions aimed at closing the black–white achievement gap. We are presented with a great opportunity with national significance. By closing the black–white achievement gap, we will be eliminating many disparities between blacks and whites, thereby creating a better America. To make progress in this area we need the engagement of all, but most especially authentic African American leadership. Our nation has made tremendous progress in its efforts to build a nation worthy of the grand vision set forth in its Declaration of

Independence. We have progressed from a social culture where chattel slavery was broadly accepted, legally supported, and vigorously defended, to the election of an African American as President of the United States. This is significant progress by any measure. But even as we accept the election of President Barack Obama as evidence of our progress, and as we celebrate that progress toward greater racial equality, we must bear in mind that it is only a step along the way. The goal is still beyond our reach. The opportunity to go further, much further, is before us. Currently, a lot of good work is underway. The efforts in California led by State Superintendent of Instruction Jack O'Connell, Colorado's Department of Education's Closing the Achievement Gap Initiative, the scholarly work of Harvard University's Achievement Gap Initiative led by Dr. Ronald Ferguson, and the remarkable work of Geoffrey Canada and the Harlem Children's Zone are just a few examples. What is missing from these valuable but scattered efforts is the high-level involvement and coordination of the African American national leadership community. Although closing the black–white achievement gap will require the efforts of all Americans, it will especially require authentic African American leadership. We need authentic African American leadership to lead the greatest civil rights issue of our time: closing the black–white achievement gap.

APPENDIX A

Sources for Quality Information on the Black–White Achievement Gap

Harvard Achievement Gap Initiative (AGI): The mission of the AGI is to help raise achievement for all children while narrowing racial, ethnic, and socioeconomic gaps. AGI serves a variety of audiences including policymakers, educators, researchers and parents, by working with scholars worldwide to produce and disseminate research and distill its implications for raising achievement levels and closing achievement gaps. Website: http://www.agi.harvard.edu/

LevelTen: LevelTen is a nonprofit grassroots organization aimed at eliminating the nation's achievement gap through innovative solutions, effective support initiatives, and mobilized community engagement. Website: http://www.level-ten.org/

Education Trust: The Education Trust works for the high achievement of all students at all levels, with the goal of closing the achievement gaps that separate low-income students and students of color from other youth. Its basic tenet is that all children will learn at high levels when they are taught at high levels. Websites: http://www2.edtrust.org/edtrust/; (The Education Trust West) http://www2.edtrust.org/edtrust/etw/

Minority Student Achievement Network (MSAN): MSAN is a national coalition of multiracial, suburban and urban school districts that have come together to study achievement gaps that exist in their districts. Since its inception in 1999, MASN has worked to change school practices and structures that keep these achievement gaps in place. Website: http://www.msan.wceruw.org/

Education Testing Service (ETS): ETS works to advance quality and equity in education by providing fair and valid assessments, research, and related services. Its products and services measure knowledge and skills, promote learning and educational performance, and support education and professional development. Website: http://www.ets.org/

American College Testing (ACT): ACT is an independent, not-for-profit organization that provides more than a hundred assessment, research, information, and program management services in the broad areas of education and workforce development. Website: http://www.act.org/news/ data.html.asp

National Center for Education Statistics (NCES): The National Center for Education Statistics (NCES), located within the U.S. Department of Education and the Institute of Education Sciences, is the primary federal entity for collecting and analyzing data related to education. Website: http://www.nces.ed.gov/

The College Board: The College Board is a not-for-profit membership association whose mission is to connect students to college success and opportunity. Each year, the College Board serves students and their parents, high schools and colleges through major programs and services in college admissions, guidance, assessment, financial aid, enrollment, and teaching and learning. Website: htttp//www.collegeboard.com/

Education Commission of the States (ECS): The mission of the Education Commission of the States is to help states develop effective policy and practice for public education by providing data, research, analysis and leadership; and by facilitating collaboration, the exchange of ideas among the states, and long-range strategic thinking.Website: http://www.ecs.org/

National Center for Educational Achievement (NCEA): The National Center for Educational Achievement is a nonprofit, nonpartisan organization and the national sponsor of Just for the Kids (JFTK). Its goal is to support efforts to reach excellence in education, to raise academic expectations, and to promote the practices that will help more students reach college/career readiness. Website: http://www.just4kids.org/en/

Your Commissioner of Education and State Board of Education: Each state has a chief state school officer—usually called the Commissioner of Education—and a State Board of Education (SBOE) whose responsibility, generally, is to oversee the public education system of their respective state in accordance with rules adopted by their state legislature. The offices of your Commissioner of Education and SBOE are good sources of information about educational achievement in your state. Website: Go to their Web pages.

APPENDIX B

SUGGESTED READING LIST ON AFRICAN AMERICAN LEADERSHIP

Carlton-Laney, Iris. *African American Leadership: An Empowerment Tradition in Social Welfare History*. Atlanta, Ga.: NASW Press, 2001.

Childs, John Brown. *Leadership, Conflict, and Cooperation in Afro-American Social Thought*. Philadelphia: Temple University Press, 1989.

Gordon, Jacob U. *Black Leadership for Social Change*. Westport, Conn.: Greenwood Press, 2000.

Hawkins, Hugh. *Booker T. Washington and His Critics: Black Leadership in Crisis*. Lexington, Mass.: D. C. Heath, 1974.

Hutchinson, Earl Ofari. *The Disappearance of Black Leadership*. Los Angeles: Middle Passage Press, 2000.

Marable, Manning. *Black Leadership: Four Great American Leaders and the Struggle for Civil Rights*. New York: Columbia University Press, 1998.

Nelson, H. Viscount. *The Rise and Fall of Modern Black Leadership: Chronicle of a Twentieth Century Tragedy*. Lanham, Md.: University Press of America, 2003.

Peterson, Jesse Lee. *Scam: How The Black Leadership Exploits Black America*. Nashville, Tenn.: WND Books, 2005.

Phillips, Donald T. *Martin Luther King, Jr. on Leadership*. New York: Warner Books, 1999.

Smith, Robert Charles. *Black Leadership: A Survey of Theory and Research*. Washington, D.C.: Mental Health Research and Development Center, Institute for Urban Affairs and Research, Howard University, 1983.

Smith, Robert Charles. *We Have No Leaders: African Americans in the Post–Civil Rights Era*. Albany: State University of New York Press, 1996.

Verney, Kevern. *The Art of the Possible: Booker T. Washington and Black Leadership in the United States, 1881–1925.* New York: Routledge, 2001.

Walters, Ronald W., and Cedric Johnson. *Bibliography of African American Leadership: An Annotated Guide.* Westport, Conn.: Greenwood Publishing Group, 2000.

Walters, Ronald W., and Robert C. Smith, *African American Leadership.* Albany: State University of New York Press, 1999.

West, Cornel. *Race Matters.* New York: Vintage Books, 2001.

White, John. *Black Leadership in America, 1865–1968: From Booker T. Washington to Jesse Jackson.* New York: Longman, 1990.

Williams, Juan. *Enough: The Phony Leaders, Dead-End Movements, and Culture of Failure That Are Undermining Black America—and What We Can Do About It.* New York: Crown Publishers, 2006.

Williams, Lea E. *Servants of the People: The 1960s Legacy of African American Leadership.* New York: Palgrave Macmillan. 1996.

E N D N O T E S

PREFACE

1. Percentile is defined as one of a set of points on a scale derived by dividing a group into its parts in order of magnitude. For example, if a score is equal to or greater than 97 percent of those attained on an examination, it is said to be in the 97th percentile. Percentile rank is very similar. The percentile rank of a score is the percentage of scores in its frequency distribution that are lower. For example, a test score that is greater than 90 percent of the scores of people taking the test is said to be at the 90th percentile.

2. Median is the middle value of the entire distribution once it has been ordered.

CHAPTER 1

1. Christopher Jencks and Meredith Phillips, eds., *The Black-White Test Score Gap* (Washington, D.C.: Brookings Institution Press, 1998), 1.

2. *Grutter v. Bollinger,* 539 U.S. 306 (2003).

3. There have been changing preferences among those who trace their roots to the African continent regarding the term that describes their group-identity. During the early seventeenth century, the term most used was "African." "Negro" gained currency during the early nineteenth century and was popular until the term "Black" became more preferred. Finally, "African American" came into majority use in the late twentieth century. We use the terms generally associated with the time period under discussion.

4. Bill George, "Truly Authentic Leadership," *U.S. News & World Report,* October 30, 2006, http://www.usnews.com/usnews/news/articles/061022/30authentic_print.htm (accessed August 18, 2008).

5. Ibid.

6. John McWhorter, *Authentically Black: Essays for the Black Silent Majority* (New York: Gotham Books, 2003).

7. William Julius Wilson, *The Declining Significance of Race: Blacks and Changing American Institutions* (Chicago: University of Chicago Press, 1978).

8. G. M. Fredrickson, review of *The End of Racism* by Dinesh D'Souza, in "Demonizing the American Dilemma," in *The New York Review of Books,* October 19, 1995, http://www.pierretristam.com/Bobst/library/wf-85.htm (accessed August 12, 2008).

9. Glenn Loury, *The Anatomy of Racial Inequality* (Cambridge, Mass.: Harvard University Press, 2003), 10.

10. Ibid., 167.

11. Jeff Howard and Ray Hammond, "Rumors of Inferiority: The Hidden Obstacles to Black Success in America," *The New Republic,* September 9, 1985, 17–21.

12. Ibid.

13. J. B. Coleman, E. Q. Campbell, C. J. Hobson, J. McPartland, A. M. Mood, F. D. Weinfeld, and R. L. York, R. L., *Equality of Educational Opportunity* (Washington, DC: U.S. Department of Health, Education, and Welfare, US Government Printing Office, 1966).

14. Richard J. Herrnstein and Charles Murray, *The Bell Curve: Intelligence and Class Structure in American Life* (New York: Free Press, 1994).

15. Jencks and Phillips, *The Black-White Test Score Gap,* vi.

16. *No Child Left Behind Act of 2001,* Public Law 107–110, 107th Cong. (January 8, 2002), http://www.ed.gov/policy/elsec/leg/esea02/107-110.pdf.

17. Laurence Steinberg, *Beyond the Classroom: Why School Reform Has Failed and What Parents Need to Do* (New York: Simon & Schuster, 1996).

18. Malcolm Gladwell, *Outliers* (New York: Little Brown and Company, 2008).

19. Paul E. Barton, *Parsing the Achievement Gap* (Princeton, N.J.: Policy Information Center, Educational Testing Service, 2003), http://www.ets.org/Media/Research/pdf/PICPARSING.pdf.

20. Lowell C. Rose and Alec M. Gallup, The 36th Annual Phi Delta Kappa/Gallup Poll of the Public's Attitudes Toward the Public Schools. *Phi Delta Kappan.* 86 (1) , 2004, 41–56.

21. James Traub, "What No School Can Do," *New York Times Magazine,* January 16, 2000, http://www.nytimes.com/2000/02/06/magazine/l-what-no-school-can-do-618950.html.

22. Richard Rothstein, *Class and Schools: Using Social, Economic, and Educational Reform to Close the Black–White Achievement Gap* (San Diego, Calif.: Economic Policy Books, 2004).

23. Steve Eubanks, ed., *Quotable King: Words of Wisdom, Inspiration, and Freedom By and About Dr. Martin Luther King, Jr.* (Nashville, Tenn.: TowleHouse Publishing, 2002), 20.

24. This statement does not imply that the school does not have some assistance from parents. Clearly, many schools have strong and well-developed parental involvement programs. The statement should be understood to mean that the school was the program's initiator and controlling entity.

CHAPTER 2
1. Dan Seligman, "Gapology 101," *Forbes,* December 12, 2005, 120–122, http://www.forbes.com/forbes/2005/1212/120_print.html (accessed August 13, 2008).

2. William J. Mathis, "A Special Section on the Achievement Gap—Bridging the Achievement Gap: A Bridge Too Far?," *Phi Delta Kappan,* 86, 2005.

3. Jim Collins, *Good to Great: Why Some Companies Make the Leap . . . and Others Don't* (New York: HarperCollins Publishers, 2001), 70.

4. Dan Princiotta, Kristin Denton Flanagan, and Elvira Geromino Hausken, *Fifth Grade: Findings from the Fifth Grade Follow-up of the Early Childhood Longitudinal Study, Kindergarten Class of 1998–99* (ECLS-K), report for the U.S. Department of Education, National Center of Education Statistics, NCES-2006-038, March 2006, http://nces.ed.gov/pubs2006/2006038.pdf (accessed September 4, 2008).

5. Scale scores make it possible to compare the achievement of a particular group of students (for example, white students, black students, female students, etc.) to that of the student population as a whole. Thus, for example, a high scale score mean for a particular group indicates that this group's performance is high in comparison to other groups. It does not mean that all members of the group have mastered a particular set of skills, however.

6. U.S. Department of Education, National Center for Education Statistics, "The Nation's Report Card (Reading) National Assessment of Educational Progress at Grades 4 and 8," 2007, http://nationsreportcard.gov/reading_2007 (accessed August 13, 2008).

7. Three levels of proficiency are defined on the NAEP reading scale: Basic, Proficient, and Advanced. These achievement levels are cumulative. Thus, students performing at the Proficient level, for example, also display the competencies associated with the Basic level.

8. U.S. Department of Education, National Center for Education Statistics, "The Nation's Report Card (Mathematics) National Assessment of Educational Progress at Grades 4 and 8," 2007, http://nationsreportcard.gov/math_2007 (accessed August 13, 2008).

9. U.S. Department of Education, National Center for Education Statistics, "The Nation's Report Card (Mathematics) Trial Urban District Assessment Results at Grades 4 and 8," 2007, http://nationsreportcard.gov/tuda_math_2007 and http://nationsreportcard.gov/tuda_reading_2007 (accessed August 13, 2008).

10. Jay P. Greene, "High School Graduation Rates in the United States" (report for Black Alliance for Educational Options, Washington, D.C., April 2002), 9.

11. All figures cited throughout the remainder of this section are from: Jay Greene and Greg Forster, "Public High School Graduation and College Readiness Rates in the United States," Education Working Paper Number 8, Manhattan Institute, February 2005, http://www.manhattan-institute.org/html/ewp_08_t01.htm and http://www.manhattan-institute.org/html/ewp_08_t06.htm (accessed September 3, 2008).

12. U.S. Census Bureau, "School Enrollment Surpasses Baby-Boom Crest," [News Release], June 2005, http://www.census.gov/Press-Release/www/releases/archives/education/005157.html (accessed September 3, 2008).

13. ACT, Inc., "ACT High School Profile: Graduating Class of 2008 National Report" Section 1, Executive Summary, 2008, http://act.org/news/data/08/pdf/National2008.pdf (accessed September 3, 2008).

14. College Board, "College-Bound Seniors, 2008, Demographic Information: SAT Reasoning Test Mean Scores by Gender Within Race/Ethnicity," Table 8, 2008, http://professionals.collegeboard.com/profdownload/Total_Group_Report.pdf (accessed September 3, 2008).

15. "Large Black-White Scoring Gap Persists on SAT," *Journal of Blacks in Higher Education* 53 (2006): 72–76.

16. College Board, "College-Bound Seniors, 2008."

17. ACT, Inc., "ACT High School Profile Report: The Graduating Class of 2008 National Report," 16–17, http://www.act.org/news/data/08/pdf/National2008.pdf (accessed September 3, 2008).

18. U.S. Department of Education, National Center for Education Statistics, *Digest of Education Statistics,* 2007, Table 192, 2007, 284–285.

19. U.S. Department of Education, National Center for Education Statistics, *The Condition of Education,* 2008, Table 25–3, 2008, 145.

20. "The Widening Racial Scoring Gap on Standardized Tests for Admission to Graduate School," *The Journal of Blacks in Higher Education* 51 (2006): 8–11.

CHAPTER 3
1. American Anthropological Association "Statement on 'Race' and Intelligence," adopted December 1994. http://www.aaanet.org/stmts/race.htm (accessed August 13, 2008).

2. American Psychological Association, "The View of the American Psychological Association," American Psychological Association, http://www.iq-tests.eu/iq-test-The-view-of-the-American-Psychological-Association-1120.html (accessed on August 14, 2008).

3. Ian F. Haney Lopez, *The Social Construction of Race: Some Observations on Illusion, Fabrication, and Choice,* 29 Harvard Civil Rights–Civil Liberties Law Review (Winter 1994), 1–62, 6–7, 11–17.

4. Paul M. Sniderman and Thomas Piazza, *The Scar of Race* (Cambridge, Mass.: Belknap/Harvard University Press, 1994).

5. Ibid.

6. Claude Steele and Joshua Aronson, "Stereotype Threat and the Test Performance of Academically Successful African Americans," in Jencks and Phillips, *The Black-White Test Score Gap,* 401–427.

7. Pedro Carneiro, James J. Heckman, and Dimitriy V. Masterov, "Understanding the Sources of Ethnic and Racial Wage Gaps and Their Implication for Policy," in *Handbook of Employment Discrimination Research,* eds., Laura Beth Nielson and Robert L. Nelson, (Dordrecht, The Netherlands: Springer, 2005), 99–136.

8. Derek A. Neal and William R. Johnson, "The Role of Premarket Factors in Black-White Wage Differences," *Journal of Political Economy,* 104, no. 5 (October 1996): 869–895.

9. Carneiro, Heckman, and Masterov, "Ethnic and Racial Wage Gaps," 100.

10. Jencks and Phillips, *The Black-White Test Score Gap,* 480.

11. The data referred to in this and subsequent paragraphs was developed from the U.S. Census Bureau, "Current Population Survey, 2007 Annual Social and Economic Supplement," http://www.census.gov/hhes/www/cpstc/cps_table_creator.html (accessed August 8, 2008). All the figures cited in this section actually underestimate the true income and employment differences between high school dropouts and graduates because they're based on U.S. Census data that lump together GED recipients with those who have high school diplomas. Research has shown that GED recipients earn much less than those with diplomas, so the real difference a high school diploma makes will be greater than these figures show (Stephen Cameron and James Heckman, "The Nonequivalence of High School Equivalents," *Journal of Labor Economics,* 11, no. 1 [January 1993]: 1–47; and Jay P. Greene, *Education Myths: What Special Interest Groups Want You to Believe About Our Schools—and Why It Isn't So* [Lanham, Md.: Rowman & Littlefield, 2005], 96–98).

12. U.S. Department of Education, National Center for Education Statistics, *Digest of Education Statistics 2005,* Chapter 5, Table 368 (August 10, 2006), http://nces.ed.gov/pubs2008/2008022.pdf, p. 547 (accessed July 17, 2009).

13. Calculations are based on *Digest of Education Statistics 2007,* Table 368, http://www.census.gov/popest/datasets.html.

14. Calculations are based on *Digest of Education Statistics 2005,* Table 368, and U.S. Census Bureau monthly population estimates, http://www.census.gov/popest/datasets.html (accessed August 8, 2008).

15. All health insurance coverage data in this section are based on calculations from data from the "2007 Annual Social and Economic Supplement of the U.S. Census Current Population Survey Health Insurance Coverage Status and Type of Coverage by Selected Characteristics: 2006 Black Alone," http://www.census.gov/hhes/www/cpstc/cps_table_creator.html (accessed on August 8, 2008).

16. Brian Gottlob, "The High Cost of Failing to Reform Public Education in Texas," (study released jointly by the Milton and Rose D. Friedman Foundation, the National Center for Policy Analysis, and the Hispanic Council for Reform and Educational Options, February 2007), http://www.friedmanfoundation.org/downloadFile.do?id=107 (accessed August 14, 2008). Gottlob's estimates are lower than those produced by some other studies; this makes them useful as a conservative estimate. If the actual chances of an African American dropout going to prison are actually higher, then addressing the achievement gap will be all the more important. The particular value of Gottlob's work is that he breaks out the incarceration rate by educational attainment levels.

17. This is the number of eighteen-year-old African American males according to the U.S. Census Bureau's monthly population estimates, http://www.census.gov/popest/datasets.html (accessed August 8, 2008).

18. These mortality rates are age-adjusted to ensure valid comparisons. Mortality rates by education are taken from the U.S. Department of Health and Human Services, National Center for Health Statistics, *Health, United States 2007,* Table 34, 212–213, http://www.cdc.gov/nchs/data/hus/hus07.pdf (accessed August 11, 2008).

The general mortality rate for the population ages 25–64 was calculated using these data and data on the proportion of the population in each educational category, taken from the U.S. Census Bureau, Current Population Survey 2007 Annual Social and Economic Supplement, http://www.census.gov/hhes/www/cpstc/cps_table_creator.html (accessed August 11, 2008).

19. Calculations are based on U.S. Department of Health and Human Services, National Center for Health Statistics, *Health, United States 2007,* Table 35, 214–217, http://www.cdc.gov/nchs/data/hus/hus07.pdf and U.S. Census Current Population Survey www.census.gov/poptest/datasets.html (both accessed on August 11, 2008).

20. U.S. Census Bureau, Current Population Survey 2007 Annual Social and Economic Supplement, http://www.census.gov/popest/datasets.html (accessed on August 11, 2008).

CHAPTER 4

1. Mano Singham, "The Canary in the Mine," *Phi Delta Kappan,* 80, no. 1 (September, 1998): 9–15.

2. Jill Davidson, "A Review of Rothstein's *Class and Schools: Using Social, Economic, and Educational Reform to Close the Black–White Achievement Gap,*" *Horace Book Review,* 21, no. 2 (Winter 2005), http://essentialschools.org/cs/cespr/view/ces_res/362 (accessed August, 2008).

3. Betty Hart and Todd R. Risley, *Meaningful Differences in the Everyday Experience of Young American Children* (Baltimore, Md.: Paul H. Brookes Publishing Company, 1995).

4. Richard Rothstein, *Class and Schools.*

5. Matthew 26:11, New International Version.

6. Richard Rothstein, "Class and the Classroom," *American School Board Journal,* 191, no. 10 (October 2004), 16–21.

7. David J. Armor, *Maximizing Intelligence,* (New Brunswick, N.J.: Transaction Publishers, 2003), see Chapter 4, "Race, Family, and Intelligence"; and Hart and Risley, *Meaningful Differences.*

8. Robert Rosenthal and Lenore Jacobson, *Pygmalion in the Classroom: Teacher Expectation and Pupils' Intellectual Development* (New York: Holt, Rinehart & Winston, 1968).

9. Alfred Binet, *The Development of Intelligence in Children: (The Binet-Simon Scale).* (Baltimore: Williams & Wilkins Co., 1916).

10. American Anthropological Association, "Statement on 'Race' and Intelligence."

11. American Psychological Association, "The View of the American Psychological Association."

12. John Ogbu, "Racial Stratification and Education in the United States: Why Inequality Persists," *Teachers College Record,* 96: 264–298.

13. Signithia Fordham and John Ogbu, "Black Students' School Success: Coping with Burden of 'Acting White,'" *Urban Review,* 18, no. 3 (1986): 176–206.

14. John McWhorter, *Losing the Race: Self Sabotage in Black America* (New York: Harper Perennial, 2001), 135.

15. Ibid., 83.

16. Ibid.

17. Barack Obama, "The Audacity of Hope" (speech, 2004 Democratic National Convention, Boston, Mass., July 27, 2004). http://www.americanrhetoric.com/speeches/convention2004/barackobama2004dnc.htm, (accessed August 14, 2008).

18. Roland G. Fryer (with Paul Torelli), "An Empirical Analysis of 'Acting White,'" October 7, 2006, http://www.economics.harvard.edu/faculty/fryer/files/fryer_torelli.pdf (accessed August 14, 2008).

19. Jason W. Osborne, "Testing Stereotype Threat: Does Anxiety Explain Race and Sex Differences in Achievement?" *Contemporary Educational Psychology,* 20 (April 2001): 291–310.

20. Ibid., 293.

21. Irwin Katz, "Alternatives to a Personality-Deficit Interpretation of Negro Under-Achievement," *Psychology and Race,* ed., Peter Watson (Chicago: Aldine Publishing Company, 1973), 385.

22. Teach for America, "About Us," http://www.teachforamerica.org/about/index.htm (accessed August 14, 2008).

23. "Equity Within Reach: Insights from the Front Line of America's Achievement." (report, Teach for America, 2005), http://www.teachforamerica.org/assets/documents/equitywithinreach.pdf#search="equity within reach (accessed on August 14, 2008).

24. The Education Trust, "What is the Education Trust?" The Education Trust, http://www2.edtrust.org/edtrust/about+the+ed+trust (accessed on August 14, 2008).

25. Ibid.

26. Russlynn Ali, (presentation, Commission on No Child Left Behind, Washington, D.C., April 11, 2006), http://www2.edtrust.org/EdTrust/ETW/RAtestimony_April06.htm (accessed August 19, 2008).

CHAPTER 5

1. Carter G. Woodson, *The Mis-Education of the Negro* (1933, reprinted, Trenton, N.J.: Africa World Press, Inc., 1990), 9.

2. Jencks and Phillips, *The Black-White Test Score Gap,* 15–16.

3. Ivan Van Sertima, *They Came Before Columbus: The African Presence in Ancient America* (New York: Random House, 1976).

4. Lerone Bennett, Jr., *The Shaping of Black America: The Struggles and Triumphs of African-Americans, 1619–1990s* (Chicago: Johnson Publishing Company, 1975), 17.

5. Ibid. John Pory, Secretary of Virginia, to Sir Dudley Carleton, September 30, 1619, 45.

6. Ira Berlin, interview by Tavis Smiley, National Public Radio, August 18, 2003, (accessed August 19, 2008).

7. Catherine Clinton, *The African American Experience: American History Series* (Fort Washington, Pa.: Eastern National, 2004), 3.

8. T. R. Davis, "Negro Servitude in the United States: Servitude Distinguished from Slavery," *The Journal of Negro History* (1923): 247–283.

9. Melvin R. Sylvester, "The African American: A Journey from Slavery to Freedom," Black History Month exhibit at B. Davis Schwartz Memorial Library, C.W. Post Campus of Long Island University, February 1998, http://www.liu.edu/cwis/cwp/library/aaslavry.htm#beginning (accessed August 19, 2008).

10. Bennett, *The Shaping of Black America*, 62. As fascinating as this area of inquiry is, its full development lies beyond the scope of this book. Readers who wish to pursue these ideas further are encouraged to read Bennett's extensive writings on this subject.

11. Ibid., 71.

12. Dinesh D'Souza, *The End of Racism: Principles of a Multiracial Society* (New York: Free Press Paperbacks, 1996).

13. Michael Phillips, *Dream of Freedom* (Carol Stream, Ill.: Tyndale House Publishers, 2005), 56.

14. Ira Goldenberg, *Oppression and Social Intervention: Essays on the Human Condition and the Problems of Change* (Chicago: Nelson, 1978).

15. Kenneth M. Stampp, "To Make Them Stand in Fear," in *Turbulent Voyage: Readings in African American Studies,* ed. F. W. Hayes, III (Lanham, Md.: Rowman and Littlefield, 2000), 295.

16. Goldenberg, *Oppression and Social Intervention*, 3

17. Bennett, *The Shaping of Black America*, 148.

18. Woodson, *The Mis-Education of the Negro*, 84–85.

19. Edgar W. Knight, *A Documentary History of Education in the South Before 1860* (Chapel Hill: The University of North Carolina Press, 1950), 461.

20. Peter Irons, *Jim Crow's Children: The Broken Promise of the Brown Decision* (New York: Viking, 2002), 274–275.

21. Harry Morgan, *Historical Perspectives on the Education of Black Children* (Westport, Conn.: Praeger, 1995), 36.

22. Carter G. Woodson, *The Education of the Negro Prior to 1861: A History of the Education of the Colored People of the United States from the Beginning of Slavery to the Civil War* (1919; New York: Arno Press, 1968), 57.

23. Carter G. Woodson, *The Negro in Our History* (Washington, D.C.: Associated Publishers, 1922), 56.

24. Woodson, *The Education of the Negro Prior to 1861*, 93.

25. Ibid, 6.

26. Jon Meacham, *American Gospel* (New York: Random House, 2006), 105.

27. Samuel Johnson, *Taxation No Tyranny: An Answer to the Resolutions and Address of the American Congress,* http://www.samueljohnson.com/freedom.html (accessed August 15, 2008).

28. http://afroamhistory.about.com/od/davidwalker/a/bio_walker_d.htm.

29. Abraham Lincoln, (Message to Special Session of Congress, Washington, D.C., July 4, 1861), Internet Modern History Sourcebook, http://www.fordham.edu/halsall/mod/1861lincoln-special.html (accessed August 27, 2008).

30. Shelby Foote, interviewed in Ken Burns' *The Civil War,* Public Broadcasting System, 1990.

31. Eric Anderson and Alfred A. Moss, Jr., *Dangerous Donations: Northern Philanthropy and Southern Black Education, 1902–1930* (Columbia: University of Missouri Press, 1999), 4.

32. Manning Marable, "An Idea Whose Time Has Come . . . Whites have an obligation to recognize slavery's legacy," *Newsweek;* August 27, 2001, 22–23.

33. Bill Sammon, "In Senegal, Bush denounces legacy of slavery," Washington Times, July 9, 2003, http://www.washtimes.com/news/2003/jul/09/20030709-121051-3342r/ (accessed August 15, 2008).

34. Walter Williams, "The Legacy of Slavery Hustle," *Capitalism Magazine,* July 16, 2001, http://www.capmag.com/article.asp?ID=968.

35. Sniderman and Piazza, *The Scar of Race,* 107.

36. Stephan Thernstrom and Abigail Thernstrom, *No Excuses: Closing the Racial Gap in Learning* (New York: Simon & Schuster, 2003).

37. James Horton, interview on the legacy of slavery in *Africans in America, Part 4,* Public Broadcasting System, 1998, http://www.pbs.org/wgbh/aia/part4/4i3088.html (accessed on August 15, 2008).

38. Ibid.

39. Sniderman and Piazza, *The Scar of Race,* 45.

40. Loury, *The Anatomy of Racial Inequality,* 5.

41. Ibid, 10.

42. Howard and Hammond, "Rumors of Inferiority."

CHAPTER 6
1. Felicity A. Crawford, "Why Bother? They Are Not Capable of This Level of Work: Manifestations of Teacher Attitudes in an Urban High School Self-Contained Special Education Classroom with Majority Blacks and Latinos," *2007 E-yearbook, Urban Learning, Teachings and Research,* American Educational Research Association (AERA) Special Interest Group, and presentation to AERA Conference April 11, 2007, http://www.aera-ultr.org/Web%20Site%20Files/Images/PDF%20files/2007_eYearbook_final.pdf (accessed August 15, 2008).

2. Rosenthal and Jacobson, *Pygmalion in the Classroom;* Rhona S. Weinstein, Hermine H. Marshall, Lee Sharp, and Meryl Botkin, "Pygmalion and the Student: Age and Classroom Differences in Children's Awareness of Teacher Expectations," *Child Development,* vol. 58, no. 4 (Aug. 1987):1079-93.

3. Thomas Sowell, *Race and Culture: A World View* (New York: Basic Books, 1994).

4. Thomas Sowell, "Race and IQ," *Capitalism Magazine,* October 8, 2002, http://www.capmag.com/articlePrint.asp?ID=1958 (accessed August 14, 2008).

5. Ibid.

6. Bradford R. White, Jennifer B. Presley, and Karen J. DeAngelis, *Leveling Up: Narrowing the Teacher Academic Capital Gap in Illinois,* Illinois Research Council, Policy Research Report: IERC 2008-1, http://ierc.siue.

7. "Issues in Brief: The Best Studies Show that Vouchers Work," The Friedman Foundation For Educational Choice, June 16, 2008. http://www.friedmanfoundation.org/friedman/downloadFile.do?id=301 (accessed August 14, 2008).

8 http://www.kipp.org/01/resultsofkippsch.cfm

9. Melanie Markley, "Studying our Schools: Faculty/Many believe 'your school is as good as your principal'," *Houston Chronicle,* October 4, 1996, http://www.chron.com/CDA/archives/archive.mpl?id=1996_1371116 (accessed July 17, 2009).

10. Karin Chenoweth, *"It's Being Done": Academic Success in Unexpected Schools* (Cambridge, Mass.: Harvard Education Press, 2007).

11. Samuel Casey Carter, *No Excuses: Lessons Learned from 21 High-Performing, High Poverty Schools* (Washington, D.C.: The Heritage Foundation, 2000).

12. American College Testing Program, "Rigorous Courses Close Achievement Gaps Between Urban and Non-Urban Students, Study Reveals," http://www.act.org/news/releases/1998/01-15-98.html (accessed on August 28, 2008).

CHAPTER 7

1. Susan R. Komives, Nance Lucas, and Timothy R. McMahon, *Exploring Leadership: for College Students Who Want to Make a Difference* (San Francisco: Jossey-Bass, 1998), 30.

2. Ibid, xi

3. Ronald W. Walters and Robert C. Smith, *African American Leadership* (Albany: State University of New York Press, 1999), 8.

4. Elliott Sober and David Sloan Wilson, *Unto Others: The Evolution and Psychology of Unselfish Behavior* (Cambridge, Mass.: Harvard University Press, 1998), 251.

5. James MacGregor Burns, *Leadership* (New York: Harper & Row, 1978), 4.

CHAPTER 8

1. W. E. B. Du Bois, "The Talented Tenth," *The Negro Problem: A Series of Articles by Representative Negroes of To-day* (New York, 1903), http://www.teachingamericanhistory.org/library/index.asp?document=174 (accessed on August 13, 2008).

2. Most scholars say that the Reconstruction era ended in the late 1870s, but the period of African American development that it spurred can reasonably be extended until 1915, the year of Booker T. Washington's death.

3. Library of Congress, African American Odyssey: Reconstruction and Its Aftermath, Part 1, http://memory.loc.gov/ammem/aaohtml/exhibit/aopart5.html (accessed on August 18, 2008).

4. William Julius Wilson, *The Declining Significance of Race.*

5. The Achievement Gap Initiative, Harvard University, http://agi.harvard.edu/ (accessed on August 18, 2008).

6. LevelTen Web site, http://level-ten.org/ (accessed on August 18, 2008).

7. NAACP, "Our Mission," http://www.naacp.org/about/mission/ (accessed on August 20, 2008).

8. Congressional Black Caucus Foundation, "ALC Preliminary Schedule," 2008 Annual Leadership Conference, Congressional Black Caucus Foundation. http://www. alc2008.org/index.php?option=com_content&task=view&id=29&temid=53.

9. National Urban League, "Our Mission," http://www.nul.org/mission.html (accessed on August 20, 2008).

10. "Thousands Protest on King Day in South Carolina to Remove Flag from Statehouse," *Jet*, 96 no. 9, February 7, 2000, 16–18.

11. Carol Sears Botsch, "The Confederate Flag," http://www.usca.edu/aasc/Flag.htm (accessed on August 27, 2008).

12. Jencks and Phillips, *The Black-White Test Score Gap*, 3–4.

13. Daniel Patrick Moynihan, *The Negro Family: The Case for National Action*, Office of Policy Planning and Research, U.S. Department of Labor, March 1965, http://www.dol.gov/oasam/programs/history/webid-moynihan.htm (accessed on August 18, 2008).

14. Brent Staples, "On the Sidelines of the Most Important Civil Rights Battle Since 'Brown,'" *New York Times*, April 18, 2005, http://www.nytimes.com/2005/04/18/ opinion/18mon4.html?_r=1&scp=2&sq=&st=nyt.

15. Ibid.

16. S. A. Miller, "Party Trumps Race," *Washington Times*, November 2, 2005, http://washingtontimes.com/news/2005/nov/01/20051101-104932-4054r/print/ (accessed on August 13, 2008).

17. Walters and Smith, *African American Leadership*, 27.

18. Robert C. Smith, *We Have No Leaders: African Americans in the Post–Civil Rights Era* (Albany: State University of New York Press, 1996), 278.

19. H. Viscount Nelson, *The Rise and Fall of Modern Black Leadership: Chronicle of a Twentieth Century Tragedy* (Lanham, Md.: University Press of America, 2003).

20. John White, *Black Leadership in America, 1865–1968: From Booker T. Washington to Jesse Jackson* (New York: Longman, 1990).

21. Earl Ofari Hutchinson, *The Disappearance of Black Leadership* (Los Angeles: Middle Passage Press, 2000).

22. Manning Marable, *Black Leadership: Four Great American Leaders and the Struggle for Civil Rights* (New York: Columbia University Press, 1998).

23. Walters and Smith, *African American Leadership.*

24. John Brown Childs, *Leadership, Conflict, and Cooperation in Afro-American Social Thought* (Philadelphia: Temple University Press, 1989).

25. W. E. B. Du Bois, *In Battle for Peace: The Story of My 83rd Birthday* (Millwood, NY: Kraus International Publications, 1952), 76.

26. Education Equality Project, "Mission Statement," http://www.edequality.org/what_we_stand_for/our_mission (accessed on July 30, 2009).

27. Al Sharpton. Radio interview with Joel Klein. June 12, 2008.

CHAPTER 9
1. Southern Education Foundation, "Promising Practices," http://sefatl.org/practices.asp (accessed on August 21, 2008).

2. Eric A. Hanushek and Steven G. Rivkin, "The Evolution of the Black-White Achievement Gap in Elementary and Middle Schools," http://edpro.stanford.edu/hanushek/admin/pages/files/uploads/w12651.pdf; and Ronald Ferguson, *Racial and Ethnic Disparities in Home Intellectual Lifestyles,* accessible through Harvard Achievement Initiative website, http://www.agi.harvard.edu/Search/SearchAllVideo.php.

3. Howard and Hammond, "Rumors of Inferiority," 21.

4. Ibid.

5. Ibid.

6. Shelby Steele, *The Content of Our Character: A New Vision of Race in America* (New York: Harper Perennial, 1991), 34–35.

7. Seymour B. Sarason, *Political Leadership and Education Failure* (San Francisco: Jossey-Bass, 1998), 132.

8. Ibid.

9. Max De Pree, *Leadership Is an Art* (New York: Dell Publishing, 1989), 9.

10. Thompson, Cobb, Bazillo & Associates, PC, "DCPS Enrollment Census SY 2003-2004," http://www.seo.dc.gov/seo/frames.asp?doc=/seo/lib/seo/information/school_enrollment/DCPS_Enrollment-FINAL.pdf (accessed on July 17, 2009).

11. Calculations are based on NCLB State Report Card for DCPS Schools, http://www.nclb.osse.dc.gov/reportcards.asp (accessed on August 1, 2008).

12. Diana Jean Schemo, "Program on Vouchers Draws Minority Support," *New York Times,* April 6, 2006, http://nytimes.com/2006/04/06/education/06voucher.html?_r=1&scp=1&sq=Program%20on%20Vouchers%20Draw%20Minority%20Support&st=cse&oref=slogin# (accessed on August 12, 2008).

13. Data compiled from NAEP Data Explorer website, http://nces.ed.gov/nationsreportcard/naepdata/dataset.aspx (accessed on August 5, 2008).

14. Schemo, "Program on Vouchers Draws Minority Support."

15. College Board, "College-bound Seniors: A Profile of SAT Program Test Takers," 9, 2003 http://www.collegeboard.com/prod_downloads/about/news_info/cbsenior/yr2003/2003_DIST_OF_COLUMBIA.pdf (accessed on August 7, 2008).

16. Data compiled from NAEP Data Explorer website, "Percentage of Students at or Above Each Achievement Level," http://nces.ed.gov/nationsreportcard/naepdata/dataset.aspx (accessed on August 5, 2008).

17. Data compiled from NAEP Data Explorer website, "State Comparisons," http://nces.ed.gov/nationsreportcard/nde/statecomp/ (accessed on August 5, 2008).

18. Schemo, "Program on Vouchers Draws Minority Support."

19. A. T. LeFevre, *Report Card on American Education: A State-By-State Analysis: 1981–2003,* (Washington, DC: American Legislative Council, 2004), 116, http://www.alec.org/AM/Template.cfm?Section=Search&section=Education_Reports&template=/CM/ContentDisplay.cfm&ContentFileID=145 (accessed on August 27, 2008).

20. District of Columbia Public Charter School Board, "10 Years of Exploration and Discovery," 2007, 23, http://www.dcpubliccharter.com/publications/docs/10thAnniversary.pdf (accessed on August 11, 2008).

21. National Center for Educational Statistics, "Table 174: Current Expenditure Per Pupil in Fall Enrollment in Public Elementary and Secondary Schools, by State and Jurisdiction: Selection Years, 1969–1970 through 2004–05," *Digest of Educational Statistics,* http://nces.ed.gov/programs/digest/d07/tables/dt07_174.asp (accessed on August 12, 2008).

22. NAEP data show that 10 percent of the D.C. eighth graders scored at or above proficient on the 2003 reading assessment, 6 percent of eighth graders scored at or above proficient on the 2003 math assessment, and 7 percent of fourth graders scored at or above proficient on both the reading and math assessments. http://nces.ed.gov/nationsreportcard/naepdata/dataset.aspx (accessed on August 12, 2008).

23. Editorial, "D.C. Vouchers," *Washington Times,* September 2, 2003, http://www.washingtontimes.com/news/2003/aug/30/20030830-104300-5031r/print/ (accessed on August 25, 2008).

24. Schemo, "Program on Vouchers Draws Minority Support."

25. Lynette Holloway, "Making It Work: This Just In: May 18 School Board Election Results," *New York Times,* June 19, 1999, http://www.nytimes.com/1999/06/13/nyregion/making-it-work-this-just-in-may-18-school-board-election-results.html?scp=1&sq=%22This%20Just%20In:May%2018%20School%20Board%20Election%20Results&st=cse (accessed on August 19, 2008).

CHAPTER 10
1. Quote by Dr. Martin Luther King, Jr., Quoteworld, http://www.quoteworld.org/quotes/7839 (accessed on August 25, 2008).

2. Victoria Thorp, "The Achievement Gap: Is Your School Helping All Students Succeed?" June 2008, http://www.greatschools.net/cgi-bin/showarticle/99 (accessed August 15, 2008).

3. Black Alliance for Educational Options, Strategic Plan, presented at meeting of the advisory committee for BAEO. 2007.

4. Edmund W. Gordon, "Establishing a System of Public Education in Which All Children Achieve at High Levels and Reach Their Full Potential," *The Covenant with Black America*, ed., Tavis Smiley (New York: Doubleday, 2006), 23–31.

5. Hugh B. Price, *Achievement Matters: Getting Your Child the Best Education Possible* (New York: Kensington/Dafina Publishing, 2002).

CONCLUSION
1. http://www.demarestnaturecenter.org/index.php?page=6education.

2. http://www.quotesandpoem.com/quotes/showquotes/author/malcolm-x/19615.

INDEX

p.7. defn of authentic A+A leadership

p.59   no universally accepted answer to what
       causes the gaps.

p.108 gap has narrowed under NCLB, gap
       K-8 math + reading.

p.137 leaders must come from within the
       "community of trust"

p.139~ parenting programs

p.150~ national social movement.

p.172~ call to service.

p.181, massive social movement.
SRQ: is the research here adequate ??